Boys, Young Men and Violence

Boys, Young Men and Violence

Masculinities, Education and Practice

Ken Harland and Sam McCready

School of Sociology and Applied Social Studies, Ulster University , UK

First published 2015 by
PALGRAVE MACMILLAN

Palgrave Macmillan in the UK is an imprint of Macmillan Publishers Limited, registered in England, company number 785998, of Houndmills, Basingstoke, Hampshire RG21 6XS.

Palgrave Macmillan in the US is a division of St Martin's Press LLC, 175 Fifth Avenue, New York, NY 10010.

Palgrave Macmillan is the global academic imprint of the above companies and has companies and representatives throughout the world.

Palgrave® and Macmillan® are registered trademarks in the United States, the United Kingdom, Europe and other countries.

ISBN 978–1–137–29734–1

This book is printed on paper suitable for recycling and made from fully managed and sustained forest sources. Logging, pulping and manufacturing processes are expected to conform to the environmental regulations of the country of origin.

A catalogue record for this book is available from the British Library.

Library of Congress Cataloging-in-Publication Data
Harland, Ken, 1955–
   Boys, young men and violence : masculinities, education and
   practice / Ken Harland, Sam McCready.
      pages cm
   ISBN 978–1–137–29734–1 (hardback)
   1. Young men—Northern Ireland—Social conditions—Longitudinal
   studies. 2. Boys—Northern Ireland—Social conditions—Longitudinal
   studies. 3. Youth and violence—Northern Ireland. 4. Masculinity—
   Northern Ireland. 5. Men—Northern Ireland—Identity. I. McCready,
   Sam, 1949– II. Title.
   HQ799.G72N643 2015
   305.242′109416—dc23   2015021437

We would like to thank Anne and Libby for their love and support not only during the writing of this book but throughout our careers

Contents

Tables and Figures

Tables

Figures

Acknowledgements

There are many people we would like to thank for their support and encouragement. William Mitchell and Colm Walsh helped us to carry out literature reviews and identify some of the key themes that informed the original research that underpins the book. Colm Walsh and Karen Glass helped us carry out some of the original interviews with young men as part of this research.

Thanks also go to those agencies and institutions who gave us access to the young men and gatekeepers such as Matt Crozier. We are deeply indebted to the many boys and young men, now numbering over 1,000, who have taken part in our research over the past 18 years and shared their stories and experiences so openly and honestly. Their insights into everyday experiences of violence kept the research grounded and on many occasions humbled us as a research team.

We would also like to thank those who have contributed to the work of the Centre for Young Men's Studies over the past number of years: Gary Bradley; Garry Prentice; Karen Beattie; Trefor Lloyd; the Boys Development Project, London; YouthAction Northern Ireland; and in particular the team leader of the Young Men's Unit, Michael McKenna, and staff members Peter Wray, Colm Walsh, Jonny Ashe, Barry McGinley, Bernard O'Shea and Gary Donnelly.

Thanks also go to our Community Youth work colleagues at Ulster University for their support and comments and Ulster's Institute of Research in Social Sciences (IRiSS) for encouragement and practical support.

We would like to acknowledge the funding support that the Centre for Young Men has received in the past from the Joseph Rowntree Charitable Trust, and the Departments of Education and Justice for Northern Ireland.

Introduction

In writing this book we draw upon data collected by the authors over an 18-year period with over 1,000 boys and young men aged 11–23 from a range of community backgrounds and cultural traditions across Northern Ireland. During this period we have gathered extensive data in regard to young men's lives and development through their life stories and experiences that has taken us deeper into their world and helped us to understand better their issues, concerns and behaviour. We have been privileged to explore themes that boys and young men say they rarely get an opportunity to discuss with others. Central to all aspects of our approach has been our commitment to ensuring the voices of boys and young men inform and influence research, practice and policy. This book is a further example of this commitment.

We believe this book is important for two reasons. Firstly, the subject of young men's experiences of violence and masculinities from their own perspective is seriously under-researched; secondly, there is a general absence of the voices and 'gritty' everyday lives and experiences of boys and young men within the scholarly literature.

The book addresses five broad areas: original and previous research and practice carried out with boys and young men; violence and violence-related issues associated with boys and young men; issues surrounding masculinity and the transition from boy to man; reflections on education and learning; and considerations for educators and practitioners working with boys and young men.

Perhaps surprisingly, while much has been written about violence and in particular male violence, the actual voices and everyday experiences and opinions of boys and young men remain relatively silent in the literature and research. Academic studies tend to be dominated by documenting trends pointing to possible causes and identifying antecedents or contributory factors that may exist in relation to violence. While this is undoubtedly valuable, this book is heavily influenced and shaped by the voices and stories of boys and young men who have experienced violence as witnesses, victims or perpetrators.

From the onset we acknowledge that girls and young women across the world also experience many forms of violence as victims, witnesses and perpetrators. Our focus on young male violence is not to condone or ignore female experiences of violence. What follows however is a lens through which we present the voices and experiences of boys and young men within a local social-ecological framework. Lomas (2014:19–20) speaks of how 'understanding local contexts can promote particular formations of gendered behaviour' that can help us to understand better 'not only diversity among men, but within individual men'.

Despite violence having shaped our history and evolution as human beings, it remains a vague and ambiguous phenomenon. In regions/countries such as Africa, the Balkans, Israel, Palestine, Iraq, Lebanon, Russia, Syria, Ukraine and Northern Ireland, to name but a few, young people have grown up in war zones experiencing atrocities such as homicide, shootings, bombings, suicide bombers, victimisation, exploitation, rape, human trafficking, neglect, physical attack, domestic abuse, bullying and race and various other hate crimes. Media coverage of war and myriad forms of violence are available on news channels 24 hours a day. We see graphic images of the devastation of violence on our television sets as if we were watching a movie blockbuster.

As we reflect upon the society in which each of us lives, it is perhaps difficult to think of a time when violence has not been in some way part of that society's existence and experience. Throughout the history of the world violence has been used, and frequently legitimised, during periods of war. Since 9/11 the face and threat of terrorism has become a global security concern. In modern warfare those who kill in the name of war are often portrayed as fanatical extremists or as having been radicalised. Yet in Northern Ireland, for example, many of those who engaged in the 'Troubles' were often perceived as 'local heroes' who were prepared to defend, and even die for, their communities, cultural identities and long held traditions. After 40 years of war in Northern Ireland, it is still unclear to many what the conflict was about and whether or not it actually was a war or a terrorist campaign.

It can appear perhaps that violence is a phenomenon that we all simply have had to come to terms with. Certainly we have found this is a common experience amongst the boys and young men in our studies. History and Hollywood can show us that war was, and is, the terrain of men. Stories of war are typically stories about men. While there is acknowledgement of the role that women played, for example during World War II, typically this was 'at home' and not on the front line. Accounts of war are pregnant with stories of sacrifice, and part of this narrative is the accepted cost of war to countries, families, women and men, in particular young men. Undoubtedly this was the reality of casualties during global conflicts such as World War I. Men fighting, dying or being wounded during war and other conflicts appears to have been embedded in the human psyche from the beginning of time, and has been a central feature of the recent history in Northern Ireland.

While we may speculate about evolutionary processes and the 'survival of the fittest' it is likely that, historically, certain men benefited from being physically stronger than women (and other men). Men also benefited from high-status social roles such as gatherer/hunter/provider/protector, and it is perhaps understandable why, in fulfilling such roles, violence was deemed necessary to ward off threat from others, including wild animals. Courage and bravado elevated the social status of 'brave men' due to their prowess and ability to protect their family and community, including their wives and children. While this may not be true of every community, this type of social stratification continues to exist in many societies that have experienced the horrors and realities of war and other forms of conflict.

We know statistically that across the globe those in prisons and caught up in the criminal justice system, for example, are predominantly male. We also know that individuals are not born violent. We perhaps know less about why individuals become violent or indeed why so many males are attracted to violence or see violence as a legitimate way to deal with conflict. Exploring violence raises complex questions in regard to why certain boys and young men may become violent and challenges us to ponder if violence is actually a broader 'problem of men'.

Boys struggling to become men

Getting 'beneath the surface' of young men's beliefs and experiences reveals the extent to which they experience many complexities and paradoxes between their expectations of masculinity and their actual lived experiences. In this book we share with the reader what boys and young men have told us about their feelings and emotions, their fears and aspirations. We hear how not 'matching up' to certain beliefs about men and masculinity can lead to feelings of personal inadequacy that can influence heavily a young man's mental health, self-efficacy and self-confidence. We identify motivating factors such as shame and respect and explore why certain boys believe it is by *acting tough* they will gain acceptance and status. Despite vulnerabilities and insecurities within their personal lives, we will hear, paradoxically, why boys believe pain and certain other emotions must remain buried as part of 'what men do'. We will also hear voices that appear to challenge stereotypes of men and seek other expressions of masculine identity and what it means to be a man.

Our journey through the world of the boys and young men to whom we have spoken will show how violence and the fear of violence are perceived as a normal part of male youth and male subculture – as a central part of growing up and learning to become a man. Boys and young men have talked to us as victims, perpetrators and witnesses of violence. They speak of contradictions such as the *blur* between what they believe are actual acts of violence and what they perceive as boys just 'messing around'. This book will focus on what boys and young men had to say about violence and masculinity. Our conversations were much broader than our key themes and reflected much of the fun, hopes and aspirations in boys' lives. However, the focus of the book is on violence and masculinity, and this will be the dominant narrative.

As we will see, however, boys' understanding and attitudes towards violence, like many other aspects of their lives, are not addressed formally as part of their education and learning. Therefore, boys learn about issues such as violence and masculinity in an ad hoc way, often without any support or guidance from adults. Indeed boys have consistently told us that as they get older they feel increasingly distant from the world of adults and are often treated with higher levels of suspicion and distrust by adults who attach labels to them such as 'troublesome' or 'problematic'.

Speaking to boys and young men about their experiences of family, school and community we find, perhaps shockingly, that these established social structures are often perceived and experienced as violent places. Boys have told us that they do not feel connected to their communities and are not involved in, or aware of, local decision-making processes. In school, boys have told us that the subjects they are taught are often unrelated to the realities of their everyday lives and experiences.

We hear of struggles that boys and young men experience living in a society that has consistently experienced high levels of socio-economic deprivation and industrial decline. We hear of challenges and threats associated with living in a society emerging from 40 years of political conflict and community violence through what is known as the 'Troubles'. We will hear how, despite 20 years of peace-building and paramilitary ceasefires, paramilitary organisations remain an everyday threat which leaves young men confused about policing and law and order. We will hear how in many working-class communities images of war and paramilitary members in balaclavas brandishing guns are still being painted on the gables, walls and streets as a reminder of where power lies and is administered. Therefore, while young men may seek to express new representations of men and masculinity, the legacy of the Troubles and the industrial heritage of Northern Ireland are powerful reminders of its patriarchal working-class history and working-class masculinities. Yet, as we will also see, there is no one type of masculinity that captures the experiences of all boys and young men. Rather, young men's experiences of violence and masculine identities are negotiated, and renegotiated, through local contexts that have produced different types of men at particular times in history.

What has become increasingly apparent from our studies, however, is the fact that boys and young men do not appear to be encouraged or supported to reflect critically upon many of the complex and contradictory aspects of their lives and development. Certainly we have found this to be the case within formal education. Subsequently many of the boys and young men we have spoken to are left clinging, sometimes desperately, to traditional and outdated notions of 'doing masculinity' that leaves them feeling 'squeezed' somewhere between masculine myths and the reality and struggles of their everyday lives.

While the boys and young men whose voices are presented throughout this book are from Northern Ireland, this is not a book about Northern Ireland or the Northern Ireland 'Troubles'. Rather, it is a book that locates certain boys and young men's everyday experiences within broader socio-economic and political conditions within a divided and contested society that is moving, albeit cautiously, towards peace-building.

We anticipate that this book will be of value to educators, academics, researchers, students and youth-orientated organisations from a range of disciplines working with boys and young men, such as youth workers, social workers, health workers and probation workers, and those involved in youth justice, restorative practices, as well as conflict and peace-building studies. While the context of this book is set within the region of Northern Ireland, we believe the content will be applicable to other parts of the world.

How we have organised this book

This book is divided into seven chapters. Chapter 1 discusses how the context of violence in Northern Ireland has informed and influenced the development of the Centre for Young Men's Studies and in particular orientates the reader towards early research carried out by the authors.

Chapter 2 critically examines the findings from our five-year longitudinal study 'Taking Boys Seriously' which provides an in-depth exploration of adolescent boys' school and life experiences and their attitudes and experiences of violence and masculinity.

Chapter 3 examines the international literature and theoretical perspectives of violence, while Chapter 4 examines the literature and debate surrounding men and masculinities. Both these chapters aim to provide a deeper understanding of the wider social-ecological context in which boys and young men live and exist.

Chapter 5 will offer a critical reflection on education and learning and in particular will discuss youth work methodology as effective in engaging boys and young men in addressing issues not typically part of the formal education curriculum, such as violence and masculinity. This chapter highlights the importance of the educator as a facilitator of learning for boys and young men. It also emphasises the centrality of 'relationship' in regard to boys' attitudes towards education and learning.

Chapter 6 presents our latest data from the composite voices of boys and young men, specifically exploring issues surrounding violence and masculinity. The purpose of this is to provide the reader with a clearer and deeper sense of their world, their hopes and aspirations, their experiences, their views, their prejudices and their values.

Chapter 7 examines practice, and in particular we present an 'integrated social ecological approach' to working more effectively with boys and young men. This chapter explores relationships between young men, their communities and formal and non-formal education. Finally, we present some of the practical lessons from our evidence-based research made over the past 18 years that we believe will be of value to educators and practitioners aiming to engage and work more effectively with boys and young men.

1
Context for Our Research Work with Boys and Young Men

At this point it is important to acknowledge the context in which our work with boys and young men has developed over the past 18 years. For over 40 years boys have grown up in Northern Ireland facing particular difficulties that have impacted upon their development and behaviour. The sphere of cultural, political and individual identity has been fiercely contested with young people developing their sense of ethnic identity in the midst of widespread social, economic and political upheaval through a period of prolonged conflict. The fact that young people growing up in Northern Ireland live in a multi-problem, multi-stress and divided region has been well documented (Cairns and Cairns, 1995; Muldoon, 2004; Browne and Dwyer, 2014) with 93 per cent of children attending schools that are wholly or predominantly Catholic or Protestant (Sommers, 2015).

During the latter part of the 20th century, the history of Northern Ireland, like many other regions, was profoundly affected by acute social, political and economic change. The decline of traditional industry, a weak economy and high levels of regional unemployment alongside an articulate voice of feminist argument clashed with the onset of what became known as the 'Troubles' (Ashe and Harland, 2014). With a population of just 1.74 million living in Northern Ireland, few lives have been unaffected in some capacity by the conflict and the extremities of violence that was inflicted upon quite a small geographical region. During the Troubles there were some 3,700 deaths. In terms of population size this would be the equivalent of 115,000 fatalities in the United Kingdom as a whole or 600,000 in the United States (Hargie et al., 2003). In essence, the prolonged political conflict was primarily inflicted upon working-class communities by working-class men and entailed young men dying at the hands of other young men (Shirlow and Coulter, 2014). Typically these men were members of paramilitary organisations who instigated brutal forms of violence that struck terror into the heart of communities throughout Northern Ireland. This is not surprising as during the Troubles there were around 34,000 shootings, 35,000 injuries, 14,000 bombings, over 3,000 punishment shootings and over 2,500 punishment beatings/paramilitary style attacks administered by paramilitary organisations. Of the deaths 91 per cent were male with 32 per cent amongst young males aged 17–24 (Smyth and Hamilton, 2003; Muldoon et al., 2008). Of all paramilitary punishment attacks 25 per cent were on those 19 years old and younger, a form of child abuse which has received insufficient attention (Kennedy, 2001) and which, as our studies will show, still appears to be tolerated to this day.

In 1994 there was a breakthrough towards peace when the Irish Republican Army (IRA) announced a cessation of military operations that was later reciprocated by some of the Loyalist paramilitary groupings. This was followed by the 'Good Friday (Belfast) Agreement'[1] in 1998 when the Irish and British governments and the political parties in Northern Ireland reached a consensus. Shirlow and Coulter (2014:716) note that 'while the Agreement sought to deal with the totality of relationships between the peoples of Ireland and Great Britain, its principal concern was to mend the troubled relations between the two main ethno-national communities within Northern Ireland'. The Agreement included a devolved, inclusive government; prisoner release; troop reductions; targets for paramilitary decommissioning; provisions for polls on Irish reunification; civil rights measures; and parity of esteem for the two communities in Northern Ireland. In a referendum held in May 1998, 71.2 per cent of people in Northern Ireland and 94.4 per cent of people in the Republic of Ireland voted to accept the Agreement. The definitive end of the troubles came in 2007 following the St Andrew's Agreement in October 2006. This was followed by elections in March 2007 and the formation of a government in May 2007 by the Democratic Unionist Party and Sinn Fein. In July 2007, the British Army formally ended their mission in Northern Ireland which began 38 years earlier in 1969.

Northern Ireland now entered its peace-building phase. This is not to say peace-building did not exist before these events in either the government's or the people's agenda up to this point, but the vocabulary relating to the Troubles has changed and Northern Ireland has become a place referred to as post-conflict and in transition from conflict to peace. Peace-building processes encompass security, demilitarisation, humanitarian assistance, power-sharing governance and elections, human rights, minority protection and reconstruction aid (Wallensteen, 2002). In countries such as Bosnia and Kosovo peace-building was assumed by external stakeholders whereas in Northern Ireland there was a functioning state and administration to facilitate it (Oberschall, 2007). The pathway towards peace has necessitated engaging in post-conflict transformation work. This process has included addressing complex issues such as reconciliation, reintegration, decommissioning, police reform, prisoner release, security, an end of paramilitarism, economic investment and the administration of a new Local Assembly. It was clear from the start of the ceasefires, however, that resolving these issues would not be straightforward. For example, Northern Ireland continues to find it difficult to establish acceptable ways to help victims feel that they have obtained justice from atrocities that occurred throughout the Troubles. There is also the issue of segregation. Northern Ireland remains a polarised society with its population continuing to live in areas that are either exclusively Catholic or Protestant (Northern Ireland Census, 2011).

The concrete barriers constructed between communities divided on religious grounds are known as peace walls. This is largely an urban phenomenon that affects the way in which people move and interact and directly impacts upon daily activities such as going to work, meeting friends and relatives and getting access to health and recreation services (Murtagh, 2003). As in other parts of the world, such as China, Israel and Palestine, Mozambique, South Africa and East and West Berlin, these structures were erected to keep people and communities apart. Towering peace walls built to keep Catholics and Protestants safe from attack from one another remain in many areas as a cold reminder of the physical barriers still necessary in a deeply divided and contested society. Research into peace walls by Byrne et al. (2012) shows that 58 per cent of people would like to see the peace walls come down now or at some point in the future. However, 58 per cent of people were very or fairly worried about their personal safety if they were removed, and 69 per cent believed that they are still necessary because of the potential for violence. These findings concur with a previous study (*Belfast Telegraph*, 2008) with long-term residents which found that, while 81 per cent of people said they would like to see peace walls demolished, 60 per cent believed it was not safe enough to remove them at present. This trend highlights the fact that, despite the optimism of a peace process, old fears and distrust still exist amongst people living in areas most affected during the Troubles. As noted by Shirlow and Coulter (2014:717), 'twenty years after the cease-fires, Northern Ireland may no longer be at war with itself, but nor does it feel quite like a society that has genuinely found peace'; and as cautioned by Aughey (2014:822) while Northern Ireland is now perceived as a region at peace, its future is 'inextricably linked to uncertainty'.

While violence is by no means a Northern Ireland phenomenon, the province does have a unique voice in attempting to understand political and community violence and more recently the drive towards peace-building. In 2013, Northern Ireland experienced the lowest record of crime for over 20 years (Nolan, 2014). However, the Northern Ireland Crime Survey 2012/13 claims that only 52 per cent of crimes are actually reported to the police (Nolan, 2014). To suggest, however, that Northern Ireland is a society at peace is to ignore the continued high levels of political violence and paramilitary activity (Gormley-Heenan and Monaghan, 2012) and the fact that so many young people face continued risks and high levels of marginalisation within a supposedly post-conflict society (McAlister et al., 2009; Haydon et al., 2012; Browne and Dwyer, 2014). More than 20 years after the 1994 ceasefires, paramilitaries, particularly dissident republicans, continue to be a 'severe' and viable threat to peace-building (Nolan, 2014:37). Certain young men also remain susceptible to certain forms of paramilitary assaults (Lloyd, 2009; Harland, 2011; Harland and McCready, 2014) in what Topping and Byrne (2012:1) term 'new paramilitary policing' in the post-Troubles era of Northern Ireland. Throughout the Troubles there was a highly localized distribution of deaths and other forms of violence in urban areas (i.e. Derry/Londonderry and West and North Belfast) which correlated to those areas with the highest levels of family poverty, social deprivation, educational under-achievement and higher rates of drug and substance misuse (Browne and Dwyer, 2014:801). A Review of Health and Social Care in Northern Ireland (2011) revealed that levels of death by suicide increased by 64 per cent between 1999 and 2008, mostly carried out amongst young men. In 2010, 77 per cent of all suicides in Northern Ireland were male, with 40.5 per cent amongst those aged 15–34 (Scowcroft, 2012). Tomlinson (2012) in a detailed study of suicide in Northern Ireland found strong links between suicide levels and the legacy of the Troubles. In particular he found that 'children and young people who grew up during the Troubles had the highest and most rapidly increasing suicide rates' (cited in Nolan, 2014:111).

It had previously been argued that the extent of sectarian and paramilitary violence suppressed other forms of violence and contributed to the under-reporting of violence against the person, intimate partner violence, vandalism, and race and hate crime (Connolly, 2002). The

Chief Constable's Annual Report (Police Service of Northern Ireland (PSNI), 2009) further indicated that increases in the use of knives, race and hate crimes, and continuing sectarianism were particular concerns. This trend is also reflected in PSNI statistics showing that between 1970 and 2013 total recorded crimes relating to violence against the person had risen from 737 to 30,305, remaining at around 30,000 since 2005 when it had jumped from around 20,000 in the late 1990s (Police Service of Northern Ireland, 2013). In 2014, the Chief Constable's report noted that ordinary people may be at increased risk from organised crime such as counterfeit goods, laundered fuel, illicit cigarettes, fraud, identity theft, drugs and human trafficking. In a further statistical report published in 2014, it was reported that violence against the person continues to represent the highest proportion of convictions in Northern Ireland with young men aged 18–25 accounting for almost 90 per cent of those convicted (Graham et al., 2014).

Appreciating the changing yet complex social, political and economic context of the region is critically important as it helps us to understand better the backdrop through which our work with boys and young men has been carried out over the past 18 years. Our findings reveal the extent to which the local context of these boys and young men's lives had a strong bearing upon their thoughts, beliefs and attitudes towards their communities, education, experiences of violence and what it means to be a man.

Spano et al. (2010:1161) argue that 'exposure to violence is a strong predictor of violent behaviour for children and adolescents'. Internationally, young people who live in areas of high and protracted conflict are, by virtue of their residence, exposed to a range of ecological influences that gives rise to an increased propensity towards violence (Goeke-Morey et al., 2013:244). One common argument is that exposure to violence leads to the 'assimilation of aggressive attitudes, as well as the replication of aggressive behaviour' (Meghan-Davidson and Canivez, 2012:3662). Witnessing violence during the formative years of adolescent development has a 'direct impact on the perpetration of violence' (Flood and Pease, 2009:131). What is witnessed is learned and what is learned is more likely to be practised.

The Troubles, the political arrangements, the peace process, the underpinning uncertainty represent the backcloth to the lives of the boys and young men from Northern Ireland that we met and interviewed over the 18 years of our work. A society in transition from conflict to peace offers hope of normality, but the long reach of conflict, its pervading influence and legacy sits uncomfortably and heavily on the shoulders of the young men in this study as they are asked to reflect on being a man, masculinity and violence.

The Centre for Young Men's Studies

The Centre for Young Men's Studies is located in the field of Community Youth Work which resides within the School of Sociology and Applied Social Studies at Ulster University. It was set up by the authors in 2004. It aims to promote the voice, needs and interests of boys and young men through research that will inform practice, training and policy. The Centre also aims to raise awareness of boys' and young men's issues through their life stories, experiences, opinions and issues.

Our work before and within the Centre for Young Men's Studies has focused heavily on boys and young men who are perhaps recognised as marginalised or vulnerable within society. In preparing to write this book we have spoken to over 1,000 young men, over a period of 18 years, in different contexts including schools, communities, young offenders' centres, prisons and youth clubs. We talked with victims and perpetrators of violence, in particular young men vulnerable to the brutal manifestations of paramilitary[2] 'justice' as a form of community policing that strikes fear into those boys and young men who do not comply with their sense of law and order. We have spoken with young men of their enjoyment of fighting, being involved in riots and being the 'hard man'. These are typically young men who find ways to exist despite carrying negative labels that can potentially block their future development and life opportunities. These are young men who present themselves as 'troublesome' to adults in authority roles: young men who do not seek emotional support and exist without male mentors and therefore look to their peers and other perhaps more sinister individuals for guidance. However, we have also spoken to young men who, on first appearance, would appear to be doing well: those from middle-class backgrounds who perform well at school and do not necessarily present themselves as 'problematic'.

Across all of our studies young men speak of the normality of violence. Some boys also speak of the excitement of violence and the 'buzz' they get from engaging in certain forms of violence. They also talk about everyday life experiences and about what it is to be a man and what they understand about masculinity.

Common to all our studies however, regardless of backgrounds, are boys and young men who are struggling to find their place and value in this world. Their experiences appear to be full of complexities and

contradictions. As we will see, young men increasingly find it difficult to find their way in a world that they perceive as being 'out of
touch'. A world where they feel disconnected from adults, fearful about
their personal safety, vulnerable within their communities and often left
clinging to outdated notions of what it means to be a man.

Our research and the setting up of the Centre for Young Men's Studies

This section highlights some of the earlier research that shaped, influenced and continues to influence the work of the Centre for Young
Men's Studies. Both authors had extensive previous experience of working directly with boys and young men as practitioners in communities
throughout Northern Ireland. An ethnographic study carried out by one
of the authors (Harland, 1997, 2000) attempted to contextualise masculinity in working-class areas of inner city Belfast with adolescent boys.
The findings highlighted the extent of complexities, paradoxes and contradictions that were part of contemporary male experience in a society
emerging from conflict. In 2002 both authors were separately engaged in
an EU Special Support Programme for Peace and Reconciliation commissioned by YouthNet (the voluntary youth network for Northern Ireland).
This research focused on understanding the links between young men
and violence.

In 2003 the authors secured a prestigious grant from the Joseph
Rowntree Trust to carry out an investigative study into the lives of boys
and young men living in Northern Ireland and to examine the factors
that impacted upon their development. This led to the establishment
of the inaugural Centre for Young Men's Studies at Ulster University in
2004 followed by a one-year pilot study with 299 boys to examine their
experiences of school, masculinity and violence (Beattie et al., 2006a).
In 2006, the Centre for Young Men's Studies was commissioned by the
Northern Ireland government departments of Education and Justice to
carry out a five-year longitudinal study into 378 adolescent boys' school
and life experiences (Harland and McCready, 2006–2012). During this
time research was also carried out with 130 young men by Lloyd (2009)
that aimed to give a voice to their attitudes and experiences of violence,
conflict and safety. In 2014/15 additional research was carried out with
180 young men specifically in preparation for this book. In total we have
worked with over 1,000 boys and young men over the past 18 years.
We have developed partnerships with organisations such as the Boys
Development Project, London and YouthAction Northern Ireland, the

North Eastern Education and Library Board, and the Regional Training Unit which supports the professional development of leaders and senior managers in schools across Northern Ireland. The following section provides an overview of findings from each of the above studies that have shaped and influenced our work and commitment to understanding and appreciating better the lives of boys and young men in the context of a society emerging from conflict towards peace.

The journey through the years of research with 1,000 boys and young men

Talking and listening to boys and young men

In writing this book we draw upon the findings of new and previous data collected by the authors over an 18-year period with over a 1,000 boys and young men aged 11–23 from a range of community backgrounds and cultural traditions across Northern Ireland. During this period we have gathered extensive data in regard to young men's lives and development. Central to our research strategy has been a methodological approach that is committed to ensuring the voices of young men inform and direct all aspects of our work. The data we present is drawn from a range of conversations with boys and young men and different studies including:

- ethnographic studies (Harland, 1997, 2000);
- a pilot study into boys' school and life experiences (Beattie et al., 2006);
- research with young men around the theme of violence (Lloyd, 2009; Harland and McCready, 2010; Harland, 2011);
- the findings of a five-year longitudinal study (Harland and McCready, 2012) funded by the Departments of Education and Justice for Northern Ireland that explored adolescent male school and life experiences;
- new, ethically approved research, with 180 young men specifically gathered in preparation for this book (Harland and McCready, 2014/15).

The work before and during the early days of the Centre for Young Men's Studies 1997–2009

To enable us to get deeper into the reality of boys and young men's lives and everyday experiences we begin our journey listening to some of the first voices of the young men we have worked with over the past 18 years. During this time we have been privileged to explore themes which the boys and young men tell us they rarely get an opportunity to discuss with adults. Talking to them provides us with valuable insights and lessons into their lives and experiences. Listening to young men enables us to understand better their attitudes, beliefs and behaviour. It is important to note, however, that on occasions the stories we hear can be deeply challenging to an adult listener. This can be because as adults we may already possess deeply ingrained views of young men and listening to their stories can, at times, reinforce these perceptions. On many occasions talking to boys and young men has triggered deep emotions and concerns that left us oscillating somewhere between empathy, sorrow, joy, feelings of frustration and even anger. These emotions are not directed at young men, but at the apparent lack of support many boys and young men receive from adults as they struggle to cope with a wide range of emotional and developmental needs. This creates a void which appears to leave adolescent boys believing that they must find their own solutions to the complex issues they face at a critical period in their development.

Ethnographic studies (1997 and 2000)

Harland's ethnographic studies (1997 and 2000) with adolescent boys living in inner city areas of Belfast was carried out between 1997 and 1999. This includes the period during and after the signing of the Belfast (Good Friday) Agreement in 1998. Findings revealed the extent to which these boys appeared to be struggling at every level of their experience and development. In school, for example, boys expressed a sense of hopelessness as they were falling behind in most subjects and failing to see any benefits from being there. This was evidenced by comments such as:

> I was never any good at school so I didn't learn.
> Ya' feel wick [feeling bad about something] when
>   everything goes over your head.
> It makes you feel shit 'cause school is where you are
>   supposed to learn.

Other boys took some responsibility for what was happening to them in school:

> I'm a messer and always get detention.

Boys typically directed their frustration at teachers:

> Teachers have no time for you, so you just mess about,
> and they think we're just wasters. This gets you
> angry and you get into more trouble.

The fact that these boys felt powerless to influence change at school led to more aggressive responses:

> Who the f*** do they think they are? They think
> they know everything and we know nothing. So we just
> sit here and say nothing.

Boys spoke of frustrations they felt at school contributing to them on occasions getting angry in school and 'kicking tables or throwing schoolbags around'.

The sense of powerlessness that these boys felt was further evidenced by how they spoke about life in their communities. Sectarianism and the fear of paramilitary violence was a daily concern to their health and well-being. They feared brutality from paramilitary organisations living in their communities and often in the same street as themselves. These young men were able to talk knowledgeably about other young males they knew who were victims of paramilitary violence such as shootings and other forms of punishment beatings.

> I hate those bastards – you can't trust them. They tell you what to do.
> There's no getting away from them and if they are after you – you've
> had it.

> They go around knocking the shit out of everyone and you've just
> gotta take it. Who wants to walk about on one leg for the rest of your
> life?

These experiences provide us with disturbing yet valuable insights into the reality of young men's lives at this point in time within inner city urban communities. They identify a range of pressures and dangerous situations they have to cope with and negotiate on a daily basis. The apparent inevitability of paramilitary violence as a form of community justice and the use of violence as the primary means of local law enforcement led them to accept and, occasionally, offer some resistance to the perpetrators of this 'justice'. In the end the research showed a reluctant, but inevitable, acceptance of the situation in these communities. The young men felt it was something they just had to put up with, cope with and learn to live with. The story of life with the paramilitaries was not unanimous in that not every boy spoke negatively about them:

> If some shit-head gets what's coming to him that's not my problem – some people deserve what they get.

Some boys spoke of preferring to contact paramilitaries if a crime was committed against them, rather than go to the police. These young men spoke of how 'paramilitaries got things sorted'. Listening to the young men in this early study revealed the extent to which they had to deal with a range of problematic and potentially dangerous situations in their daily lives. Violence was perceived as something they thought about all the time, as something normal, inevitable and most likely to happen when they left their own community.

These young men also spoke of fears they had about getting involved in crime. They felt susceptible to the influence of other boys and young men who took drugs or engaged in anti-social behaviour. Most boys spoke of feeling a pressure to be able to 'take care of themselves' through their own violent or aggressive methods as this appeared to be the community norm for boys and young men. However, it was apparent that not every young man felt comfortable using violence to resolve issues.

In this study, as well as asking young men to reflect on violence in their lives, the researcher was keen to understand what they understood about being a man and masculinity. Over half of them were unfamiliar with the concept:

> I've never heard of the word before.

For those who ventured a response the association was strongly linked to their need to *prove* to others that they are no longer children, or that they were not gay. The inclination was not to say what they thought masculinity was, but rather what it was not. They talked about the importance of men being in control and how they should exercise different aspects of *power*:

> A man has to be emotionally strong so he can overcome
>   his problems at work.
> A weak or shy man doesn't really get anywhere.

Some young men had more reflective perceptions:

> You don't have to be hard to be a man and you don't have to drink
> every night. It's in the mind that you're a real man.

It was also apparent, however, that their notions of power were also
directly linked to feelings of superiority, particularly in relation to
women:

> It's men who sort out the problems. Women want men to protect
> them. If you can't protect your family then you're not a man.

Talking about men and masculinity appeared to make the boys feel
awkward and at times uncomfortable as they attempted to describe
what they believed it meant to be a man. While they may not have
consciously contemplated masculinity, it was very apparent that from
childhood these young men had been bombarded with forceful messages about what it means to be a man. These messages were reinforced
in the family, in school, by the media, by paramilitary activities and
influences, paramilitary murals painted on the gable walls and in the
streets where they lived. Typically these messages embodied a type of
hyper-masculinity that portrayed men as violent, brave and defenders of
their communities and homes. There was a glorification of violence and
violent men. This was reinforced by the status ascribed to paramilitary
groups and its members within many of these working-class communities. When talking to these young men about paramilitary violence
and justice the extent of dichotomies and contradictions in their mental processing were very apparent. These young men had grown up
experiencing (and possibly believing and accepting) that violence was
a normal and necessary part of their daily lives. The use of violence
as a means of resolving conflict was seldom questioned and their perceived threat and fear of violence was the foremost concern they had
in regard to personal safety. One consequence of this was that violence,
and violence-related behaviour amongst men, was not only perceived as
normal, but an important aspect of male youth culture. For these young
men their ideas and ideals of men and masculinity were constructed
within the values, beliefs and traditions of a society deeply steeped in
violent political conflict. They were living in a society where violence
was inflicted upon its people through bombings, shootings and other
extreme forms of state and paramilitary brutality. Violence was therefore not only perceived as normal, but a legitimate way of dealing with
personal threat. This localised socio-political context made it extremely

difficult for these young men to consider or even begin to comprehend alternative ways of resolving conflict or violent situations. Therefore the types of violence they experienced living in a society at war with itself powerfully shaped their beliefs, attitudes and behaviour. Whether as victims, perpetrators or witnesses, violence was an everyday concern and perceived as 'something to just have to deal with'.

Yet it was very apparent that these young men struggled with other aspects of their development. For example, the fear of appearing 'unmanly' disconnected these young men from sharing the pain they experienced in their lives with others. They poured scorn on other males displaying what they perceived to be 'feminine traits' such as being tender or gentle, typically branding such men with homophobic labels as 'gay' or 'fruits'. Despite, at times, speaking of feeling depressed and 'fed up with life', these boys rarely spoke to anyone about how they felt. Whilst acknowledging the possibility of men needing emotional support they mocked at the idea of males actually asking for support:

> Men don't go around asking for support. It's only girls need it.
> You can't go around showing people that you can't cope –
>   you would get your bollocks[3] kicked in
> You see around here there is a lot of crime and violence,
>   and if you can't handle yourself it's bad for you.
> If one of my mates cried I would just laugh at them
>   and call them a fruit.
> Even if you want to cry, you can't.

The perceived need for these young men to demonstrate a dominant type of normative masculinity resulted in repulsion and disassociation with perceived notions of femininity. Through their positive association with hegemonic masculinity and rejection of subordinate notions of femininity, these young men openly displayed a range of homophobic attitudes and beliefs. This narrow interpretation of masculinity necessitated a belief that men must deny, or conceal, other aspects of their personality. By being dismissive of pain in their lives and separated from their internal world of feelings and emotions, the young men often appeared 'unemotional' and at times desensitised and intimidating in their responses.

Aggressive and violent behaviour amongst fathers was a common occurrence for these boys and few mentioned their fathers as positive role models. Although they did not seek or expect emotional support from their fathers, boys displayed an enormous sense of loyalty and unquestioned respect towards their fathers. This has been a consistent finding across all our studies. For most boys, time spent with their fathers was scarce and some laughed in reaction to the question as to whether they would speak to their fathers about emotional issues or personal problems:

> Wise up – me and my dad do not go around talking about how we feel.

Most young men spoke positively of their fathers as 'working hard and trying to provide for the family'. Speaking about their fathers was a subject that appeared to affect the young men deeply and revealed some strongly felt needs and emotions. It was within this subject that many boys opened up and revealed a different side of themselves:

> I wish I could get closer to my dad. But he doesn't do anything with me.

> My dad doesn't really bother with me. In the house we hardly
>   ever talk.
> If I ask my dad to do something with me he just says he
>   can't be bothered.
> My da' doesn't talk about how he feels. He doesn't go about
>   saying I love you or anything.
> My da' doesn't cry – he can take it.
> I seen my dad cry at my granny's funeral but that was the
>   only time.
> My da' is a hard man who has a reputation in the community.

Being able to deal with potentially aggressive and threatening situations was esteemed more highly by these boys than their father's capacity to be caring or loving. Harland's work from 1997 to 2000 (he undertook his research work as the youth worker in the community where he had established rapport and good working relationships with the subjects), whilst specific to inner city Protestant and Catholic working-class communities, is set within a timeframe when political change was occurring in Northern Ireland. The Good Friday Agreement and paramilitary ceasefires offered a potential game changer for people. The voices of young men at this point and place in time did not reflect the hope or the prospects of an immediate peace dividend for these young men. Their early formative and teenage years were lived almost exclusively within one community in a deeply divided and contested society. At this stage the authors were known to one another professionally but had not, as yet, collaborated on any research on boys and young men.

Research into the lives of young men and violence (2002, 2006 and 2009) and the birth of the Centre for Young Men's Studies

In 2002, both authors were engaged in two of three separate programmes that lasted for just over a year and attempted to develop a broader and deeper understanding of the link between young men and violence in communities across Northern Ireland. We also wanted to address the consequences of violence and violent related behaviour amongst young males. A full evaluation of these programmes was carried out by Lloyd (2002:8–9). Some of the main conclusions from the evaluation of the three projects included that:

- many of the young men reported that they rarely talked about violence or had the opportunity to talk about violence in a reflective way;
- for most of the young men, violence was not 'good' or 'bad', but a complex mixture ranging from excitement to fear;
- there was a strong link between the young men's perceptions of manhood and their attitudes towards violence.

An important aspect of this joint research was a process whereby the researchers engaged young men both as subjects of the research and collectors of data. Within one of the strands (Chapman and McCready, 2002) young men were trained as interviewers in order to interview other young men around the subject of young men and violence. It was from this work that the authors (Harland and McCready) came together to discuss the potential of setting up a Centre for Young Men's Studies within Ulster University. A prestigious grant from The Joseph Rowntree Charitable Trust in 2003 paved the way for the Centre being set up in 2004; their first output built upon the early work by Harland and the European study.

In 2006 the Centre for Young Men's Studies published the findings of a one-year pilot study with 299 boys aged 11–12. This research was carried out in partnership with YouthAction Northern Ireland. The study explored boys' experiences as victims or perpetrators of violence and their interpretations and expectations of men and masculinity. The initial research of Harland relied heavily on qualitative data and worked off the statements and comments of the young men. In this pilot study the Centre developed quantitative and qualitative approaches to data collection. The findings from this study (Beattie et al., 2006) revealed a chasm between boys' perceptions and actual experiences of violence. It was found, however, that when these boys were asked about precise events or encounters of violence, levels of victimisation escalated dramatically.

- 40 per cent reported malicious damage to their belongings;
- 38 per cent of all boys said they felt safe in school;
- 30 per cent of boys were worried;
- 90 per cent of boys had been kicked;
- 82 per cent of boys had been pushed;
- 80 per cent of boys had been punched;
- 50 per cent of boys reported being bruised as a result of being attacked by other boys;
- 43 per cent of boys reported being hit with a weapon;
- 40 per cent of boys had been a victim of violence on more than one occasion by boys they perceived as 'hard men';
- 8 per cent reported some form of violence directed at them from young men in paramilitaries.

This study further revealed differences in levels of violence between boys living in rural areas compared to boys living in urban areas. For example, boys living in urban areas were twice as likely to be hit with a weapon and they placed more emphasis on 'being able to fight' than boys from rural areas. However, the data revealed slightly incongruous and contradictory attitudes towards paramilitary groups with 20 per cent of boys reporting being worried about paramilitary activity while 10 per cent reported they respected individuals who were in such groups.

Those boys reporting being 'deeply suspicious' of persons from other religious backgrounds accounted for 30 per cent, and 22 per cent spoke of being in fights with boys from a different religion to themselves. Boys living in interface[4] areas reported the highest levels of sectarianism and spoke of regular incidences of violence in their communities. Across the sample all boys reported an increase in racial violence which they believed was characterised by the perceived increase in ethnic groups that had come to Northern Ireland, particularly post-Good Friday Agreement.

While the majority of boys spoke as victims of violence that left them feeling powerless, sad or angry, there were others who spoke openly of themselves as perpetrators of violence. These boys reported that being aggressive felt 'electrifying' and provided them with a sense of possessing 'high energy'.

Every single one of us have been involved in a riot. It's absolutely mad. There's no fighting like it. See when you're about 13 or 14 and you have about 50 boys in front of you and about 50 behind you, it's just brilliant. The adrenalin rushes, you chant a bit of abuse at each other and get stuck in. It's just brilliant.

From these boys' experiences three main themes were identified as to why they justified involvement in violent acts. The first was self-preservation:

If they think you are weak and you can't fight they will just push you around.

They talked of proving their manhood:

You wouldn't be seen as a man – people would call you a wee girl ... you gotta act tough.

They affirmed male social bonds and friendships:

If there's a fight you've gotta help your friends, if you don't then no one would want to be your friend.

This study also found that 74 per cent of boys considered the use of violence as an acceptable way to resolve issues. Generally it was found that boys who had experienced higher levels of violence were more inclined to use violence to resolve issues. Hitting a parent or a girl was considered the least acceptable form of violence:

You can't hit a wee girl. If you do other fella's get pulled into it when it's nothing to do with them. Like we were at this place and a wee girl was slobbering at this fella' and he said I don't want to fight you so get your brother down here and I'll fight him. She said no so he pulled her to the ground and took her phone and called her brother and told him to come down so he could fight with him.

Boys can't hit girls, that's the worst thing you can do. I saw my
   da' hitting my ma and that taught me never to hit a girl
   or a woman.
No you never hit a girl, that's terrible.
If a girl hits you, you feel so annoyed but you can't hit them back.

Homophobic attitudes were apparent throughout interviews and focus groups. In fact 40 per cent of boys reported that homophobic violence was acceptable and the fear of being perceived as gay influenced these boys' behaviour throughout the study:

> Only fruits back down.
> I don't like gays. But I wouldn't hit someone just because they're gay.

But there were also more tolerant voices:

> Gay just means wee lads that are more girly if you get me. Look, I've got no problems with gays. I know gay people who you wouldn't mess with.

Those boys who believed it was improper for men to hug each other accounted for 62 per cent. Those boys who did not adhere to hegemonic masculine stereotypes reported being the victims of homophobic bullying and isolation from their peer group and wider society.

In regard to their understanding of men and masculinity boys adhered to strict male stereotypes, yet were not taught how to fulfil these roles. As with their experiences of violence, this resulted in feelings of confusion, vulnerability and inadequacy as they strove to fulfil narrow stereotypical gender male roles. They worried about being unable to 'match up' to certain male images and believed if they could not demonstrate these masculine characteristics they would face derision, shame and ridicule.

Findings on the theme of masculinity included:

- 96 per cent of boys believing that a man should defend and provide for his family;
- 93 per cent believing a man should be a good father;
- 89 per cent believing a man must be able to defend himself.

From Harland (1997) to Beattie et al. (2006) the pattern appeared set. Young men living within a society in conflict are overly influenced in their thoughts and behaviour on the importance and role of violence in their lives. There were significant numbers of young men experiencing some form of violence in their lives, and this was perceived as normal. Strongly held views on the *traditional* role of men as breadwinners and defenders of community and family predominate. The lack of space and opportunity to reflect on their experiences of both violence and what it means to be a man was evident.

Stuck in the Middle (2009)

Trefor Lloyd from the Boys Development project in London worked as a consultant with the Centre for Young Men's Studies during 2009. During this time he carried out an extensive piece of research with 130 young men aged 13–16 from more than 20 areas and estates across both Catholic and Protestant urban and rural areas of Northern Ireland. This study was carried out as the Centre reflected on its work to date and the relationship between violence, conflict and safety and how these continued to emerge as being critical to young men's everyday lives and experiences. In particular the study was aimed at young men who were identified as being marginalised within their communities and wider society and whose voices were not typically included within current research findings. The main findings from this study included:

- conflict and violence impacted upon these young men's lives most days and their personal safety was a daily consideration;
- violence was perceived as 'just the way it is' and not out of the ordinary;
- once again we heard young men speak of 'getting a buzz from engaging in violence';
- weekends were when the likelihood of violence would occur and the consumption of alcohol was a significant contributing factor to this;
- sectarianism, someone's ethnicity and where they came from also emerged as important factors;
- young men reported that the police seldom entered their communities and most said that they would not report incidences of violence to the police who they perceived as ineffective and often hostile towards them;
- all young men reported that paramilitaries were still active in their communities and that views of them were mixed;
- police and paramilitaries were perceived as competing forces in their communities who 'stopped us doing what we wanted to do';
- young men were victims and perpetrators of violence and drawn to riots and other anti-social activities even if meant that they were only observers;
- as they got older they found that there were less organised activities available to them and there was a dearth of age-specific activities in

their areas that would be supervised by adults who could provide them with an alternative to the street;

- a key finding of this study was that very little appeared to have changed for these young men who appeared to be 'stuck' somewhere between ceasefires and a peace process.

Listening to the voices and experiences of boys and young men requires us to lay out the findings from our studies in a substantive way in order to bring the reader through the journey travelled by the authors. The 'Ethnographic Studies' (1997, 2000); Young Men and Violence (2002), the Pilot Study (2006); and Stuck in the Middle (2009) were critically important in shaping and informing the methodology, the direction and the momentum of our five-year longitudinal study (Harland and McCready, 2012). These findings will be presented in Chapter 2.

2

Taking Boys Seriously (2006–2012): A Longitudinal Study

A significant development for the Centre in 2006, in the form of a £141,000 grant from the Department of Education (Northern Ireland) and the Department of Justice (Northern Ireland), enabled us to undertake a longitudinal study to examine concerns about boys' academic attainment in school and wider concerns about the health and well-being of boys and increases in local suicide rates amongst young men.

Prior to the establishment of our Centre for Young Men's Studies in 2004, previous research into the lives of boys and young men in Northern Ireland was relatively scarce, and tended to focus on socio-economic conditions and how young people were particularly susceptible to psychological distress as a result of the Troubles (e.g. Trew, 1995). Also notably missing from academic studies was the actual voices of the boys and young men who were being investigated. Furthermore despite critical studies of masculinities being an important and growing part of global social enquiry, there has been a dearth of studies into masculinities and its association with violence in Northern Ireland (Ashe and Harland, 2014).

Ethical approval for all the work of the Centre for Young Men's Studies was approved by Ulster University's Research Ethics Committee. This is a rigorous process whereby Ulster expects the highest standards of integrity to be adhered to by its researchers. Governance of research is defined as: setting standards; defining mechanisms to deliver standards; monitoring and assessing arrangements; improving research quality and safeguarding the public (by enhancing ethical and scientific quality, promoting good practice, reducing adverse incidents, ensuring that lessons are learned and preventing poor performance and misconduct).

Building on the work of the previous research of the authors, 'Taking Boys Seriously' (Harland and McCready, 2012) followed the same cohort of 378 boys aged 11–16 from nine post-primary schools across Northern Ireland for each of the five years (2006–2011). We discuss this particular longitudinal study in detail as it was significant in shaping our thinking and conclusions about the practice of work with boys and young men and fundamental in creating a platform for their voices. The specific objectives of the research were to increase our understanding of:

- Factors that may contribute to concerns in regard to male academic attainment levels and finding practical ways to address this.
- The value of education and how school can become a more positive learning experience.
- Non-formal educational approaches.
- Male transitions through post-primary school; beyond post-primary school to higher education/work and factors that impact upon future employment aspirations; and transitions from boy to man.
- Experiences of violence in a post-conflict society.

These objectives were to be investigated through identifying and exploring factors that impacted upon the social, physical, psychological and emotional well-being of boys during their five-year experience of post-primary education. This required a methodological approach that would be true to the principles of the Centre and be suitable for addressing the different, but complementary, requirements of the funders.

From the outset, the Centre for Young Men's Studies placed firm emphasis on listening and responding to the voices of the boys who participated in this study. While we cannot know for certain what the boys told us of their feelings and their situations were true, we took a position of high trust within our process. Returning each year to the same group of boys and young men in the longitudinal study provided us with the opportunity to establish relationships within which we would listen to what they were telling us and also offering a challenge when necessary. Our focus was on giving recognition to 'what works' (as identified by boys themselves) and on looking to find practical ways that would enable them to develop to their full potential in school and in the other parts of their lives. Until now our previous research had been entirely qualitative. The longitudinal study enabled the development of a mixed and creative methodology utilising both quantitative and qualitative data. Nine schools from across Northern Ireland participated in the study. The sample of 378 boys consisted of two major religious groups, which averaged 54 per cent Catholic and 36 per cent Protestant and 10 per cent classifying themselves as 'Other'. The schools in the study were selected from the Department of Education schools database to include a mix of schools that were: Controlled (mostly Protestant), Maintained (mostly Catholic) or Integrated (mixed religion); urban or rural; grammar or non-grammar; co-education or single sex (all boys).

In order to inform the initial research topics, three distinct measures were put in place. Firstly, as highlighted above, a pilot study was carried out one year before the longitudinal study (Beattie et al., 2006a) with 299 boys aged ten across five primary schools who were entering post-primary school the following year to enable the research team to anticipate and identify issues and concerns they had. As well as school experiences, the pilot study informed the research team in regard to these boys' thoughts and experiences of school and violence. For example, boys offered reasons as to why they felt violence occurred, and the purposes served by aggression. In addition, their thoughts and expectations of manhood were sought as was their understanding of masculinity. This pilot study strongly illustrated the depth of complexity in regard to how boys understand and experience different forms of violence. It also demonstrated the normality of violence and exposure to violence in young boys' lives and the fact that from the age of ten they appeared to have constructed concrete ideas about men, masculinity and violence.

Secondly, the research team were advised by a 'gapper' who worked as a volunteer within the Centre for Young Men's Studies during the pilot study.[1] The 'gapper' influenced the research by suggesting areas for exploration including attitudes towards schooling and assisting with the design, content and analysis of the qualitative questionnaires and focus-group interview schedules.

Thirdly, 12 young men aged 16–22 from YouthAction Northern Ireland's 'Young Men's Forum' were invited to provide feedback and help steer the direction of the longitudinal study and research design. The young men came from a variety of backgrounds and were all involved as youth volunteers in a number of different communities. All group members had received training in working with boys as part of being a member of the forum. They also worked in their own communities as well as representing young fathers, individuals working with boys and young men at risk of anti-social behaviour, and those working with excluded boys and young men living in rural areas. The input from the Young Men's Forum enabled the longitudinal research questionnaires to reflect better the diverse range of young adolescent male experiences.

Over the years, we are often asked when carrying out research with boys and young men if it is better that an interviewer is male. Feedback from boys over the years has convinced us that the skills, qualities and knowledge of a researcher are more important factors than gender. From the beginning of our work, we consciously determined this would not be an all-male research team. The first research assistant within the Centre for Young Men's Studies was female. She worked on the pilot study for the longitudinal study and early questionnaire design and data collection. One of the focus group team was also female. Finally, an advisor throughout the project was female. This provided us with a necessary and valuable female perspective for our work in the Centre.

Methodology

Six questionnaires with different themes were used to collect the quantitative data each year of the study during one visit to each school in May or June:

- the About Me Questionnaire, which concerned background and family information;
- the KIDSCREEN Quality of Life Questionnaire for adolescents (Rajmil et al., 2004);
- the Strengths and Difficulties Questionnaire (SDQ) (Goodman, 1997) was used to assess emotional and behavioural issues;
- the Schools Questionnaire inquiring about school experiences, preferences and post-school aspirations;
- the Being a Man Questionnaire exploring perceptions of 'masculinity and what it means to be a man';
- the Violence Questionnaire seeking to understand how adolescent males conceptualise their perceptions and personal experiences of violence, being in trouble and bullying.

Quantitative data was supplemented by a number of qualitative approaches, including an average of ten focus groups held every year with an average of six to eight boys from six of the nine participating schools. Typically these focus groups concentrated on themes that were emerging from the quantitative questionnaires and enabled boys to discuss in more detail the broader contextual issues that impacted upon their lives and development. In-depth interviews were also held with six head-of-year teachers, each with over ten years teaching experience. An in-depth case study was also conducted in an all-boys post-primary school that was not participating in the longitudinal study. This school had been particularly successful in improving attainment levels amongst boys for a number of years in a catchment area that included a number of urban wards where unemployment, poverty, educational under-achievement and the effects of the Troubles had impacted for more than a generation.

Creatively engaging boys and young men in research

As part of the overall methodology, non-formal youth work interven-tions (this is explained in more detail in Chapter 5) were delivered three times per year in classrooms consisting of approximately 30 boys in two of the participating schools. This enabled the research team to take advantage of an experimental design that underpinned the initial research aims. These 'youth-work sessions' lasted two hours each time. Their purpose was to elicit how the themes emanating from the quan-titative questionnaires could be further explored through non-formal educational youth-work approaches and to increase the opportunities for the researchers to interact with the participating young men in the study. While the primary researchers, Harland and McCready, directed the research, members from YouthAction Northern Ireland's 'Work with Young Men's Unit' designed and led these classroom interventions based upon adaptations and methods that had previously been delivered and tested on adolescent males. These sessions involved small and large group work, work in pairs, kinaesthetic approaches, artistic expression, storytelling and role playing. All sessions were designed to encourage discussion and increase participation – through a methodology that encouraged safe risk-taking and personal disclosure from the boys – and were underpinned by a willingness of the workshop organisers to use experimentation.

Our earlier work had identified as significant the fact that boys and young men lacked space and opportunity to talk about and reflect upon their feelings about violence and about growing up as a man. We were determined that this research would provide that facilitated space and opportunity.

From year one of the study there was strong emphasis placed on a rela-tional approach to the boys (developed in Chapter 7) which encouraged honesty and trust building. This led to more in-depth issue-based inter-ventions in subsequent years focusing on increasingly complex aspects of adolescent development such as violence, conflict and safety issues and what it means to be a man. While masculinity was addressed as a specific theme in year one of the study, this focus underpinned sessions throughout the subsequent four years. The themes addressed in these sessions were:

- conflict and violence;
- masculinity and becoming a man;
- young men and emotions;
- personal safety and aggression;
- risk taking;
- education and learning;
- young men's health and well-being;
- male transitions and life skills.

From the outset, the approach was to push tables and chairs to the side of the classroom to introduce a non-formal aspect to the sessions and to allow for movement while doing icebreakers and energisers. Classes were also set up to be interactive and enable small group work, large circles and work in pairs. Teaching staff were encouraged either to take part in or observe the discussions in the working groups. In years three and four of the study, one of the schools moved the sessions to three mobile classrooms, which again were adapted to suit the type of sessions that were being delivered. Therefore, regardless of the setting, consideration was given to the physical learning environment.

The youth-work-style interventions demonstrated the value of taking time to build relationships with boys. The themes were intentionally connected to their everyday lives and the skills of the youth workers were focused on encouraging the boys to share feelings and emotions and engage with subjects at a deeper level. Boys who reported 'not being good at school work' often displayed other qualities during sessions which made them feel good about themselves. On occasions when this did happen youth workers reinforced the value of the boys' input. Feedback also revealed that boys looked forward to the sessions. They remembered the names of the youth workers and asked about those who were not attending on that particular day. They clearly enjoyed the content, were highly motivated and engaged actively with the subjects.

Feedback from the boys across the study about the process and purpose of the interventions was very positive. They really enjoyed the interactive style and liked the fact that icebreaker games were used to orientate them to the subject matter. They believed this broke up the intensity of the sessions and made learning more fun. It was consistently demonstrated that boys were highly motivated by interventions that combined energy, activity, creativity and fun to address issues. They also enjoyed learning by visualising situations rather than memorising information, which gave them a strong sense of personal achievement in contrast to learning solely through intellectual capabilities. The boys also believed that the sessions made school more connected to their actual lives and everyday experiences.

Boys reported learning new skills and thinking more about situations. Storytelling about 'other boys' was adopted to make controversial issues (e.g. violence, aggression, attitudes, alcohol misuse and behaviour) less personal, yet nevertheless something with which they could readily identify. The boys very quickly connected this to their own lives and experiences and were able to add their personal story to the scenario. This gave them a sense of control over content and increased their confidence to participate in class discussions. What was particularly striking was the way in which they listened attentively to the stories. For example, there was total silence as the storyteller outlined a scenario where young men were confronted with potentially violent situations. Each time the story reached a potentially threatening situation, the story was paused and boys were asked to break into small groups and consider what they would do in that situation. This methodology fully captured the imagination of the boys and led to intense class discussions. They were encouraged to think of the types of skills they could use to try and alleviate potentially violent situations. Skills development was a key outcome of the interventions.

While many boys noted the importance of schooling and qualifications they also reported frustration at the more formalised aspects of school such as: having to wear uniforms; the teaching day being too long and repetitive; expectations placed upon them being too high; some male teachers acting 'hard'; and 'teachers giving you the work but not teaching you the work'.

While throughout this longitudinal study there were occasional incidences of bravado and messing around, boys were enthusiastic and engaged actively in all aspects of the research. They applied themselves attentively when filling in questionnaires and became more measured in their responses each year. In focus groups, and in particular in the classroom interventions with youth workers, boys were willing to discuss sensitive and potentially controversial issues with honesty, openness and maturity. As they got older their thinking and understanding matured and deepened. It was also apparent that as these boys moved from one year to the next in the school they had formed strong and deeply held beliefs and opinions on many issues, and when asked or encouraged to speak, they had lots to say.

We believe that this relational-driven approach within 'Taking Boys Seriously', alongside creative and innovative quantitative and qualitative methods of data collection, played an important part in producing the richness of data we gathered. Having experts in working with boys and young men, as well as young men already engaged in their community, involved in the design and delivery of data collection, along with the results from a pilot study, were key factors in ensuring the research team stayed connected to the real life and developmental experiences of the boys and young men from whom we wanted to learn.

Data analysis

Quantitative questionnaire responses were uploaded and analysed using the 'Statistical Package for the Social Sciences', and data were investigated using the appropriate statistical tools. Each interview and focus group was taped using digital recording equipment, and then transcribed and analysed using Content Analysis to summarise the main contents of data and their messages (Cohen et al., 2011). Information from the youth-work-intervention sessions was collected through direct feedback from participants, materials produced by the participants on flip charts, researcher observation, the recorded documentation from the youth workers and direct verbal feedback from teachers. The analysis of data enabled the research team from year to year to reflect more deeply upon issues emanating from the questionnaires and identify themes for further investigation the following year.

Taking boys seriously: Overview of findings

Before we have a more focussed discussion on the findings of this longitudinal study, and in particular before we present a three-factor analysis model of masculinity and violence, we would like to make some general comments on the overall findings. This is to assist us in better understanding and appreciating the wider social-ecological context in which these boys lived. Table 2.1 highlights how percentages are used to present qualitative data from this longitudinal study.

Table 2.1 Key to the use of percentages within qualitative data

Minority	Less than or equal to 20% of boys
Significant minority	More than 20% but less than or equal to 50%
Majority	More than 50% but less than or equal to 80%
Significant majority	More than 80%

While the majority of these boys came from working-class backgrounds and socio-economic influences were critical factors, the sample also included boys from middle-class backgrounds. We would stress however that many of the issues raised by boys in this study were similar regardless of their community background or cultural traditions. We therefore would caution against any assumption that issues associated with boys and young men's lives, and in particular experiences and attitudes towards violence and masculinity, should be viewed as the preserve of working class and poor young men. Furthermore, we would highlight this as an important area for future study into violence and masculinities.

As boys got older, significant changes occurred with regard to how they perceived relationships with parents and their peers. From mid-adolescence in particular they increasingly desired a relationship with adults based on mutual respect and recognition of their own qualities and talents other than their educational capabilities. Boys also desired to be given more responsibility and to be more involved in decision-making processes that affect their lives and the society in which they live. This was particularly true in regard to peace-building processes in Northern Ireland. Not one boy in our study was involved in any type of peace-building activity, or spoke of being asked to participate in such activities. This subject was not addressed in school. Nor were these young men involved in any political debate about shaping the future of the society in which they lived.

- Physical changes over the five years were very apparent to the research team as these boys developed into young men. Rapid increases in size, shape, body hair and levels of maturity were very evident from year to year.
- Less apparent were the internal emotional pressures these boys experienced during early to mid-adolescence.
- Across all five years these boys consistently self-reported they were closer to their mother than their father. At age 16 almost half (41.8 per cent) of boys reported being closest to their mothers compared to 24.7 per cent reporting being closest to their fathers. Closeness to fathers did increase by 6 per cent across the five years in comparison to an 8 per cent increase in boys reporting closeness to their mothers.
- Across the study, boys also spoke of many school subjects being unconnected to the reality of their everyday lives and experiences and reported being easily distracted and lacking concentration in the classroom.

- Boys were ambivalent about seeking personal support and struggled to know what to do when they got into trouble.
- It is noteworthy that levels of misbehaviour amongst the boys dropped significantly across the years which contradicted many of the negative and alarmist stereotypes often directed at adolescent boys.

While the majority of boys reported feeling happy and healthy at school, the percentage of boys reporting 'abnormal' levels of 'hyperactivity' and 'conduct problems' was higher than the UK percentage norm (see Table 2.2).

Table 2.2 shows that in relation to the 'emotional' and 'peer relations' dimensions of the Strengths and Difficulty Questionnaire, the percentage of boys in the 'normal', 'borderline' and 'abnormal' categories remained relatively similar to the UK average. In contrast, a noticeably higher percentage of boys in the sample reported 'abnormal' levels of 'conduct' problems compared to the UK average, particularly in age 11–12. At the age of 15–16 the 'conduct' dimension more closely reflected the UK norm. The higher levels of abnormal conduct during early adolescence suggest that boys at this age may need a different and more creative approach to engage them in school than at the age of

Table 2.2 Comparison of the strengths and difficulties scores across years compared to UK norms

	Age School	Percentage of sample					UK norm percentage
		11 Year 8	12 Year 9	13 Year 10	14 Year 11	15/16 Year 12	
Emotional	Normal	92.5	90.7	90.8	94.3	93.4	91.0
	Borderline	3.8	4.8	4.0	4.1	3.9	5.7
	Abnormal	3.7	4.5	2.1	1.6	2.7	3.2
Conduct	Normal	60.7	58.4	60.4	71.5	76.5	74.6
	Borderline	12.2	16.2	14.8	11.1	9.3	11.9
	Abnormal	27.1	25.4	23.2	17.4	14.2	13.5
Hyperactivity	Normal	70.5	65.6	63.9	67.7	68.2	77.0
	Borderline	14.9	14.8	13.7	13.5	13.0	10.3
	Abnormal	14.6	22.7	20.3	18.8	18.8	12.6
Peer relations	Normal	85.8	82.0	85.2	87.0	84.4	89.2
	Borderline	10.5	12.6	9.0	9.2	11.7	9.3
	Abnormal	3.7	5.4	2.9	3.8	3.9	1.5
Pro-social	Normal	78.0	67.9	60.9	64.7	70.4	86.1
	Borderline	12.5	17.3	20.8	19.1	16.5	11.0
	Abnormal	9.5	14.9	16.2	16.2	13.2	2.8

15–16. It may be that conduct levels at this age are reduced because of boys naturally maturing, or perhaps they are becoming more focussed due to their perceiving the importance of school exams in regard to their future aspirations. If the latter is true, this suggests that adolescent boys benefit from approaches that have a clear and specific focus and are deemed important to their education and future careers. Either way it is noteworthy that during early adolescence certain boys in this study presented extremely high levels of abnormal conduct in comparison to UK averages.

There were also noticeably higher percentages of boys with 'abnormal' levels of 'hyperactivity' compared to the UK norm across Years 9 to 12. This suggests that certain boys in this study were displaying types of behaviour that would have a significant and perhaps negative effect upon their school experience and the value they place on education. Conversely, it could be that school does not stimulate these boys, or it is perceived by them as irrelevant, or unconnected to their lives, or that they cannot cope with the educational demands placed upon them. While hyperactivity levels did reduce during Years 11–12, they still remained much higher than UK averages.

Behaviour in school

Boys were asked to interpret and assess their own behaviour at school. When examining self-reported misbehaviour across the five years, findings revealed a significant reduction in misbehaviour levels amongst boys (see Figure 2.1). The 42.6 per cent of boys who said they had been misbehaving and got into trouble in the final year of post-primary school was noticeably lower than previous years, reflecting a continued

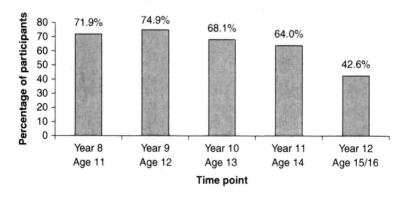

Figure 2.1 Levels of misbehaviour across the five years

downward trend in reported levels of misbehaviour across the years from 74.9 per cent in Year 9. This trend suggests that as adolescent boys mature they may be less likely to misbehave or get into trouble in school. These findings contradict the often negative perception of boys and young men that is portrayed in the media.

Personal safety

Boys' perceptions of their personal safety also shifted across the years. The insecurities and excitement boys initially felt about the transition from primary to post-primary school did not cause them too much concern, particularly when processes were in place to support this transition. In post-primary school, however, boys spoke of the playground being the place where they felt most insecure. They suggested having their morning and lunchtime breaks separate from older boys as they perceived most bullying and other forms of violence in school occurred during these times. They also suggested they would benefit from more opportunities for older boys to support and mentor younger boys in school and during playground breaks.

As in other findings from our previous research (Lloyd, 2009; Harland, 2011), boys spoke of feeling increasingly alienated within their communities and experiencing higher levels of suspicion and distrust directed towards them by adults. They also spoke of knowing and fearing members of paramilitary groups and having strained relationships with the police. While not all boys came into conflict with the police, they were perceived as 'distant and not welcome in our communities'. Another consistent finding from our previous work was the way in which boys perceived acts of violence as 'normal and acceptable' – an inevitable part of being male and male youth culture. However, what became more apparent and complex from this particular study was the judgement boys made in distinguishing between what constitutes bullying from an act of violence. Violent acts were viewed by boys as typically one-off incidences and therefore less traumatic than bullying, which can occur on a daily basis. While quantitative data analysis showed a reduction in reported incidents of bullying as boys progressed through school, in focus groups boys spoke of their need to feel safe and free from bullying in school. All boys agreed that being bullied was the most significant barrier to their education and learning. This issue was very important to them. The *blur* between different acts of violence was further complicated by what they perceived as 'messing around', which although it may result in injury, was accepted as part of everyday life.

The distinctions between acts of violence, bullying and messing around are further complicated by the location of acts of violence and the way in which these boys interpret where they feel safe. While boys believed school could be at times intimidating, and bullying and different forms of prejudice did occur, school was generally perceived as a safer place than their local communities. This was because school was perceived as providing boundaries and that teachers provided some form of discipline and order whereas what happened in their communities was much more unpredictable and uncontrolled.

Feelings about getting into trouble

Table 2.3 reveals how boys felt about being in trouble across the five years of post-primary school. Once again they could indicate more than one answer. Throughout the study the boys' most frequent response was 'I didn't care', which was an increase of almost 25 percentage points, culminating in over half the sample, indicating this choice in the final time point in Year 12. The second most frequent choice, which remained consistent across time points was, 'I just wanted to get it sorted out, just get it over with'. Notably, these most frequent choices are opposites, with 'I didn't care' interpreted as avoiding the trouble-related issues, while the other suggests that the boys wanted to tackle the problems directly and quickly.

The fact that so many boys have been in trouble, particularly during the formative years in post-primary school and the wide range of responses to this question, would suggest that interventions to help boys process and reflect upon misbehaviour and its consequences would be

Table 2.3 Feelings about being in trouble across the five years (%)

	Age 11 (Year 8)	Age 12 (Year 9)	Age 13 (Year 10)	Age 14 (Year 11)	Age 15/16 (Year 12)
I didn't care	30.8	43.0	39.6	34.4	54.4
I felt sad	10.2	19.0	9.8	6.3	7.1
Angry with myself	21.7	29.8	20.8	13.2	18.3
No-one to talk to	5.1	9.7	5.0	4.0	5.9
I felt stupid	15.9	31.8	22.7	15.1	24.9
I felt sorry	12.9	2.4	12.9	20.3	12.4
I felt scared	9.5	16.3	5.3	4.0	2.4
Wanted to get it sorted	24.7	32.2	25.3	20.6	37.9
I felt ashamed	11.5	18.3	8.4	6.9	7.7
Angry with someone	10.8	23.6	20.1	16.4	21.9
I felt good	5.4	8.9	4.5	2.4	3.6

beneficial to them and their schools. Addressing the consequences of misbehaviour could begin in Year 8 (age 11) and be reinforced during subsequent years. This would encourage boys to question and reflect upon certain types of behaviour and help them to appreciate better the benefits of talking to someone when they need support. This process may also enable boys to develop empathy towards others and explore practical and restorative ways to resolve conflict. Hence schools might reflect on their behaviour management policies and perhaps consider replacing them with relationship policies.

Boys seeking support

It should be noted that each school in this sample had appropriate and supportive pastoral systems in place, and boys consistently reported finding this service extremely beneficial. However, it should also be noted that not one boy admitted or recorded in questionnaires that they had gone to see a counsellor during the five years of the study in any of the schools that offered this particular service. They said they refused to use this service as they perceived it as revealing weakness and an inability to cope.

Boys were asked who they confided in when they got into trouble at school – they could select one or more answers (see Table 2.4). Across the five years the most commonly cited choices were friends and one or both parents. While the number of boys confiding in their mother and father increased across the years, the most significant increase was a shift towards confiding in a friend which almost doubled across the years. This suggests that during adolescence boys develop a different and more intimate relationship with friends than when they were in primary school. By the time they reached Year 11 (aged 15) friends had become

Table 2.4 Individuals who boys confided in when in trouble across the five years (%)

	Age 11 (Year 8)	Age 12 (Year 9)	Age 13 (Year 10)	Age 14 (Year 11)	Age 15 (Year 12)
Friend	16.3	19.5	23.7	31.6	31.3
Mother	22.4	28.9	29.6	28.9	28.2
Father	13.9	15.9	13.2	12.9	18.9
Parents	15.9	24.4	16.4	13.7	11.9
Teacher	5.4	2.9	2.1	0.8	1.3
Other family member	6.4	6.1	10.9	8.2	5.3
Professional	0.7	1.2	0.7	3.1	1.8

the most likely individuals they would confide in when they were in trouble. This does not mean that they confide less in their mother or father or both parents, just that they are more willing to share personal issues with others as well as parents. As this question focused on whom boys confided in when in trouble, responses may have been different if they had been discussing a different issue. It is worth noting that across the years boys' willingness to talk to adults other than parents about issues relating to being in trouble dropped considerably from Year 8 (aged 11) to Year 12 (aged 16).

Notably there was a significant decrease in the number of boys confiding in their teacher across the years, from 5.4 per cent in Year 8 (aged 11) to 1.3 per cent in Year 12 (aged 16). This is perhaps understandable as the focus of the question was boys getting into trouble in school and therefore participants may have been reluctant to discuss this with a teacher. However, because boys' liking for teachers did increase across the years, it would appear that as they mature they become more selective about the type of support they need from teachers and the types of relationships they expect from different individuals.

Relationships with teachers

A key finding, that was consistent across the sample and across all years, was that relationships with teachers were the most determining factor in regard to how well a boy believed he would do at school. This relationship was also powerfully associated with levels of motivation towards, and engagement with, the learning process. The majority of boys appreciated it when teachers took time to get to know them as individuals, showed interest in their lives outside of school, and treated them more like adults as they matured. For a significant minority of boys, relationships with teachers were typically strained and examples were given of how certain relationships broke down because of an incident of conflict that was unresolved at that particular time, or a belief that a teacher had 'over-reacted' to a situation. A minority of boys believed that once they had conflict with a teacher the relationship could not be maintained. However, this did not deflect from the overall desire that the majority of boys had to have a more positive relationship with their teacher. It was also apparent that the majority who had a conflict with a teacher were reluctant, or perhaps unwilling, to acknowledge their role in why the relationship may have broken down. In focus groups boys aged 14–16 became more reflective about the importance and value of their relationships with teachers, and even with those boys who had reported on occasions 'having difficulties with a particular teacher' there was an underlying sense of regret that this particular relationship had not developed, despite the conflict.

Throughout the study it was found that the nature of a boy's relationship with a teacher was closely correlated to the extent to which he liked and expected to do well in a particular subject. The relationship with a teacher also strongly influenced boys' levels of aspirations for the future. The stronger the relationship was with a teacher the more confident a boy felt about his future life and well-being.

The 3 Rs: relationships, respect and responsibility

As these boys matured through adolescence *relationships, respect* and increased opportunities to be given more *responsibility* became much more important to them. As in our previous studies boys perceived that teachers did not appreciate the different pressures of male youth culture and were 'out of touch'. Boys aged 12–14 reported frustration at still being treated like children rather than maturing adults. While these boys acknowledged that they were not quite adults, they appreciated the times when teachers and other adults treated them as if they were. They found it extremely patronising and disempowering when teachers, and other adults, did not consult with them or involve them in decision-making processes and believed that more recognition should be given to other qualities and abilities they possessed. A significant majority of boys felt strongly that teachers and other significant adults should make more effort to let boys know they are valued within school and treat their views, opinions and ideas with respect.

Relationships with peers also had an important influence on boys' behaviour and attitudes towards learning, particularly in the classroom. While the majority of boys appeared to appreciate 'having fun and banter' within their peer group, they expressed concern when teachers were unable to exercise control within the classroom. Teachers who could manage the classroom environment were perceived as the 'better teachers'.

Lowering of aspirations meets high expectations

Over the five years of the study there was a noticeable 'lowering of aspirations' in regard to the type of future boys expected, particularly if they did not believe they would attain the necessary academic benchmark qualifications at school. The majority of boys reported feeling unprepared for life beyond school. They desired skills that would help get them a job and be better prepared for the future, yet felt pessimistic about ever getting a job in a slowing economy during a time of savage government austerity cuts and high levels of youth unemployment. In focus groups, the majority of boys spoke of a dawning reality that 'even with academic qualifications you may not get a job'. It was noticeable that in Year 10 (aged 14) of our study the lowering of aspirations was most dramatic. It was at this point that low aspirations met high expectations as boys prepared to sit GCSE exams that they believed would ultimately determine their future options. Those boys who did not expect to get good grades questioned the very purpose of going to school for 12 years when they could potentially leave with no formal qualifications and therefore produce no evidence whatsoever of ever having been in school.

Constructing masculinities: A three-factor analysis

Studying the lives of adolescent boys for five years generated an enormous amount of data which needed to be analysed and ultimately disseminated to others. In the following sections we delve deeper into two core areas of the longitudinal study and indeed of this book – boys' experiences of violence and their expectations of masculinity and becoming a man. We would like to note that from the beginning of the longitudinal study we were guided by our previous research findings which had identified that research on masculinity, particularly in Northern Ireland, was light. Therefore we constructed one self-reporting questionnaire that focused specifically on the theme of 'What is a man?' (see Appendix 1). Using a Likert Scale (rated on a range of 0 for strongly disagree to 5 strongly agree), the 20-item questionnaire aimed to identify attitudinal change and the pressures adolescent males may experience in regard to their perceptions of becoming a man through each of the five years of the study. We then asked boys each year to rate the items which would enable us to group the items into clusters. From these we developed our own language for interpreting boys' beliefs about what it means to be a man. From this a *three-factor masculinity* analysis was developed and the clusters were labelled 'hegemonic', 'duty' and 'dissonance'.

- **Factor one: hegemony.** Representing a type of normative masculinity associated with competitiveness, toughness, aggressiveness and wealth. This reinforces male power and domination over women and other more subordinate masculinities that conform to the idea of a generic (stereotypical), dominant or exclusive masculine typology. These correspond to an idealised, self-oriented, stereotyped male image as may be portrayed by the popular media. As such, they are simple, unambiguous attributes that connect to powerful core emotions. Factor one contains items which are most salient to a boy's mental view of 'what a man is' and relate to assertiveness, competitiveness, success and power.

- **Factor two: duty.** Representing a type of masculinity associated with men being responsible, having moral and ethical standards and a sense of duty to the family and community, demonstrating caring traits and acceptance of others who are different. This implies moral importance in the construction of becoming a man and as such would not be concrete or easily observable constructs but more abstract and hidden or latent. Being based in more complex, abstract values, these would require more personal reflection, perhaps dependent on the presence of strong family relationships or role models such as a father, mother, brother or other male, but would be less easy to communicate with other peers, though perhaps not having the language to express themselves well enough (hence could inadvertently be complicit with dominant notions of masculinity). These values are less easy to articulate and may not be readily observed in young boys and even suppressed by the need to conform to the dominant masculine behaviour displayed in their localities.

- **Factor three: dissonance.** Representing a type of masculinity that is more uncertain, controversial and with identity-challenging attributes that present emotional challenge or threat through contemplations such as 'a man hugging another man', 'a man being someone who shouts', 'a man is lonely' and a man 'has a boyfriend'. As such, these would be viewed as attributes that would be at odds with the idea of manhood as suggested by factors one or two. Boys who verbalise or display such views may find themselves ridiculed by others who conform to the dominant stereotype. Factor three does not represent hegemony or homophobia, but rather the uncertainty or threat that leads boys and young men to reject these items as viable masculine attributes.

Findings around masculinity

During early adolescence aged 11–13, irrespective of school type, association with hegemonic masculinity, as outlined in factor one, was relatively high across the whole sample, with the majority of boys believing that men should for example be dominant, aggressive, a good fighter, competitive, powerful, heterosexual and able to stand up for themselves. At this age boys appeared readily to accept and reinforce masculine stereotypical notions of men and openly display homophobic attitudes. Those who scored high in hegemony also displayed higher levels of misbehaviour and were more inclined to be perpetrators of violence and conflict. In contrast, those boys with low misbehaviour levels also self-reported the lowest levels of hegemony. Boys from all-boys schools displayed higher levels of hegemony than boys in co-educational schools. This would suggest that when boys are in all-male company hegemony levels are highest and consistent and these boys are much more likely to reject other masculine types or association with femininity.

By mid-adolescence some of the male stereotypes held by boys became less acceptable to them and increased thought was given to the more intellectual, abstract and moral themes of masculinity, which are not determined by stereotypes. Our findings show that as these boys matured they began to challenge some of the behaviour and stereotypical hegemonic attitudes they had formed during early adolescence.

Figure 2.2 shows that while hegemony levels decreased across the years, duty remained a strong and consistent element of being a man across all years, suggesting that a man having moral and ethical responsibility and providing for his family was important to these boys throughout adolescence. This suggests that moral and ethical development has been firmly established in these boys during pre-adolescence and is firmly cemented during early to mid-adolescence. Figure 2.2 further shows a significant increase in dissonance levels up to Year 4 of the study (age 15) with a slight dip towards Year 3 (age 13), with

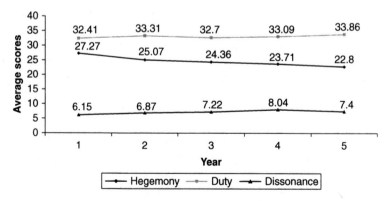

Figure 2.2 Mean plot showing change in 'hegemony', 'duty' and 'dissonance' levels across the five years

the average level in the final time point Year 5 (age 16). These scores indicate a moderately high level of dissonance – that is uncertainty and confusion about the more controversial, identity-challenging factors about what it means to be a man. This suggests that during early adolescence these boys become increasingly confused/uncertain about particular aspects and expectations of male behaviour. The increase in dissonance levels up to Year 4 (age 15) of the study suggests that up to mid-adolescence boys appear to struggle with male behaviour that is contrary to the typical masculine hegemonic stereotype. The dip in dissonance levels in Year 5 (age 16), however, suggests that as these boys approached late adolescence their views had broadened and they presented a more maturing attitude about controversial and identity challenging aspects of being a man.

So, in relation to hegemony, there were higher levels when:

– it was an all-male environment;
– there was lower academic motivation;
– there were higher levels of misbehaviour.

The more hegemony was present:

– the less likely there would be change in the young man during mid-to late-adolescence;
– the more likely they would be in trouble with the law and/or paramilitaries;
– the more they lacked direction and support.

There was a general trend for boys' increasing dissonance in the sample irrespective of academic motivation/preference and misbehaviour levels. In Year 1 those boys with low academic motivation/preference or low levels of misbehaviour had the lowest dissonance levels at Year 5, suggesting they had constructed narrower (hegemonic) perceptions of what it means to be a man. Those boys with high levels of misbehaviour and high academic motivation/preference groupings had the highest dissonance levels.

Findings reveal the extent to which boys' understanding of what it means to be a man during adolescence is complex, negotiated and renegotiated according to age and other social factors. What is not clear is how the school and its curriculum influences, assists or enables them to reflect upon the movement between hegemony, duty and dissonance. Evidence from this study suggests that from early to mid-adolescence, boys are capable of at least beginning to consider the kinds of issues, values and beliefs that are important to their future development as responsible young men who have begun to process complex and emotionally challenging issues. Findings further suggest that perceptions of masculinity can and do shift over time and that the nature of becoming a man becomes more complex during mid- to late-adolescence as boys begin to form their own, rather than predefined, stereotypical masculine identities.

Understanding these complexities will enable educators to make better connections between the different types of behaviour that may be evident amongst boys. For example, the pressures boys feel to be seen as 'cool' or 'able to stand up for themselves' amongst their peers. Fear of being 'shamed' or 'put down' in front of their peers may also help to explain why a boy will 'stand up' to a teacher. These internal pressures are strong motivators for understanding adolescent male behaviour and point towards reasons why many boys willingly 'mask' their true feelings and emotions.

As boys mature their understanding of what it means to be a man changes. So for example, if a boy behaves or holds certain attitudes in early adolescence, this does not necessarily mean he will continue to behave this way during mid- to late-adolescence. This maturing aspect of male development can be overlooked, which means that certain boys may be ascribed negative labels that they find difficult to remove as they get older. In addition, as boys mature they look for and expect a different type of relationship with adults, one that acknowledges that boys can, and do, change during adolescence.

Findings from qualitative questionnaire data on men and masculinity

Throughout the longitudinal study, boys in focus groups consistently spoke about the pressures and confusion of moving away from childhood behaviours to becoming, and being accepted as, young men. As they matured they felt increasing frustration when they attempted to engage maturely with adults through conversations, contesting, questioning, taking risks and accepting consequences, yet felt they were still treated as children. When parents and teachers trusted and respected boys, they believed this strengthened those relationships. Boys also responded extremely positively to being given freedom within the parameters of a secure and supportive setting (i.e. school and the family home). For these boys becoming a man was not defined by a timeline or rite of passage. Rather it represented a time when adults would treat them as young adults and show them respect. These comments are from 15-year-old boys:

> We don't like being treated like children, that really
>   annoys us.
> You want to be treated with respect and trusted
>   more as you get older.
> Being a man is about taking responsibility and standing
>   up for what's right – but you need to be given
>   responsibility and trusted to do things right.

Changing patterns of masculinities

Our findings suggest that the construction of masculinity can be seen as a developmental process where young males are active agents in the development of their own constructions of personal and social masculinities that are shaped by a complex mix of biological and social-ecological factors. Importantly however, if we acknowledge that masculinities are socially and locally constructed, then there must be conditions under which they can change. Our findings reveal a complex and shifting analysis by boys and young men of their understanding of masculinity and what it means to be a man. This is an important consideration because, as Moller (2007) explains, men's practices and motivations are often much more complex than the concept of hegemonic masculinity allows.

Perceptions of violence questionnaire

As with the masculinity data, a self-reporting questionnaire was designed whereby boys were asked to rate a series of aggressive acts from a list where three separate factors were derived concerning how violence and violence related acts were perceived (see Appendix 2):

- The first factor suggested physical forms of violent acts such as punching, hitting, pushing and kicking as well as shouting and calling others rude names. These are labelled 'physical verbal' acts of aggression.
- The second factor characterised 'non-physical' violent actions such as ignoring, spreading rumours, spitting, texting, threatening and damaging others belongings. These are labelled 'verbal/demeaning' acts of violence.
- The third factor related to the most violent actions that are characterised by the use of weapons, stabbings, bullying and smacking a child. These are labelled 'extreme/aggressive violence'.

Comparison of violent action-related issues across years

Table 2.5 reveals that across the years:

Table 2.5 Prevalence of self-reported violent incidents committed against boys across the five years (%)

	Age 11 (Year 8)	Age 12 (Year 9)	Age 13 (Year 10)	Age 14 (Year 11)	Age 15/16 (Year 12)
Violent acts committed against them	74.6	84.4	80.9	74.9	72.3
Did not talk about violent incident	48.8	46.9	44.1	68.9	66.8

- An average of 73 per cent of boys reported that a violent act had been committed against them.
- The majority of boys, reporting high levels of violence directed towards them, scored low in academic motivation/preference and high in levels of misbehaviour.
- Those boys who reported at least one act of violence against them, the majority reported low levels of academic motivation/preference (57.5 per cent).
- Of those who had violent acts perpetrated against them, a relatively large proportion of them did not talk to anyone about the incidents. This was particularly high in the final two years of the study at age 15 (68.9 per cent) and age 16 (66.8 per cent), suggesting that as adolescent boys get older they are more reluctant, or find it more difficult, to talk to someone when they experience being the victim of a violent act. This may be due to perceived cultural norms whereby males are not supposed to show weakness. Conversely, it may be that boys believe certain forms of perceived violent acts are accepted as part of normal adolescent male experience.

Boys' perceptions of violence and bullying

Boys differentiated between what constitutes a violent act and bullying. For the majority of them violent acts were viewed as less traumatic than bullying:

- Bullying was primarily perpetrated by a proportionately small minority of boys (12 per cent) on a relatively small number of boys (11.1 per cent).

- Throughout all of our previous studies and similarly in this longitudinal study, boys reporting being victims or perpetrators of bullying consistently averaged between 10 and 13 per cent.
- Boys reporting being a victim of violent acts over the five years was consistently higher, averaging at 73 per cent.
- In further investigation of this trend with boys in focus groups we discovered that judgements and distinctions were being made between bullying and acts of violence. It was evident that boys struggled to differentiate between acts of violence and acceptable levels of 'messing around' which, although it may result in injury, was perceived as an acceptable and normal part of everyday life for these adolescent boys.
- Whereas bullying was perceived primarily as unacceptable in school, 'messing around' was considered as both an acceptable and normal aspect of school life.
- When boys spoke of certain factor one types of violent acts in school this was typically described as 'messing around'. However, when boys spoke of factor one types of violence in their community this was typically perceived as violence.
- When boys spoke of factor two and factor three types of violence these were typically described as more personally threatening and potentially dangerous types of violence. However, once again there was complexity and confusion as some demeaning acts were also perceived by boys as 'messing around' while others perceived such acts as 'extremely violent'.
- Similarly to masculinity, as boys progressed through adolescence more considered thought was given to violence and its place in their lives. During early adolescence, at ages 11–13, a significant minority of boys spoke of 'getting into fights and being picked on by older boys'. These boys expected there to be times when they would get 'picked on' and appeared to accept that this is what happens when you go to 'big' school. They spoke of being a victim of verbal/demeaning abuse at times which they found difficult to resolve. However, once again boys were unclear of the boundaries in regard to whether the perpetrators of such acts viewed this as healthy 'male banter' or purposeful acts of violence. It was clear, however, that this type of violence caused victims much concern.

From our findings it was very apparent that boys are left to their own devices, or the influences of more sinister forces, to discover and negotiate how they should respond to different acts of violence. While the majority of boys had no specific way or indeed awareness of how to respond to acts of violence, they spoke enthusiastically about their need to learn avoidance strategies and skills that would help them cope with the threat of violence. Distinctions between acts of violence, bullying and messing around were further complicated, however, by the location of perceived acts of violence and the way in which these boys interpret where they feel safe. While violent incidents and messing around did occur primarily at school, boys perceived school as a relatively safe place in comparison to their community.

Boys views on the location of violence

Concerns about the nature and location of violence became more of an issue for these boys as they got older. Consistently, they described their homes and schools as relatively safe and their own communities often as being unsafe. There was acknowledgement that while certain types of violence did occur in school, the fact that there were teachers, school rules with clear boundaries, as well as punitive forms of discipline for perpetrators, they felt more secure in school. Boys across the study and from all school types reported that paramilitaries were still active in both sides of the community. As in our previous studies, a minority of boys saw paramilitaries as a positive force in their community, while a significant majority said they were 'harassed and threatened' on a regular basis, particularly by older boys representing paramilitary groups. Boys reported knowing who these young men were and where they lived and were able to talk about the types of threats paramilitaries made towards them. Stories were told of how they were encouraged to join paramilitary organisations and verbally threatened if they refused. They also spoke of boys they knew who had been victims of paramilitary punishment beatings and being 'kneecapped'. They also spoke of concerns about older young men in their communities who offered drugs to them.

While boys spoke of their communities as often being unsafe, they also spoke of a reluctance to travel outside of these communities. However, as in previous studies, there were a minority of boys who spoke of times when they went into other areas looking for conflict and viewed this as 'a bit of fun'. These boys spoke openly of being perpetrators and instigators of violence within their own and other communities which included:

- getting into and starting fights;
- being drawn to riots;
- their involvement in sectarian attacks;

- throwing stones at passing cars;
- getting 'high' and taking away and driving stolen cars;
- organising gang fights through social media.

For these boys, engaging in such activities provided them with a 'buzz' which they defined as a mixture of excitement and fear. They acknowledged that they were perceived by people in their communities as 'anti-social'. While there was clearly bravado in how these boys described some of their behaviour, their vulnerability was very apparent. In particular these boys spoke of receiving threats and, on occasions, after several warnings, actually being a victim of paramilitary justice. They spoke of ongoing conflict with the police whom they perceived as 'always giving us hassle'. Typically these boys did not perceive themselves as doing well at school and reported frequently getting into trouble with teachers. They also spoke of their concerns about the future, particularly in relation to gaining employment.

Throughout this longitudinal study boys spoke of feeling alienated from their communities and distant from the world of adults and decision-making processes which is consistent with our previous studies. Despite this disconnect, boys sought acceptance into the community and the adult world, but were unaware of any processes that enabled this to happen.

From 1997 through to 2015 the authors have been engaged in various research programmes and interventions with boys and young men that provide the database for this book. These first two chapters have followed their journey and documented the various processes and approaches in collecting this data as well as some of the key findings.

Looking ahead

The next three chapters will examine the literature, research and under-pinning theory in regard to violence (Chapter 3) and masculinities (Chapter 4) and education and learning (Chapter 5). These chapters aim to provide a deeper understanding of the wider social-ecological context in which boys and young men live and exist.

In order to reflect the primary aim of the Centre for Young Men's Studies, we will return to the voices of boys and young men in Chapter 6 where we will present our latest data from the composite voices of young men from our 2015 study.

Chapter 7 will discuss and explore practice with boys and young men and in particular will present a 'balanced approach' that aims to make stronger connections between young men and their communities and education and learning. This chapter will also offer some practical considerations for educators and practitioners to consider in their work with boys and young men.

3
Research with Boys and Young Men: Critical Reflections on the Theme of Violence

Defining violence

Definitions of violence can be vague and ambiguous, tending to revolve around the specific types of problem behaviour with which a particular organisation or project is concerned. The World Health Organisation (WHO, 2014) defines violence as 'the intentional use of physical force or power, threatened or actual, against oneself, another person, or against a group or community that either results in or has a high likelihood of resulting in injury, death, psychological harm, mal-development, or deprivation'. The first World Report on Violence and Health (WHO, 2002:4) divided violence into three broad categories according to who commits the violent act:

- self-directed violence, in particular self-harm and suicide;
- interpersonal violence which involves family/partner;
- collective violence, a categorisation that differentiates between violence a person inflicts upon himself or herself, violence inflicted by another individual or by a small group of individuals, and violence inflicted by larger groups such as states, organised political groups, militia groups and terrorist organisations.

Dictionary definitions of violence typically refer to 'the use of great physical force', which does not take into account any aspect of either emotional or threat factors, or relate to any damage or injury that may result from this force. For example, there is confusion in distinguishing aggression from violence. While violence is defined as a threat or use of physical force that causes physical injury, damage to or intimidation of another person, aggression is a broader concept, involving efforts to harm or control another person. Some forms of aggression employ physical force while others do not, and some forms seem less concerned with harming than with controlling another person (Lawson, 2005:5).

What is perhaps missing from these definitions is the extent to which more subtle and harmful forms of violence and exploitation are being perpetrated upon young people. Compared with previous generations, young people today face additional personal risk through increased access and exposure to technology. While the internet and other digital content, such as chat rooms, have created great opportunities for advances in growth, development and communication, they have also increased the potential for more sinister types of violence such as cyberbullying, trolling and online sexual exploitation through activities such as 'grooming'. Between 2011 and 2012 young people aged 13–14 represented the largest percentage (35 per cent) of victims of online sexual exploitation, with 80 per cent being female victims in all reports (Child Exploitation and Online Protection Centre, 2013:11). A survey of almost 25,000 European children and young people found that whilst only 50 per cent of those surveyed recognised risks online, which is concerning in itself, one-fifth of respondents cited having been exposed to potentially harmful content (Livingstone et al., 2014:272).

Violence: A global concern

Few reading this book will disagree that the subject of violence is both a concerning and disturbing aspect of modern societies. We are particularly shocked when we hear of young people suffering as victims of violence, but we are similarly shocked when we hear of young people as perpetrators of violence. This section of the book provides a brief consideration of trends of international violence. This is not meant to be an analysis of conflict between countries, but a reflection upon how the local contexts in which young people grow up affects their lives, experiences and attitudes. We will see, later, how the local context of over 40 years of conflict in Northern Ireland, and the drive towards peacebuilding in a post-conflict society, significantly shapes and influences the everyday lives of young people, and in particular boys and young men from working-class and inner-city areas.

When presenting data on violence and political conflict it is important to be aware of the fact that official statistical analysis and surveys can be highly inaccurate. We also know that many incidents of crime, war and violence go unreported and, depending on where data is collected, each 'different set of statistics can tell divergent stories' (Furlong,

2013:189). The WHO (2002:7) highlights how 'rates of violent deaths vary according to country income levels with rates of violent death in the low-to middle-income countries being more than twice as high as those in high income countries'. It reveals, however, that the overall rates of violent deaths conceal wide variations. For example,

in the African Region and the Region of the Americas, homicide rates are nearly three times greater than suicide rates, whereas in South-East Asia and European Regions, suicide rates are more than double homicide rates, and in the Western Pacific Region, suicide rates are nearly six times greater than homicide rates. (p. 7)

Despite obvious limitations, statistical information provides extremely useful contextual insights into understanding global and local patterns and types of violence and violence related behaviour.

In the First World Report on Violence and Health, the WHO (2002:2) stated that 'no country or community is untouched by violence and because it is so pervasive, violence is often seen as an inevitable part of the human condition'. Violence is therefore a universal problem (Krauss, 2006) with youth violence presenting a huge challenge and cost to societies around the world. Globally, interpersonal violence impacts upon millions of people each year and this is exacerbated by intra- and inter-state conflict which impacts upon whole populations, presenting huge psychological and socio-economic costs to the populations it affects. Indeed the trauma of violence and loss can continue to affect victims for many years after the defined conflict.

Since the end of World War II, there have been almost 300 armed conflicts, most of which have been intra-state (Themner et al., 2012:566). Akin to the statistical patterns related to interpersonal violence, global conflicts appear to, in many ways, mirror these trends with a spike in activity in the early 1990s, followed by a gradual decline in the number of reported conflicts during the early years of the new millennium, followed by a trajectory which denotes a rise in armed conflict (Harbom et al., 2006). Indeed, since 2010 this appears to have significantly increased, partly due to what has been commonly coined the 'Arab Spring' (Allansson et al., 2012): the collective community and grass-roots' action aimed at challenging existing power structures in the Arab world. In the year that followed the Arab Spring (2010–2011) there was almost a 20 per cent increase in armed conflict (Themner et al., 2012) on the previous year. Like the conflicts reported on by Themner et al. (2012), many are protracted or appear to ebb and flow, dissipate or escalate, particularly those which are intra-state and often fought along ethno-religious lines. These authors note that in 2012 there were 32 armed conflicts in 26 locations worldwide which is, in fact, a relatively low level in the context of the post-World War II period (p. 509). Of these 32 active conflicts, 31 were fought within states (p. 510).

A United Nations report (February, 2015) estimates that since the conflict erupted in Ukraine in April 2014 more than 5,486 people have been killed and 12,972 injured with 5.2 million people estimated to be living in conflict areas. Conflicts continue in Palestinian and Israeli territories which ripple throughout the Middle East and indeed the Western world. Pre-dating the establishment of the Israeli State in 1948, the conflict currently centres on two very polarised positions. On one hand, the Palestinian people have struggled for an independent state, initially during the Turkish Ottoman occupation of the area which now includes the state of Israel, later during the British occupation of the land, as well as Jordanian (West Bank) and Egyptian (Gaza Strip) rule, and currently under the Israelis who brokered an international deal to secure an independent state following the pogroms against the Jews during World War II. The Israeli perception, however, is that they, as a small state surrounded by other states overtly opposed to them, must defend their existence and have the right to challenge that opposition in whichever form it takes. With strong military might, Israel over recent years has responded violently to what it perceives as a threat to its security. During 2014, the huge military onslaught on Gaza was predicated upon a moral right to protect its people and resources and prevent missiles being launched from the refugee camps into the Israeli state. Regardless of the historical accuracies or contemporary paradigms, what has been verified in that region is the death of countless people, the destruction of basic utilities and infrastructures and what appears to be a disregard for human rights. This trauma, akin to that experienced during many conflicts, impacts greatly on the populations well beyond the completion of a military exercise, preparing generation after generation to take up arms willingly in the name of basic rights and defence. Whilst there are no verified statistics following the 2014 incursion into Gaza, it is estimated that one in five Gazan youths have experience of losing a family member as a direct result of the conflict and that as many as two-thirds of young Gazans have reported to have been shot at least once (Barber, 2008:301). More recent figures estimate that 99.8 per cent of young people living in conflict territories indicate that they had witnessed community violence (Haj-Yahia et al., 2013:2225).

Many studies have documented the effects of war and violence on children and young people across the world (Muldoon, 2004; Reilly et al., 2004; Barber, 2008; Haydon and Scraton, 2008; Schubotz and Devine, 2008; McAlister et al., 2009; Werner, 2012; Bernard van Leer Foundation, 2014; Browne and Dywer, 2014). Barber (2008) has critiqued the complexities in understanding ethno-political conflict and violence in Bosnia and Palestine and how this became a critical aspect in the formation of a child's identity. Dubow et al. (2010:104) exploring exposure to conflict and violence across contexts found that the way in which children were impacted upon by ethno-political violence depended significantly on 'a child's social ecology (the child's family, peer group and larger society) and the attributions the child made about violence'. These authors further argue that while 'the social environment is a serious and significant risk factor for the development of psychopathology in children and adolescents', relatively less research has investigated 'the cumulative or unique effects of specific forms of violence at multiple ecological levels' (p. 103).

Whilst each conflict is premised upon its own nuances and intricacies which can make sense in the context and culture within which it occurs, there are patterns which appear to be similar as core components of conflict and that include notions of justice, power, control and access to what are perceived as basic resources (food, education, health-care and employment). Whilst it is not always necessary or sufficient to have each of these components in place as a catalyst for conflict, South Africa pre- and indeed post-apartheid had many of these features. Combatants, who used armed struggle for decades to challenge the apartheid regime and fight for civil and political equality, used the gun as a means to address the inequalities (Maringira, 2014). The South African experience tells us how young people grew up in militarised communities, fighting a well-defined foe, having access to weapons and an identity akin to the 'warrior hero' (Woodward, 2000). Young people in South Africa, as in Northern Ireland, during the conflict had a place and position with defined roles and responsibilities (Cock, 2001; Harland and McCready, 2007). With negotiated settlements come the challenges of changing conflict-orientated paradigms and transforming what was normal into a new normal where identities so previously bound with conflict must be renegotiated (Woodward, 2000; Ashe and Harland, 2014). In South Africa, almost two decades following the introduction of democratic rule, these identities continue to be blurred. Communities where combatants lived can still hold a degree of respect, having evolved roles in mediating community based disputes. However, the paradigm challenges for the individual extends to the community. For example, in areas of South Africa communities can perpetuate conflict identities by setting expectations for ex-combatants and providing them with 'peace time' roles such as the settling of community disputes; but implicit are also expectations that 'mediators can and will employ force if perceived as necessary, both to maintain peace and perpetrate community justice' (Maringira, 2014:7).

So integrated are psychologies of aggression in South Africa that broader society continues to ponder what has fundamentally changed in regards to exposure to violence and crime. South Africa continues to have one of the highest violent crime rates in the world (Parkes, 2007:402). Official statistics for recorded crime, covering the period 2012–2013, suggest that violent crime has increased for the first time in six years with incidents of murder rising by 5 per cent (or two more murders per day, taking the toll to 45 per day from 43, which is four and a half times the global average); attempted murder charges have risen by 10 per cent and the number of sexual offences has risen by almost 2000 more reported cases (Africa Check, 2013).

Parkes (2007) attempted to understand young people's experiences of violence in the context of South African culture through a study of young people attending primary school in a working-class urban setting. Some of the most striking outcomes of the study were that young people, whilst exposed to much violence and aggression, had complex ways of understanding and making sense of those experiences and risks: 'who enacted the violence, where it took place, the outcomes and the perceived intentions each influenced the multiple ways in which children understood violence' (Parkes, 2007:406). When aggression was perceived as necessary or justified, it was not necessarily defined as violent; where aggression was objectively considered more serious (such as rape and murder) it was often perceived as unjustified. What was common throughout the study was a continuum of justified and illegitimate violence which served to position young people both as perpetrators and resisters of violence in their everyday lives depending on the situation, context and audience. What was also true was a trajectory of increased risk as the social arenas become more fluid and proximity to violence increases.

In Eastern Europe, war raged during the early 1990s in Bosnia. During the intense civil war it was estimated that 100,000 people lost their lives and almost 50 per cent of the total population were displaced (O'Loughlin, 2010). Ignited by an ethnic dispute over territory and polarised opinion around the future of the Yugoslavian Republic, the war continued for three years until the United States facilitated a peace agreement (Barber, 2008:299). During those few years, however, the impact on life was pronounced with almost one-third of young people, who engaged in a comparative study of violence in Bosnia and Palestine, reporting having their home destroyed during the conflict. Forty per cent of young people also reported having lost a family member during the war (ibid.: 301). Despite the US brokered Dayton Accords and the massive financial and aid mission of the United Nations, the European Union, NATO and other external agencies following the truce, evidence of improved community relations is scant (O'Loughlin, 2010). In the decade that followed, the UN reported their concern for the region that came after a period of political and social change (United Nations Development Program, 2006), while Fagan (2005) argued that the failure to secure a sustainable peace in Bosnia following the conflict was a result of a failure to transform the mentality of the population. As an ethnic war premised on mutual fear, distrust and resentment (Kaufmann, 2001) it has been asked, if the causes of the conflict are based on engrained and enduring social norms, whether these really can be transformed post-conflict (Whitt, 2012). A basic requirement for sustained peace and community transformation is then based on a society that recognises its needs and has the capacity to change social norms (Varshney, 2001). A recent US State Department report, monitoring social developments in Bosnia, disclosed a variety of criminal problems, some born of the civil war, which has flooded the streets of Sarajevo with military grade weapons and that are now accessible to criminal gangs (United States Department of State, 2013).

The focus of this book is on young men and violence, and while it is clear that violence is a global concern the impact of violence on young people, and in particular young men, requires closer examination. With wars and civil wars come the legacies of armed conflict and its impact on combatants and non-combatants alike. The heavily masculinised, militarised arenas of war can lead to a valorising of the heroes, mostly male, and, in the case of the Northern Ireland conflict, lives are lived within an armed patriarchy and gendered ethnic order. The inheritance for young men post-Troubles is the association of men with physical force and hyper-masculinities and confirmation of normative gendered identities. But is violence a male problem?

Violence: A male problem?

'Men's violence represents a huge problem world-wide' (Pringle, 2007:613) and is 'one of the most massive global social problems'

(Pringle and Pease, 2001:246). The WHO (2007) cites several risk factors that contribute to the likelihood of becoming a victim of violence. Being male is the most predominant, with young men (15–29) accounting for three-quarters of all victims of homicide globally. This trend is reflected in the findings of many studies investigating community violence (Haj-Yahia et al., 2011). A review of youth violence by the WHO Media Centre (2015) further found that, worldwide, 200,000 homicides occur among young people aged 10–29 and, although rates vary between countries, young males in every country constitute the majority of perpetrators and victims. From 222 countries across the world, figures show that the United States has the highest incarceration rates with men typically accounting for over 90 per cent of those in prison, with an overwhelming majority being young males (International Centre for Prison Studies, 2013). Findings from the United States suggest that, while young women and young men both perpetrate violence, distinctions exist around the context in which it is perpetrated, with young men more likely to use violence and abuse instrumentally and young women to use violence defensively (McCarry, 2007:18). Regardless of intent or motivation, statistics have shown a worrying trend in the United States with significantly increased rates of serious violence compared to the last half of the 20th century with estimates that some 100,000 school children arrive at school armed with weapons (Heilbrun et al., 2005).

Muncie (2015:31) contends that men account for 'nine out of every ten people guilty of indictable offences and are responsible for 92 per cent of convicted cases against the person'. Statistics in Western societies consistently reveal that criminal offences are overwhelmingly committed by men and that the prison population, for example in England and Wales, is constituted by only 4.8 per cent of women (Giddens and Sutton, 2013).

Being male not only increases the likelihood of being a victim of violence, but also increases the likelihood of becoming a perpetrator of violent acts. A European Union Agency for Fundamental Human Rights study (2014) shows that while violence against women, in particular sexual violence and sexual harassment, is carried out predominantly by men, the actual scale of violence against women by men is under-stated and not reflected by official data. The 2012/13 Crime Survey for England and Wales found that the relationship between victims and perpetrators also differed by gender. For example, of those in prison 95 per cent were male. The study further showed that young men are the group most likely to be a victim of violent crime, with those aged 16–24 the group most likely to suffer at the hands of strangers. In 2011/12, as in previous years, the study showed that more than two-thirds of homicide victims (68 per cent) were male. In contrast, women were more likely to be a victim of domestic abuse. Some 7 per cent of women and 5 per cent of men were estimated to have experienced domestic abuse in the previous year, equivalent to an estimated 1.2 million female and 800,000 male victims. Similarly, the survey found that young women were much more likely to be victims of sexual assault. The study also found that there was an estimated 821,000 incidents of crime experienced by children aged 10 to 15. Boys were more likely to be victims, with 16 per cent having experienced a crime in the previous 12 months, compared to 9 per cent of girls. An overall finding of men's experiences of interpersonal violence in Germany, carried out by the Federal Ministry for Family Affairs (2004:5), found that men were overwhelmingly the main perpetrators with 90 per cent committing acts of physical violence. However, a key finding of the study was that men believed perpetrating certain forms of violence was so normal in their lives that they no longer perceived these acts as violent and had limited recollections of them.

In Northern Ireland, Smyth (1998) recorded that, between 1969 and 1997, 35 per cent of all deaths relating to the Troubles were of those under 24 years old of which 90 per cent were male. There was a highly localised distribution of these deaths in urban areas (i.e. Derry/Londonderry and West and North Belfast) which related to the areas with the highest levels of deprivation and family poverty. Apart from deaths, punishment beatings carried out by paramilitary organisations were directed almost entirely on young men, under 20, with varying degrees of tariffs applied. A Review of Health and Social Care in Northern Ireland (2011) revealed that levels of death by suicide increased by 64 per cent between 1999 and 2008, mostly carried out amongst young men. In 2010, 77 per cent of all suicides in Northern Ireland were males, with 40.5 per cent amongst those aged 15–34 (Scowcroft, 2012).

Harland and McCready (2014) show that the Youth Justice Review (2011) highlights that around 10,000 young people in Northern Ireland come into contact with the criminal justice system at some level during the course of a typical year, which represents just 5 per cent of the total population in this age group (under 18). Within this review we discover that offending patterns by gender have remained steady over a number of years and show young males committing 77 per cent of the 9,782 recorded offences in 2009 (though note that some young people will appear on more than one occasion and have committed more than one offence).

Fraser et al. (2010) have argued that despite recognition that gender is a strong predictor for aggressive and violent behaviour, little research has been carried out with boys and young men to understand the worlds they inhabit and the behaviours they use as tools to engage with that world. These authors argue that the depth of complexity and contradiction in terms of violence is currently not captured by the statistics that seek to portray an official picture of risk and public safety. Sommer et al. (2013) also note that while boys and young men are often the perpetrators and victims of certain forms of violence, 'little evidence exists from the voiced experiences of boys themselves on perceptions and interpretations of the violence around them' (Sommer et al., 2013:695). Muncie (2015) notes that 'the problem of crime may indeed be a problem of men', or more precisely a problem of what he terms 'maverick masculinity' (p. 31).

There is also increasing recognition that teenage relationship violence is widespread and research suggests that between 15 and 75 per cent of young women aged 13–17 years have experienced violence within an intimate partnership (predominantly with young men), depending on how the violence is defined (Barter et al., 2009; McCarry, 2010). The UK government has recently reviewed its definition of domestic violence to include 16- and 17-year-olds in response to research which found that 16–19-year-olds were most likely to be the victims of intimate partner violence, including psychological, physical, sexual, financial and emotional violence. What is more concerning is that the trend appears to be, if not static, increasing, despite decades of effort to address the global problem of interpersonal violence. In 2000, statistics from the WHO suggested that young people were the grouping most vulnerable to becoming the victim of interpersonal violence, citing the daily mortality rate of at least 565 young people aged 10–29 (WHO, 2000). Since that global research collective, it appears that this trend has continued, with violence remaining the second leading cause of death among adolescents (see also Patton et al., 2009). International reports estimate that violence accounts for almost 1.5 million deaths per year (WHO, 2014). In addition to the obvious and immediate medical implications of interpersonal violence, secondary consequences such as psychological and mental health problems are almost harder to measure and more difficult to remedy (Haj-Yahia et al., 2013:2224).

Violence amongst school-aged youth is increasingly a topic of concern for policy makers, practitioners and educators. An emerging body of research in the UK suggests that rates of violence among young people remain high and that extreme acts of violence, such as murder, are on the rise (Office for National Statistics, 2015). Understanding how youth violence is experienced and the contexts in which it takes place is crucial for early intervention and effective prevention (Hemphill et al., 2009:290).

Lawson (2005:3) discusses how criminal violence is most prominent amongst adolescents aged 14–16, while its prevalence peaks between ages 15–19. Whilst official figures vacillate, there is significant statistical and qualitative evidence that the trajectory from childhood into adulthood is one underpinned by increased risk of exposure to violence (Fagan and Catalano, 2013) the transition represents a significant upsurge in the intensity of such aggression (Elliott, 1994; Farrington, 2003).

Gender, masculinity and pathways to violence

Whilst some research with young offenders has identified three main motivations for violence, that is, excitement, status and protection (Fraser et al., 2010:9), gender norms appear to predict and influence what is considered violent and what is perceived as acceptable and not acceptable behavioural responses to stimuli (Sundaram, 2013). Further, Sundaram (2013:902) argues that the predictor of gender as the primary role in prevention science has been overlooked. The majority of perpetrators are male (Fitzgerald et al., 2004:13), and in terms of gendered experiences young men are more likely to be both victims and perpetrators of violence, 'accounting yearly for an approximate 90 per cent of offenders, and 70–85 per cent of victims, since 1989' (Fraser et al., 2010:21). Flood and Pease (2009) argue that gender, across all studies and evidence from systemic reviews, is a constant predictor of attitudes related to accepting violence as a normal behavioural response (Meghan-Davidson and Canivez, 2012:3662). Whilst in general terms women have learned to use effective alternatives to violence, men, on the contrary, firstly resort to physical aggression to resolve conflict with only limited feasible alternatives (McCarry, 2009:25). It was also found that compared to females, males evidenced higher levels of both aggressive responses to shame and comfort with aggression' (Meghan-Davidson and Canivez, 2012:3662). Even during early adolescence, normative gender expectations were found to be directly related to predictors of aggression and toleration of violence (Lacasse and Mendelson, 2007), that is, those with more traditional perceptions of gender and the expectations around behaviour that derives from those attitudes and beliefs were more inclined to be higher on the aggression scale (Sundaram, 2013:890).

> The relationship between adherence to conservative gender norms and tolerance for violence has been documented among males in a wide variety of communities and countries, both Western and non-Western, including Arab and ultraorthodox Jewish communities in Israel (Haj-Yahia, 2003; Steinmetz & Haj-Yahia, 2006), South Africa (Abrahams, Jewkes, Laubscher, & Hoffman, 2006), and adult men and young men in Australia (De Judicibus & McCabe, 2001; NCP, 2001; Pavlou & Knowles, 2001).
>
> (Flood and Pease, 2009:128)

Sundaram (2013) in their study of gendered violence found that, whilst

> there were no gender differences in terms of identifying violence as a more or less severe act, girls and boys were equally likely to name emotional or verbal acts of aggression as violence, and were equally likely to cite fighting, the use of weapons and sexual violence as forms of violence... However... contradictions in how the violence was perceived began to emerge.
>
> (Sundaram, 2013:895)

McCarry (2009) too found that whilst there was general acceptance that violence was wrong, where specific contexts of scenarios were presented, perceptions around acceptability and unacceptability became confused and much more subjective.

> A frequently invoked narrative around what constitutes violence and the acceptability of violent acts was that of 'deserved' violence vs. 'undeserved' violence. In instances where the behaviour being enacted was narrated as being 'deserved', the participants were less likely to name this as 'violence' or they defined the behaviour as violent but immediately presented caveats to explain or justify the behaviour. However, in photographs depicting violence by a man (towards women and other men), the participants produced stories around the situation in order to explain, rationalise and sometimes justify the use of violence.
>
> (Sundaram, 2013:898)

Violence, it can be argued, related to gender, fulfils a function. Violence as an integral and complex aspect of male identity (Harland, 2011:428) also 'serves to maintain group solidarity, reinforce kinship ties, affirm allegiances and enhance status within the group' (Burman et al., 1997). For others the function is related to self-protection through an attempt to use violence or aggression or threat as a means to ward off the threat from another (Fraser et al., 2010:9). McCarry (2009:19) argues that 'it is necessary therefore to understand the way in which young people conceptualise gender and how they develop their own gender identities'.

If one learns from the environment around them, to understand male violence we must understand how males experience the world and find their place within it. Richardson and Hammock (2007:419) argue that it is not primarily being male but rather it is the 'gender role that is a better predictor of aggression'. Kaufmann (2001) argues that, from an early age, boys are conditioned to behave and act in a certain way that is different to girls. He argues that, 'children are socialised into expectations of behaviour by our society at a young age' (Crooks et al., 2007:219). This includes avoiding traits that are perceived to be feminine, in order to gain the validation of others and increase self-efficacy, employing more accepted masculine traits, such as being independent and in control, but as a consequence manifest as an unemotional and aggressive risk taker (Crooks et al., 2007). Kivel (1997) concurs, arguing that traditional masculinity not only leaves many young men feeling angry and isolated but leads to the creation of a public vs. private image of the self. Seaton (2007) argues that 'rage and aggression, through forms of resistance, mask real psychological distress. Boys' experiences of psychological pain, when it cannot be articulated, may spur further harm as they inflict similar hurt on others' (p. 212). The acceptance of aggression as a legitimate form of expression is reinforced as boys develop. Familiar advice such as 'man-up', 'be a big wheel', 'be a sturdy oak' or 'no sissy stuff' (David and Brannon, 1976) ensures clarity of acceptable male behaviour.

'Research to develop scales of masculinity show high convergence with attitudes that accept violence' (Biddulph, 2003). A lack of emotional intelligence or ability to use and comfortably deal with a range of emotions, assertively and effectively, forces young men to look inward and foster an inability and fear to share those private thoughts, fears and experiences (Jakupcak et al., 2005). While there has been much speculation around the natural predisposition towards aggression, Kivel (1997) argues that gender is learned, expectations are learned and therefore behaviour as a response is learned. Since gender is learned, the attitudes and behaviour associated with aggressive male behaviour can be unlearned. This is the premise by which those that employ a cognitive behavioural model claim success. According to Crooks, one of the fundamental goals of cognitive behavioural therapy is to alter maladaptive core beliefs; and since individuals are typically not aware of their core beliefs, it is only through intervention and exploration that barriers become clear. Once barriers and challenges become apparent and accepted then attitudes and ultimately behaviour can be altered (Crooks et al., 2007:226). Harland (cited in Titley, 2003) argues that masculinity is the 'cultural expectation of male behaviour'. When one explores this conditioning commonly defined as masculinity through the gender lens, the connections between masculinity and violence are clear. According to Brown and Hogg (1992), 'masculinity is absolutely central to the question of violence'.

> There is no doubt that multiple linkages exist at hormonal, physiological, developmental and personality levels between degree of maleness or masculinity and aggression.
>
> (Weisbach, 1999)

Representations of boys and young men: A 'moral panic' from the government and the media?

Gray et al. (2014:1) posit that 'it is uncommon for academics to be funded to seek the views of young people on issues other than the problematic'. This statement in itself is concerning, yet when we delve deeper we perhaps see more sinister undertones as to why this may be the case. For generations the image of young people, and in particular certain types and groups of young men, being presented as a threat to society has become a recurring theme within studies of male youth and subcultures. The depiction of young males as 'deviant' has also become a regular feature of the popular media and the press. Media driven 'moral panics' (Young, 1971:182) have been portrayed in Britain since the 1950s and the 1960s when typically male gangs, such as Teddy Boys and 'Mods' and 'Rockers', were popularised as 'violent, depraved and sex craved' (Muncie, 2015:8–9). Stanley Cohen, in his work, *Folk Devils and Moral Panic* (1972), first coined the term 'moral panic'. He defined the concept as a sporadic episode which occurs when the values and principles of a society may be under threat. He describes its characteristics as 'a condition, episode, person or group of persons [who] become defined as a threat to societal values and interests'.

Cohen's 1972 study looked at deviancy and examined the effects of labelling within youth subcultures. His study revealed the extent to which the media's representation of young people is often sensationalist exaggeration, leading to a moral outcry that contributes to the negative stereotyping of young people. Throughout the world representations of young people continue to be associated negatively. It is not uncommon to hear references to young men as 'slobs', 'scum', 'lazy', 'wasters', 'bluebags', 'gangs', 'underachievers', 'louts', 'thugs', 'deviant', 'teenage dads', 'anti-social', 'young offender', 'troublesome' or 'delinquent'. Furlong (2013:193) contends that moral panics focus on certain activities of young people through stories that suggest generational differences and 'a breakdown in the moral fabric of society'. Muncie (2015) notes how storylines of 'feral youth', for example, reveal the extent to which 'youth powerlessness has been obscured' and how studies and surveys of youth 'fail to address questions of why, where, to whom or to what we should look for an explanation' (p. 165). Becker's (1963) seminal work previously showed how the perceptions of young people as deviant were produced through 'labelling processes rather than through deviant motivations' (Giddens and Sutton, 2013:927). Labelling 'as an infraction of some agreed upon societal rule' (Anderson, 2014:20) typically produces a negative evaluation of the person. One of the consequences of this is that others will respond to the young person as they are categorised by the label. This in turn can lead to a self-fulfilling prophecy whereby a young person's self-concept is determined by the label applied to them which may lead to further deviant behaviour (Gordon, McAlister and Scraton, 2015).

While moral panic can occur for many reasons and is neither gender specific nor exclusive to issues of sex and violence, concerns about boys' educational underachievement in the 1990s was linked to a wider moral panic about boys and young men. Authors identified that panic about working-class boys in particular translated to boys generally by the late 1990s (Foster and Brooks-Gunn, 2009). These same authors argued that this was at least in part because of the move from an education system that aimed to promote social justice to Conservative notions of 'freedom of choice', with complex league-table driven systems that brought to light the gender gap and in turn the moral panic about underachieving boys into the 21st century.

Žižek (2008), in an attempt to challenge current discourses on violence and the prevention of violence, makes a distinction between what he defines as subjective and objective violence. Subjective violence he notes as the 'perturbation of the normal, peaceful state of things', whilst objective violence is 'inherent to the normality of what people experience and expect to occur'. He also conceptualises a third position that he defines as systemic violence. This he argues helps us to gain a greater understanding of the countless crises that are communicated and streamed to us daily in a variety of ways. For instance, reporting a given tragedy, or indeed defining the tragedy, only happens within a context of complex systemic struggles that define it as such for a particular purpose. What is also true is that whatever the motivations of media reporting of tragic events, it has a great influence on our perceptions of violence and the policies that develop in order to respond to a perceived social threat. Against the backdrop of a reported rise in violence and youth crime, any associated moral panic potentially influences legislative responses which often have disregard of the fact that the drivers of violence are highly complex. High profile cases such as 'the murders of Olaf Palme, James Bulger, Ana Lindh and Theo Van Gogh ... heighten the public's awareness of the types of crime which are most frightening' (Fitzgerald et al., 2004:11). With the public outcry that followed such crimes, the media purported to represent the common voice, with a call for Britain to 'take back the streets' and the prime minister of the time, John Major, calling for a 'crusade against crime' (*Mail on Sunday*, 21 February 1993). This represented a populist response more inclined towards vote winning than a root and branch overhaul of the youth justice system to deal with what Gerald Warner described as a 'nation of vipers' (*Sunday Times*, 3 July 1994). By the late 1990s the newly elected Labour Government began to enact a range of measures it hoped would end what Prime Minister Blair described as 'the moral vacuum' of British Society (Scraton, 2004:137). The Labour Government entered the new millennium with a range of measures and interventions to combat the apparent evils of society with the intention to be 'tough on crime and tough on the causes of crime'. The White Paper 'Respect and Responsibility: Taking a Stand Against Anti-Social Behaviour' (2003) would be the government's road map in the creation of 'safe communities'. Despite the claim of the later 'Respect White Paper' to ensure the protection of the local community as a priority (Scraton, 2008:152), young people, members of the community, came under intense scrutiny. The range of interventions designed to 'take back the streets' copperfastened perceptions that a generational gap had emerged. However, those, such as Scraton and Pearson, argue that the delusion of a moral vacuum, set within a framework of increased tension and biased media coverage, only served to ignore and avoid the real issues impacting upon our children and our communities. MORI conducted a study in

2004, monitoring 17 newspapers with stories related to children and young people. They found that 71 per cent had negative coverage of young people and over one-third were related to violence and anti-social behaviour (cited in Muncie, 2009).

The Coalition Government, that followed the Labour Governments under Tony Blair and Gordon Brown, led with their 'Centre for Social Justice' (headed by Ian Duncan Smith), which they established to combat the 'alternative society' created by young people. The 'code of the street' (Centre for Social Justice, 2009:26) was to be challenged. The rioting reported in England in 2011 provoked a political response that was swift and possibly severe, but by no means new. Following the riots during August 2011 in England, the Prime Minister David Cameron called for 'concerted, all-out war on gangs', which constituted a 'criminal disease that has infected streets and estates across our country' (Cotrell-Boyce, 2013:193). The militaristic terms and emotive language was, in many ways, reminiscent of the moral message implicit in the rhetoric of those such as Warner and Major during the 1990s. It echoed the moral panic of the 1960s and 1970s identified by Cohen.

In November 2011, following the street disorders across Britain in August, the Government launched their 'Ending Gang and Youth Violence Review' into the scale of the problem of gang and youth violence. It looked at what could be done by government and other agencies to stop the violence and to turn around the lives of those involved. It examined what measures would have the biggest impact in addressing the issue of gangs. The gang culture was perceived as the driver that triggered, escalated and sustained the unrest during the summer riots. As a consequence of the review, the Home Office set up a dedicated team of people to work in the 33 local authority areas with the highest levels of gang and youth violence. The result was the 'Ending Gang and Youth Violence' programme (The Home Office, 2011:5).

Hester and Pearson (1993) had earlier argued that, in many ways, government responses to youth violence and crime usually represented a populous response to appease a growing and increased concern with youth violence. He argued that many UK policies were flawed and that they lacked any empirical basis: indeed many only served to exacerbate the issue further. The focus on blame and punishment for perpetrators prevented any meaningful understanding around the complexity of how and why violence emerged. For instance, whilst we know from empirical evidence that there is a broad consensus that violence is wrong, subtleties within and between human interaction creates conditions that change these social norms where violence, in some circumstances, can be justified. Within the objective, common and learned norms, subjective and sometimes conflicting behavioural responses can present themselves (Noguera, 1995; Daiute et al., 2003; Sundaram, 2013). It is by examining more closely these clouded contextual variables and the interplay between objective social norms and subjective environmental stimuli that our understanding of violence can be enhanced and efforts to prevent it can be informed.

However, some argue that beyond the sensational headlines there is a much more interesting story regarding youth violence. Sivarajasingam et al. (2014) also found that, despite presenting statistical evidence that violence was reducing (NHS data), there were regional variations. For example, the Police Service of Northern Ireland reported (in 2014) that violent crime had remained constant since 2007 with around 30,000 incidents per year. Attempting to understand and make sense of statistics can be further complicated by the evidence that certain populations and demographic characteristics appear to increase the likelihood of engaging in violent behaviour. Attempting to make sense of the apparent statistical conundrum, Fitzgerald et al. (2004:61) highlighted that

> the faster increase in convictions for violent offences than for the other indicators is of great relevance to debates on policy in this area. Existing academic debate in this area has tended to concentrate on whether the increase in juvenile violence is real or perceived. Our analysis suggests that it is both, although the perceived increase is greater than the real one.

At high level forums the extent and impact of youth violence is recognised and regarded as a preventable public health problem (Schnitzer et al., 2010:1095). It is clear that the way in which we perceive and define the problem goes some way in helping us to understand policies and practice that are aimed at addressing the issue of violence: 'perceptions of children and young people, and correspondingly of youth violence, are frequently coloured by factors other than experience – notably popular opinion, folk knowledge, and media coverage' (Fraser et al., 2010:40).

Despite regional variations, recent statistics appear to show that whilst some recorded offences have fallen, such as robbery which fell 11 per cent between 2007 and 2011, there are other crimes being reported and processed more frequently (Cotrell-Boyce, 2013:194). Data outlining hospital admissions due to violence, published in 2014, also reports year on year decreases, with a 12 per cent decrease or 33,000 less admissions compared to 2013 (Sivarajasingam et al., 2014). Bateman (2011:4) argues that reductions in crime is consistent with long-term trends, which is believed to be indicative of an overall decrease in youth offending since the early 1990s.

Fraser (2010:6) argues that an evolving justice system in the UK has moved towards diverting young people away from court processes and engaging victims and perpetrators within restorative justice frameworks. This emerged in the UK during the first decade of the new millennium as an attempt to navigate young and first time offenders away from the formal judicial system, thereby reducing the likelihood for recidivism. Fewer prosecutions, however, may not necessarily mean there are fewer offences. Cotrell-Boyce (2013:194) shows regional differences in serious crime offences; for example in London during 2008–2011, these offences increased by 3 per cent, whereas in other boroughs such as Enfield, Lambeth and Newham increases in serious crime were in the range 20–22 per cent.

If we are to understand how and why some people engage with the world in an aggressive way, we must first come to understand how they understand the world they inhabit (Gilling, 1997; Harland, 1997; Anderson and Bushman, 2002; Forest, 2004; Gibson, 2004; Crooks et al., 2007; Lloyd, 2009; Harland and McCready, 2012, 2014). Therefore discourse must explore the person, the individual (Whitehead, 2005), within the context of the environment with which they engage. Individuals are part of a bigger association and, regardless of their perceptions, exist within a society with socio-cultural, religious and economic norms and expectations (Baron et al., 2003). In addition, as we have seen, being male increases significantly the chance of becoming a victim or perpetrator of violence.

Titley (2003) argues that, in order to understand 'being male', masculinity must be explored within the context of any social investigation into violent behaviour. This will be the key focus of Chapter 4 but, before this, the following section offers a social ecological framework to help us better understand how local history in Northern Ireland has been inextricably linked to a period of protracted ethno-political violence.

Violence: A social ecological perspective

McAlister et al. (2013) have pointed out that violence needs to be contextualised within local, historical, political, cultural and material contexts. Schoenwald, et al. (2000:114) found a series of factors linked with serious anti-social behaviour in adolescence, ranging from individual and social attitudes, family background, parental problems, peer association and school and community experiences. In this sense behaviour can perhaps be best understood when an appreciation of the natural environment is recognised. These ideas are by no means new and are commonly associated with the 'social ecological theory of behaviour' most notably developed by Uri Bronfenbrenner (1979). Bronfenbrenner and others have argued that the influence of our environment on behaviour cannot be underestimated. Indeed the idea that people learn through observation is nothing new and can be found as far back as Plato and Aristotle (Gibson, 2004). The basic premise is that there is a natural tendency for young people to imitate what they see, repeat what they hear and think according to what they are told. Implicit within social ecology is the belief that boys and young men live within interconnected systems. Yet, as we have found in our studies, young men influence these systems as well as being influenced by them. The extension of this logic is that, in order to effectively understand, address and prevent problems such as violence and deviancy, researchers and practitioners must pay cognisance not only to the victims and perpetrators of these behaviours but also to the entire ecology within which it occurs. While Miller and Dollard in *Social Learning and Imitation* (1941) articulated these ideas further, there is general consensus that the theories of Rotter (cited in Gibson, 2004) and Bandura (1977) were the most comprehensive and far reaching.

Two theorists who greatly influenced psychological thinking and our understanding of development and formation were Erik Erickson (1994) and Jean Piaget (Baron and Byrne, 2003). Both argued that we learn through our environment and our experiences, which are limited at various stages through our physical and cognitive capacities. Vygotsky (Carlson et al., 1992) engaged with the ideas of these developmental theorists but made more explicit the role of the environment as a factor in the development of children, which existed within a symbiotic framework along with cognitive development, emotional development and identity formation. He moved the concept of cognitive development beyond that of Piaget arguing that, 'within the realm of human development, cognitive development is only one part of the story but culture is another' (Baron and Byrne, 2003). While there are natural developments affecting cognitive development, the environment around us also has a large impact not only on how we view ourselves and the world around us but how we respond to and engage with it. Studies have shown that the brain continues to develop right into adulthood with each period of life placing greater or lesser emphasis on particular areas of the brain (Skuse et al., 2003).

Studies have shown through functional MRI scanning that adolescence, in particular, is a time when the brain undergoes a period of renewal, rebuilding and pruning. The pruning of specific areas of the brain at this time occurs in the areas responsible for social behaviour and is greatly influenced by environmental stimuli (Blakemore and Choudhury, 2006). People establish perceptions of what is expected of them and behave accordingly. Particular attention is paid to the responses from others, and if certain behaviours get a predicted result, it serves to reinforce that behaviour. This reinforcement value increases the likelihood that a certain behaviour would occur again.

> Social cognition may also be expected to change during this time period. In addition, the interaction may be two way. During this time, what is perceived as important in the social world around us also changes and leaves its imprint on the pruning process.
>
> (Blakemore and Choudhury, 2006:302)

Bandura's *Social Learning Theory* (1977) explored how people use what they know to do what they do. Bandura (2006) moved the focus of learning through observation more towards cognitive processes involved in the observation. Bandura argued that social learning is governed by four separate processes – attention, retention, behaviour production and motivation. A working model of the world is perceived by persons based on what they have seen and experienced. This perception is then translated into a performance that is best matched to the model they have developed of the world around them and how they perceive themselves within it. As Gibson (2004) commented, 'as a result of direct or vicarious experiences, people learn standards of performance, which then become the basis of self-evaluation'. Berger and Luckmann 'argued that we are primarily concerned with knowledge production' (Holstein and Gubrium, 2007) and that we are guided by our everyday experiences and the socially constructed view of reality. The self is therefore constantly scanning and testing the interaction of our environments (Holstein and Gubrium, 2007). We learn to understand ourselves through practising and understanding our role, particularly through assessing opinions and gaining the validation of others. Efficacy centres upon our perceptions of our environment (Pike et al., 2006) and our understanding of how well we engage with it (Bandura, 2006).

Ecological influences as predictors of violence

Over the past 15 years, seeking to understanding the risk factors associated with violent behaviour has been at the centre of devising preventative strategies and has become a dominant discourse in prevention science (Fraser et al., 2010:10). Farrington's (1999:55) *Cambridge Study in Delinquent Development 1961–81* identified a number of 'predictors of future criminality labelled as individual family and environmental drivers'. What the *Cambridge Study* provided was a foundation to understand, and in turn potentially inform, violence prevention policy, because there came a recognition that 'most of the problems posed by groups of youths arise not because they enter into a collective that becomes immediately pathological, but derive instead from the ecology of the world in which they live' (Hallsworth and Young, 2004:12). Hemphill et al. (2009) argue that studies from the United States, the UK and New Zealand consistently show risk factors escalated within an ecological framework, the influences of which include the individual, their family, school, peers and community (Hemphill et al. 2009:291).

> Multi-level influence on individuals' attitudes, broadly termed gender and culture, [are] both multi-level in the sense that they influence attitudes at each of the four levels of attitude formation otherwise used to organize this discussion: individual, organizational, community, and societal. Both gender and culture therefore can be seen as meta-factors, influencing attitudes at multiple levels of the social order.
>
> (Flood and Pease, 2009:125–126)

In terms of individual factors, strong and convincing arguments have been made between the correlation between alcohol and violence, particularly in nightlife settings (Hughes et al., 2008). Sociological, as well as neurological, investigations have found that alcohol use directly affects cognitive as well as physical functioning, reduces self-control and the ability to process information rationally and respond logically (Peterson et al., 1990; Graham, 2003). As a consequence, this combination of deteriorated responses and cognitive understandings can lead to antisocial or impulsive behaviour, including violence (Schnitzer et al., 2010:1096). National Survey data from England and Wales show that nearly half of victims of violence believe the perpetrator to have been drinking alcohol at the time of assault (Kershaw et al., 2008).

Others, investigating these specific categories, concurred with previous general findings. Violent victimisation history (Hawkins et al., 2000), antisocial beliefs and attitudes (DHHS, 2001), exposure to violence and conflict in the family and in the community (Fowler and Braciszewski , 2009), parents' authoritarian childrearing attitudes (Chaffin, 2006), and harsh, lax or inconsistent disciplinary practices (Meghan-Davidson and Canivez, 2012:3661) all placed a young person at greater risk of becoming the victim and/or perpetrator of violent acts.

Family structure, parental practices and parenting styles are empirically proven to be important risk factors for serious crimes including violence. In terms of the family, risk, stability, abuse, domestic violence and parenting have been seen to impact upon the behavioural outcomes of young people (Olate et al., 2012:397). Whilst poverty and social status has long been cited as a risk factor associated with violence, numerous studies have found a high correlation between violence and inequality (Fajnzylber et al., 2002; van Wilsem et al., 2003). This may be partly explained by the pressure that parents experience when living in poverty (James, 1995; Weatherburn and Lind, 2001). 'It is argued that the frustration and exhaustion of life in poverty render parents more likely to be irritable, conflictual and to use harsh and inconsistent parenting. This produces violence in the sons who are exposed to it' (Fitzgerald et al., 2004:14).

> Furthermore, youth may be exposed to a substantial degree of chronic community violence that is either non-sectarian or sectarian in nature. Studies in both Northern Ireland and Palestine have shown that in the context of political conflict and community violence, the family environment is often high in stress and conflict (Cummings et al., 2010; Dubow et al., 2010) and parenting may be compromised.
>
> (Goeke-Morey et al., 2013:244)

Literature exists to indicate that increased family conflict and low family functioning is related to a range of behavioural and health problems such as mental health problems, problem behaviour, low academic attainment, violent behaviour and substance abuse (Proctor et al., 2009:593). Frequent references are made in the literature to an association and perceived correlation between parenting and youth offending, most notably characterised by violence (Proctor et al., 2009; Fraser et al., 2010), not least because families, in whichever form they exist, 'are the prime socializing influences on children' (MacDonald et al.,

2005:1513). Family conflict, cohesion and the demise of the transitional family unit have been explored. A stronger predictor of violence and conversely a protective factor in mitigating the risk of engaging in violence seems to be related to parenting style rather than the fabric of the unit within which it is practised (Smith and Stern, 1997). Parenting styles are generally regarded as the 'attitudes, behaviours, and interaction styles that, when taken together, create an emotional context in which socialization efforts and family interactions can occur' (Schroeder and Mowen, 2014:229). Since Baumrind's (1966, 1967, 1971) and Maccoby and Martin's (1983) seminal work, four styles of parenting have been identified: authoritative, authoritarian, permissive and neglectful (Alegre, 2011:57). There is consistent evidence from major international studies, such as the New Zealand *Dunedin Study* (Henry et al., 1993) and the *Pittsburgh Youth Study* (Loeber et al., 2001), that the way in which children are reared can predict future violent offending. Alegre (2011) suggests that:

> Children of authoritative parents have been found to score better than children of authoritarian, uninvolved, and permissive parents in measures of adjustment (Steinberg, Lamborn, Darling, & Mounts, 1994), attachment (Karavasilis, Doyle, & Markiewicz, 2003), resilience (Kritzas & Grobler, 2005), school achievement (Boon, 2007), social and school competence (Lamborn, Mounts, Steinberg, & Dornbusch, 1991), and pro-social behaviour (Hastings, McShane, & Parker, 2007)
>
> (Alegre, 2011:57).

Conversely, parents who provide a warm, stable, secure and loving home, are consistent in their parenting approaches, not excessively harsh in their discipline and model productive approaches to conflict and disappointment, consistently monitor the behaviour of their children at home and in the community, and who have good networks of support tend to have children who exhibit less problematic behaviours (Walden and Beran, 2010; Alegre, 2011; Goeke-Morey, 2013; Schroeder et al., 2014:229). A peaceful home environment may provide youth with both the instrumental and emotional support necessary for academic success, including 'emotional and bio-psychological regulation, adaptive sleep patterns, a sense of emotional security, self-confidence, and a culture of achievement' (Goeke-Morey, 2013:249).

Loeber et al. (2000) during their study found that the most common style of parenting was authoritative but that the most common shift was towards permissive parenting, representing a significant move in parental control and supervision as adolescents get older. Whilst parental monitoring generally declines as young people make their journey through adolescence and make the transition into adulthood, Spano et al. (2011) found that the ability of parents to monitor their children effectively (particularly in areas of high deprivation where additional risk factors exist) was a strong protective factor that enabled young people to avoid exposure to violence (p. 933).

> The transition from uninvolved and permissive parenting styles to authoritative parenting show statistically significant reductions in offending, but the decrease in offending shown by the authoritarian to authoritative group does not reach statistical significance... Importantly, however, all shifts to authoritative parenting are associated with significant increases in maternal attachment.
>
> (Schroeder et al., 2014:239)

The development of strong attachments to family, defined as the 'discriminating bond that a young child forms with his or her primary caregiver' (Walden et al., 2010:7), can have a profound impact upon the formation of children's well-being, their emotional regulation and social competence. Where conflict and trauma exist, where families are experiencing a crisis and children are experiencing multiple placement, children can develop insecure attachment styles, which, on the other hand, carry with them the expectation that others are unavailable and social exchanges are not positive or rewarding (Renken et al., 1989). This negative bias, regarding social interaction, may result in hostile interpretations of ambiguous behaviours and aggressive reactions to them (Walden et al., 2010:7). It is not of surprise that significant efforts have been made to identify families 'at risk' or indeed experiencing a crisis, not least because of the increased risk of prolonged social problems but also the potential cost incurred during a family breakdown and the behaviour that can occur as a result of the experiences that led to that breakdown.

The role of the environment it seems cannot be underestimated in how natural or innate potential is diluted or indeed set alight within the ecology in which it develops. The Social Development Model (SDM) (Catalano and Hawkins, 1996) pays particular attention to the role of the environment and how one learns to operate within it (Hemphill et al., 2009:292).

Consistent with ecological perspectives, the SDM organises risk and protective factors according to their influence in different developmental settings including communities, families, schools, peer groups and within individuals.

(Hawkins et al., 1992)

The SDM integrates the main features of crime and delinquency and argues that violence originates with unhealthy or confused attitudes and beliefs and, through the attachments that people form and the activities they are exposed to, are at greater risk or indeed, conversely, greater protection from violent behaviour (Hemphill et al., 2009:292). While many theorists have debated the when, where and how formation of identity and personal construction takes place, few would argue that we are formed by nature alone (Gibson, 2004). We are not born with a sense of self or agency, we are constructed through our experiences and the environment around us shapes us (Bandura, 2006:16). Extreme neurological development in the first four months of birth enables newborns to learn quickly the skills that will prove vital for their future. However, we are also subject to the environment around us and, however much our developing mind has the capacity to learn and develop new skills, capabilities and understandings, formation is subject to those around us and our experiences of the world, both pre- and post-natal (Baron and Byrne, 2003:11). Our contact with the world forms how we see the world and how we respond to the world in the way that best matches our perceptions: 'at present, most social psychologists believe that how people act in various social situations is strongly determined by their thoughts about these situations' (Baron and Byrne, 2003:14).

The basic premise is that there is a natural tendency for people to imitate what they see, whether in the school playground, their home or their community. While Miller and Dollard in *Social Learning and Imitation* (1941) articulated these ideas further, there is general consensus that the theories of Rotter (cited in Gibson, 2004) and Bandura (1977) were the most comprehensive and far reaching. Rotter's theory based on behaviourism, cognitivism and personality theory described four concepts to predict behaviour as:

1. behaviour potential;
2. expectancy;
3. reinforcement value;
4. psychological situation (Gibson, 2004).

People have perceptions of what is expected of them and behave accordingly. Particular attention is paid to the responses from others, and if a certain behaviour gets a predicted result, it serves to reinforce that behaviour. This reinforcement value is postulated to increase the possibility that the behaviour would occur again. It is here that Bandura's (1977) social learning theory is a useful model to understand attitude development. This theory posits that learning occurs within a social context such that individuals utilize observational learning, imitation and modelling. Additionally, the theory emphasizes cognition, affect and behaviour (Meghan-Davidson and Canivez, 2012:3661).

The concept centres on the idea that: attention is paid to the behaviour of others that is being displayed; the modelled behaviour is stored by the viewer to be retrieved when needed; the model is translated into behaviour where the response of others is interpreted and, if there are perceived gains, then the model is adopted. For instance, in the wild, particularly in harsh conditions, animals shadow, observe and mimic their parents' behaviour. Three conditions are present: instinct, necessity and a lack of alternatives. When a further condition emanates from the practice (success), the behaviour will be replicated. Even when the fourth condition is not present, however, the lack of alternatives increases the chances that even unsuccessful ventures will be replicated to the detriment of the animal. As in the animal kingdom, where we want to change patterns of behaviour, it may be necessary to create two, sometimes natural, conditions – alternatives and success. We want our young to realise feasible alternatives but, by using alternative strategies, to see the success too, thereby increasing the chances of behavioural replication. Berger and Luckmann cited in Holstein and Gubrium (2007) argue that we are primarily concerned with knowledge production. We are guided by our everyday experiences and the socially constructed view of reality. The self is therefore constantly scanning and testing the interaction of our environments (Holstein and Gubrium, 2007). We learn to understand ourselves through practising and understanding our role, particularly through assessing opinions and gaining the validation of others. Efficacy centres upon our perceptions of our environment (Pike et al., 2006) and our understanding of how well we engage with it. Bandura argues that this forms the basis of 'self-efficacy' – the belief that one can succeed, even in the face of challenges:

> Belief in one's self-efficacy is a key personal resource in personal development ... efficacy beliefs affect whether individuals think optimistically or pessimistically, in self-enhancing or self-debilitating

ways. Such beliefs affect people's goals and aspirations, how well they motivate themselves and their perseverance in the face of difficulties and adversity.

(Bandura, 2006)

Social learning theory has been used to account for the strong relationship between exposure to violence and violent behaviour. Margolin and Gordis (2004) argue that youth who are exposed to violence will learn how to engage in aggressive behaviour. Dodge et al. (1990) and Guerra et al. (2003) found that exposure to violence changes the cognitive schema of youth and increases the risk of engaging in violence: 'Gorman-Smith and Tolan (1998) also argued that youth who are repeatedly exposed to violence are more likely to (a) view violent and aggressive behaviour as normative and (b) lose their inhibitions about the use of violent behaviour over time' (Spano et al., 2010:1162).

Youth violence increasing

Analysing trends between 1980 and 2000, some authorities suggest that there has been a steady increase in violence across all areas. A report by the European Agency for Fundamental Rights in their report 'Racism and Xenophobia in the Member States of the EU' cited in 2007 that in at least eight of the member countries there had been an 'upward trend in racism and violence'. Indeed evidence taken from national surveys exploring some of the nation's most violent crimes appeared to show that, contrary to the popular notion that violence was decreasing with the advent of the new millennium, youth violence remained a serious problem and, in some cases, incidents of violent altercations was rising (Marcus, 2005:442). In Western Europe, rates of murder convictions increased by almost one-third in the early 1990s compared with the late 1980s and remained relatively stable until 2006 when it rose again to be 14 per cent higher than the initial surge in 1990. The same appears true for assault with almost a 50 per cent rise in the numbers reported compared with the pre-1990 period (Aebi and Linde, 2012).

One of the most revealing empirical findings about youth violence over the past 20 years has been the prevalence and normality of violence in the daily lives of boys and young men (Marcus, 2005:442; Harland and McCready, 2014). Young males report being exposed to multiple and varied forms of violence daily, such as verbal and physical conflicts with friends, family or siblings as well an increase in racist violence and threats from more sinister sources such as paramilitarism (Harland and

McCready, 2012). Boys experiencing violence as they grow up is common in many countries across the world. For example, Contreras et al. (2012) found that in Brazil, Chile, Croatia, India, Mexico and Rwanda up to 80 per cent of men report experiencing violence growing up in their home, neighbourhood and school. Despite such evidence the perceived normality of youth violence is often 'unseen, unrecognised and unrecorded' (Fraser et al., 2010:36), and the fear and emotional threat of personal violence does not appear to be captured or fully understood within the current analysis of youth experience in regard to violence (Lloyd, 2009; Harland and McCready, 2014).

In the UK, violence amongst young people has increasingly become a high level concern for policymakers. Whilst official figures can be clouded and present messages that vary in their meaning, an emerging body of research in the UK suggests that rates of violence among young people remain high and that extreme acts of violence, such as murder, are on the rise year on year (Office for National Statistics, 2013: 889).

It is vital, therefore, that those concerned with the impact violence has on individuals, families, communities and societies understand it and wrestle with the complexities associated with a propensity towards it as a means of having any sort of impact upon its demise.

Risk factors

With decades of research and social investment attempting to understand factors that create the conditions and sustain violence and aggression, emerging bodies of evidence have developed to create a theoretical basis from which violence could (theoretically) be prevented. One potentially important characteristic of violence is the risk associated with increased likelihood of aggressive social responses. If these could be understood and predictors of aggression could be redressed or mitigated, violence could potentially be reduced. One of the most influential studies that investigated predictors of offending behaviour was the previously mentioned *Cambridge Study* (Farrington, 1999). For instance, being male predisposes people to interfacing with the justice system (Home Office, 2001). The British Home Office reported in an overview of violent crime for 2004–2005 that young men aged 16–24 were most at risk of violence and cited 'being male' the top factor associated with offending (Coleman et al., 2006).

Other factors too have been argued to increase the risk and likelihood of engaging in violence and which, at different times, have taken precedence over cause and effect arguments. For instance, Schnitzer et al.

(2010:1095) found that in England and Wales 20 per cent of all violent crimes take place within the context of pubs or clubs and almost 50 per cent of violent altercations reported take place at the weekend, adding weight to others who have found that drinking alcohol can significantly increase the propensity towards violence (Kershaw et al., 2008).

Involvement in violent crime during childhood and into adolescence has significant implications for the individual, their families and the communities within which they reside. These include low educational attainment, constrained and conflicted social relationships, compromised mental health, and increased rates of victimization and physical injury (Fagan et al., 2013:141). Significant evidence internationally suggests that violence and abuse are routinely utilised in young people's own interpersonal relationships, particularly within the everyday lives of young men (McCarry, 2009:17). Lipsey and Derzon (1998) distilled a list of the factors most closely associated with serious and violent juvenile offending from a meta-analysis of 66 reports on 34 independent studies. Whilst most of the studies originated in the US, there were some European studies originating from Britain and Scandinavia. Through this, Lipsey and Derzon (1998) set out the different ways in which identified risk factors are prevalent within 'life course persistent' and 'adolescent onset' offending (Fitzgerald et al., 2004:20). Variables associated with a propensity towards violence, and protective variables which predict shelter from aggression, show a progression over the life course, emerging and/or becoming more significant at particular times of life. During early childhood, for example, family risk factors are prevalent and the degree to which a child is more likely to engage in violence can be correlated with the degree to which there are strong attachments, there is suitable and developmentally appropriate monitoring, and parents are able to meet basic needs. Moving into adolescence, school and peer experiences become more influential and the degree to which a young person is surrounded by positive peers and is achieving in school can predict the extent to which they are at risk of engaging in violence. Community factors too, such as availability of drugs or weapons and informal social control, tend to gain precedence during middle to late adolescence when children spend more time in the community (Farrington, 2003a). It is important to note that this tends also to correlate with reduced parental monitoring where, in high risk areas, this exacerbates risk factors. In their meta-analysis of longitudinal research on predictive risk factors for adolescent and early adult violent or serious delinquency, Lipsey and Derzon (1998) found that the best predictors of violence varied depending upon the age range a young person was situated within.

At age 6 to 11 years the most important predictor variable was committing an offence (violent or otherwise), followed by substance use (mainly tobacco or alcohol). Moderate risk factors for this age group included male gender, family socio-economic status and anti-social parents. The most important predictors for 12–14 year olds were weak social ties, antisocial peers, and committing a general offence. Other risk factors included: family factors, particularly antisocial or abusive parents and poor parent–child interactions; individual factors, particularly low intelligence and antisocial attitudes and beliefs; and contextual factors, particularly neighbourhood crime and social disorganisation.

(McKinlay et al., 2009)

Significant research, countless randomised control trials and significant efforts to understand violence has contributed to a wealth of general understanding regarding the risk factor that generally divides into distinct categories including biological, individual, peer, school, neighbourhood and situational factors (Farrington, 1995:55). Research has also identified other *protective* factors which are linked to positive outcomes, and which protect young people from difficulties, even when they are growing up in adverse circumstances and are heavily exposed to risk (ibid.:55).

Taking account of both Hirschi and Gottfredson's (1990) *General Theory of Crime* and Agnew's (1992) 'General Strain Theory', self-control is assumed to be a relative constant across time (Turner and Piquero, 2002) but can be impacted upon by extraneous variables and contextual factors such as lifestyle, activities, peers, health and relationships. As Hirschi and Gottfredson (2001:90) summarize, 'people who engage in crime are people who tend to neglect long-term consequences. They are, or tend to be, children of the moment. They have what we call low self-control'.

Experience of care and risk of violence

Whilst no concise explanation or overarching theme has emerged from a wave of recent studies exploring the lives and experiences of those looked after, and the relationship between their proximity to the care and criminal justice systems, it does appear that there is sufficient data and literature to support the assertion that risk factors associated with entry into care exacerbate those risk factors which are also associated with engagement within the criminal justice system (Convery et al., 2006; Blades et al., 2011; Pitts, 2011; Jacobson et al., 2012; Schofield et al., 2012; Summerfield, 2012). Mooney et al. (2006) highlighted that in 2003 'looked after children were fifteen times more likely to be convicted of an offence or cautioned than the general youth population'. There is strong evidence to indicate that young people aged 10–17 who are in care experienced and resided in an out-of-home placement for more than one year were three times more likely to offend and be prosecuted than the general youth population (Darker et al., 2008:135). A study of young people in custody in England during 2011 found that of 1,052 young men surveyed in custody, 27 per cent had had experience of being in care, and of the young women surveyed, 56 per cent had been looked after (Summerfield, 2012:28–31). Findings by the Northern Ireland Statistics and Research Agency corroborated Mooney et al.'s findings, indicating that 10 per cent of children between 10 and 17 who had been in care had been convicted or cautioned for a criminal offence between 2009 and 2010 (NISRA, 2012:1). The same report stressed that, as one would expect with a developmental trajectory, the likelihood of offending increases as those in care progress through adolescence. In the same year, 20 per cent of those 16 and over were cautioned or convicted for a criminal offence (NISRA, 2012:17). In 2006, a report carried out by the Criminal Justice Inspectorate for Northern Ireland, concerning bail applications for young offenders, found that of those who were refused bail, many were refused on the grounds of appropriate accommodation (CJINI, 2006), thereby increasing their time spent in custody, despite the fact that, upon disposal, only 6 per cent received a custodial sentence (NIO, 2006).

Other studies carried out in Northern Ireland have found similar patterns. A study carried out by Convery et al. (2008:255) found that within the Woodlands Juvenile Justice Centre (Rathgael, Northern Ireland), 'over half of the children in custody were committed from a residential care background'. With vulnerable, complex and sometimes volatile family ties, accommodation is more likely to be an issue for those who are care experienced. Whilst it is true that not all young people offend (Blades et al., 2011:11), the parallels between experience of care and experience of justice are profound. Being drawn into the justice system is one issue for young people in care, but even more concerning is how much more likely young people in care remain within the justice system, are remanded for longer periods than the general youth population, and, by virtue of their over-exposure to criminality, have increased recidivism rates (Convery et al., 2008:255). Sempik et al. (2008:225) found that against the general youth population (5–15), looked after children were three times more likely to have emotional problems, almost eight times more likely to have conduct disorders and almost five times as likely to have mental health problems, all of which exacerbate risks associated with offending.

McSherry et al. (2008) found that children in care are:

- 10 times more likely to be excluded from school;
- 12 times more likely to leave school with no qualifications;
- 4 times more likely to be unemployed;
- 50 times more likely to go to prison.

Challenging behaviour is fairly understandable within the context of how young people enter into the care system. Fitzpatrick et al. (2009) found that out of 1,626 young people in care for longer than one year, 77 per cent were of school age and 23 per cent were deemed to have special educational needs. The Human Rights Commission in their 2006 report 'Still in Our Care' found that custody was sometimes used as a way of dealing with problem behaviour and argued that, compared with the general youth population, care experienced young people are more susceptible to incarceration by virtue of their residential status. Of one young person, a staff member commented: 'he was in and out of the [children's home] consistently.... He's in for nuisance offences.... He has serious learning difficulties and there's a concern that this may lead to serious harm' (Convery et al., 2006:31). The report went on to highlight the link between lack of stability and entry into the justice system:

> We have had a few shocking cases...We had a boy who'd been in over 210 homes in 10 years...That was horrendous...and then you wonder why he offends.... When they go back out they want to come back in. That was true of this boy.... This is the longest period of time of stability he's had in his life.
>
> (ibid.:31)

Studies over the previous decade have indicated that care experienced young people are in fact more likely to interface with the justice system (Garrett, 1999; Taylor, 2003; Ruiz, 2005; Mooney et al., 2006; Darker et al., 2008; McSherry, 2008; Gillen, 2010).

Almost all children in care are from backgrounds of deprivation, poor parenting, abuse and neglect, factors that together create risk for a range of emotional, social and behavioural difficulties, including anti-social behaviour and offending behaviour.

(Schofield et al., 2012:2)

Fulcher and McGladdery (2011) note that:

a significant paradigm shift that has shaped contemporary child and youth services in the United States and Canada as well as in the UK and Ireland, involved a growing recognition that comprehensive ecological approaches are required in order to achieve significant developmental outcomes with children and young people in out-of-home care. (pp. 19–20)

Whilst the literature has alluded to the balancing of welfare and justice it does appear that a focus on public safety at the expense of social care vacillates with time, policy agenda and public opinion. Pitts (2011:15) highlighted the fact that in England and Wales, between 1992 and 2011, the number of young people receiving custodial sentences rose by 90 per cent and the number of young people within the age range 10–14 quadrupled, despite there being a marked decrease in offences committed in the same period. Scraton (2004) argues that in the exercise of justice, there exists a close and symbiotic relationship between the courts and public opinion. It seems that a combination of a group of young people with challenging behaviour patterns, staff who appear disempowered and lacking in morale, together with negative police attitudes towards looked after children and young people 'may unnecessarily inflate the offending rates amongst this population' (Skuse and Ward, 2003:183). However, despite the apparent evidence for care being the catalyst for crime and violence, these problems are not necessarily a consequence of having been in care per se, given the life experience many have endured before entering into the care system (Darker et al., 2008:135).

Bateman (2005) found that through a detailed analysis of 147 randomly selected case files of those involved with youth offending teams in England, nearly half of whom had no previous convictions, had high levels of vulnerability in terms of emotional health. The researchers established a checklist of factors against which to measure such vulnerability. These included bereavement, separation, rejection, impermanence of home and loss due to illness. More than nine out of ten of the sample, 92 per cent, had experienced at least one of these factors, 46 per cent three or more and 11 per cent had experience of at least four. Connotations are clear, for those in care, that issues around attachment, separation from the family, feelings of rejection and loss, lack of a consistent and secure base, and multiple placements were, for many, experiences of everyday life.

Prevention

Serious attempts to understand and prevent violence are by no means new. Whilst 19th-century efforts to mitigate the risks societies face was based upon little evidence and generalist approaches to violence prevention, by the 1950s there was a greater impetus to research antecedents of violence and also the approaches used to deter repeat acts of serious violence (Gilling, 1997). There was an increasing awareness that root causes of youth violence can be in some ways better understood within the context of the complexity of young people's social experiences and the formative influences of family, community, peers, school and social media (Jacobson et al., 2012:9). The task of preventing violence in our society, however, with its many contextual and ecological variables, is immense, although the literature suggests that any effective and sustainable response must involve multi-layered approaches supported by government departments and facilitated by a 'highly trained workforce able to provide wraparound services for children' (Sempik et al., 2008:230). Whilst there is evidence about what works in preventing violence, arguments have been made that this evidence has not been effectively communicated to practitioners who work with and support young people to achieve optimal outcomes (Kerner and Hall, 2009).

The Centre for the Study and Prevention of Violence at the University of Colorado has spent decades evaluating 'promising programmes' to assess their effectiveness in responding to interpersonal violence and the transferability of those programmes to other cultures and contexts. One of the overall findings from the Centre was that 'every programme may need to look somewhat different in order to be effective ... the assumption that identical procedures will produce the same outcomes in diverse settings cannot be justified' (Mattaini and Mcguire, 2006:188). Some evidence based programmes validated by hallmarks such as 'Blueprints' included 'Communities that Care', 'Promoting Alternative Thinking Strategies' and 'Multisystemic Therapy' (MST).

Prevention science tends to promote evidence from multi-component interventions, such as the 'Communities that Care' model, given that these programmes simultaneously work with different causes of the problem behaviours and indeed across systems that are sustaining them (Coie et al., 1993; Dahlberg and Potter, 2001), but some findings suggest that significant effects can also be achieved when a strategy or intervention is facilitated with recipients in just one system, such as the family environment or targeting the individual young person himself (Fagan et al., 2013:152). For instance PATHS (Promoting Alternative Thinking Strategies) is a model facilitated with the objective of increasing young people's self-control, emotional competence, social skills and problem-solving skills (Alegre, 2011: 58). Likewise, programmes that are longer in duration are often touted as best able to produce significant and long-lasting effects on problem behaviours (Nation et al., 2003). However, this review also indicated that some relatively short interventions (e.g. school curricula and parent training programmes lasting only a few months) can reduce violence among a universal audience of youth and families. In addition, short-term but intensive therapeutic services (e.g. MST and Multi-Dimensional Treatment Foster Care) have been shown to reduce violence among adolescents already involved with the juvenile justice and child welfare systems, with effects lasting for a number of years post-intervention (Fagan et al., 2013:152).

MST is an intensive community based model that uses evidence-based interventions to address problem behaviours and prevent criminalisation of young people (Cary et al., 2013). By increasing an understanding of the 'fit' of the problems, MST intervenes directly in the systems and processes related to those areas. Driven by a belief that programmes seeking to influence problem behaviours were at best costly and also potentially ineffective, the Family Services Research Centre at the Medical University of South Carolina developed MST within a research context during the 1980s (Henggeler et al., 2009), later being applied in field situations internationally. Henggeler et al. were motivated by the evidence at that time that the main approaches to deal with violence and anti-social behaviour involved out of home placements. The evidence, Henggeler argued, demonstrated that this approach was not only economically problematic but also ineffective in achieving behavioural change and potentially harmful to those who were incarcerated in juvenile detention centres or hospitals (Carey et al., 2013). From the inception of MST within the research setting, the model has since been developed further in the field and replicated across numerous jurisdictions. The reported effectiveness of MST has resulted in not only replication in its indigenous country, but also in its significant expansion internationally. Today there are around 250 MST teams worldwide in countries such as Chile, New Zealand, Norway, Denmark and the UK (Littell, 2005).

Schoenwald et al. (2008) highlights the fact that 'across numerous RCT's (Randomised Control Trials), MST has consistently achieved significant reductions in problematic behaviours with follow-ups ranging from 1.7 to 13.7 years' (p. 214). Carr (2005) too highlights, that of the '9 treatment outcome studies (including 3 controlled trials) have been published and for 7 of these follow-up data from 1–4 years have been reported...to be effective for those who completed the treatment programmes' (p. 429). Evaluating a pilot of MST delivered between 2003 and 2006, Painter (2009) found that 'families, who received the MST support, as opposed to services as usual, experienced...more improved treatment outcomes and less juvenile justice involvement...(and) experienced a significantly higher level of clinical improvement in mental health symptoms that did the usual service group' (p. 321). Although some would cite that a limitation of the research for European observers is that the majority of these trials were conducted in the US, there is an increasing number of studies from Europe that demonstrate that MST is effective in reducing youth re-offending, preventing out of home placement and improving individual and family functioning (Olsson, 2009; Tighe et al., 2012). Evaluating the replication of the MST model in Sweden, Olsson not only found that families in receipt of MST treatment had very low comparative drop-out rates and placement breakdown during the treatment process compared with beneficiaries of 'treatment as usual', but 'a follow up study of treatment effectiveness conducted 2 years after intake to treatment showed that MST was more effective than regular services' (p. 587). Similar results were found in Norway with 87 per cent of the 487 families referred to MST in 2005 achieving treatment goals (Ogden et al., 2009). Reflecting on the UK experience of MST implementation and outcomes of a randomised control trial, Carey et al. (2013) argued that the 'findings of the clinical and economic evaluation provide initial indications that MST may be a promising approach to tackle youth offending in the UK' (p. 5).

Schoenwald et al. (2000) found that:

> a combination of individual (attributional bias, anti-social attitudes), family (low warmth, high conflict, harsh and/or inconsistent discipline, low monitoring of youth whereabouts, parental problems, low social support), peer (association with deviant peers), school (low family-school bonding, problems with academic and social performance), and neighbourhood (transience, disorganisation, criminal

sub-culture) factors are linked with serious anti-social behaviour in adolescence. (p. 114)

In MST, it is assumed that because anti-social behaviour is caused and maintained by many factors within a youth's multisystemic social network, 'effective treatment involves identifying specific factors relevant to each case and then tailoring a multi-systemic intervention package to modify these... in this sense, MST rests on a social-ecological conceptualisation of adolescent violence' (Bronfenbrenner, 1979:428).

Violence in private and public spaces

Cameron's (2000:1) study of young men identified a range of violent activities in a variety of contexts which were part of their lives to the extent that 'there was little evidence that the young men considered they had a responsibility to society'. Such indifference to violence related to associated issues in, for example:

- antagonistic relationships between the young men and police;
- the inability to manage their anger;
- no access to affordable recreational facilities to legitimately expend their anger;
- drugs were too easy to access.

This seeming indifference is manifested in their exposure to violence, particularly in association with the hegemonic dominance of males. Therefore, the perception of violence as an occurrence in the lives of young men is exposed in a number of ways across a range of settings. For example, Moser and McIlwaine (2000) in their study of urban, low-income communities in Columbia found that the single most frequent issue was violence and that, between 25 and 60 (depending on the community), different types of violence were identified. These types of violence ranged from intra-family violence to fights between rival gangs and local militias. The various types of violence were grouped into three categories – political, economic and social – wherein specific perceptions of violence identified that:

- intra-family violence was especially important;
- gang and political violence resulted in large numbers of displaced people;
- adult men were most concerned about political and youth violence;

- adult women mostly focused on violence against children;
- young men were especially troubled about drug-related violence.

However, these issues are not exclusive to the types of communities portrayed in this study. Cameron's (2000:2), for example, does likewise. She found that violence in the family, largely as a result of enquiries about child abuse and domestic violence had been made increasingly visible since the 1970s. This included how women experienced either physical or sexual violence by a male perpetrator, the extent of violence towards children in families, the extent of sexual assault against children in families, and the high average of perpetrators in sexual assault cases being family members. She asserted that 'violence is characteristic of many families, and it has implications for how young men grow up – violence is learnt'. Whilst interpersonal violence exists in families it is not prevalent in all families and, although violence in the family is no longer considered a private issue, Day and Hunt (1996) maintain it has implications for broader social policy whereby violence in the family and subsequent social crime is a complex relationship which extends beyond the family.

Beyond the family, some young men are involved in a culture of violence which relates to a range of issues. For example, Ireland and Thommeny (1993) demonstrate that a significant amount of young men involved in violent assaults used alcohol. Tomsen (1997) claims fights can start from everyday trivial incidents since some young men simply enjoy fighting. In addition, Polk (1994) presents evidence from a study of homicide that indicates that violence which starts out as trivial evolves quickly from 'honour contests' into feuding that lasts for several months, particularly amongst working-class young men. Such violence often equates to illegal activities such as drugs, and legitimate forms of resolving conflict are often ignored. A consequence of this is that groups quickly emerge as forms of protection and, as members become immersed, they 'may view the world as consisting of the strong and the weak, and as a place of conflict and struggle. They may believe that only the strong can prosper and ritualistically convey their ruthlessness and brutality' (Shover, 1996:87–88). Sampson (1997) supports this by arguing in most situations the conventional values of groups are observed by members but in certain contexts violent behaviour becomes the norm. In this respect, young men in certain circumstances, irrespective of the violent nature of the group, feel a sense of camaraderie and belonging. This was a significant feature of Mitchell's (2012) study into young men and paramilitary membership in Northern Ireland.

Within the community, as an additional public space, schools are sites of violence for some young males. The well-publicised phenomenon of school yard shootings in the United States is a demonstration of the most extreme form of violence in schools. However, Rigby (1996:14) points out that the less extreme forms of violence are also common: 'bullying may or may not be intended to hurt and may take the form of physical, non-physical, or non-verbal action undertaken by the bully or someone co-opted to do so'. In recognising that in schools bullying is hurtful and may have health consequences, Rigby's study finds support in the Balkans region whereby fieldwork with young males identified the pervasiveness of peer violence in their lives was particularly significant in schools. This, it was highlighted, begins in primary school but extends through secondary school with the researcher claiming that 'schools are a key site of peer violence' and quoting one young male as saying that 'in the school we feel endangered' (Crownover, 2007:34).

What we are highlighting is that violence and perceptions of it are predominant in the public and private spheres of a significant number of young males in today's society. Whilst the much publicised increase in violent related incidents via social media through the development of mobile phones and the internet is a major concern, peer violence within youth culture is not a new phenomenon. Poynting in Flood et al. (2007) discusses the development of the 'Teddy Boys' in the 1950s and the 'Skinheads' in the 1970s as new modes of masculinity among working-class youth. Jefferson (1976:82) notes: 'the Teds were very "touchy" about "real or imagined" insults, especially about their clothes or style, often leading to fights'. And Clarke (1976) claims likewise with the 'Skinheads' violently exercising their resentment of 'outsiders'. The propensity for young men to become involved, particularly in peer group violence, is precipitated, according to Yablonsky (1962), by the failure to accommodate the norms and values of the middle class and is compounded by the lack of opportunities for marginalised young working-class males, leading them to demonstrate masculinity through violence.

Violence and shame

Nathanson (1992) identifies four categories that are used as defensive scripts through which an individual reacts when experiencing shame. The four poles within his 'compass of shame' are 'withdrawal', 'attack self', 'avoidance' and 'attack other'. The compass usefully illustrates techniques and strategies within each category. Nathanson posits that 'withdrawal is likely to be accompanied by distress and fear; attack self by self-disgust; avoidance by excitement, fear and enjoyment; and attack other by anger' (p. 314), a response which Nathanson argues is associated with an individual's feelings of being endangered by the depths to which his self-esteem has been reduced (p. 366). While to 'attack other' can be interpreted in many ways, it is this response to shame that Nathanson believes is key to understanding the complexity through which an individual may become violent. Gilligan (1996) has proposed that all forms of violence are precipitated by feelings of shame and humiliation. Working as a psychotherapist with violent high-security inmates in prisons in the United States, he was struck by how often, when asked why the offender had been violent, they replied that they had been 'disrespected'. Gilligan believes that early experiences of being rejected, abused or made to feel as if they did not exist predisposed them as adults to be sensitized to feeling ostracized, bullied or ignored, leading to unbearable feelings of shame and humiliation which need to be defended against by violent means. Such anecdotal data based upon self-reporting within a population of individuals known to be chronically deceptive, however, is not a firm empirical basis for such a broad theoretical formulation. Gilligan (2000:62) writes that 'understanding violence requires understanding of what thought or fantasy the violent behaviour symbolically represents'. This can be difficult however 'as most violent people express their thoughts in the form of actions rather than words'. Quoting Darwin, Gilligan adds that 'beneath shame lies a strong desire for concealment' (p. 64). For Gilligan the emotion of shame underlies all forms of violence and he sees the purpose of it 'to diminish the intensity of shame and replace it with its opposite, pride' (p. 111). Gilligan (1996) has argued that 'any factor that reduces the shame-inducing effect of...youth or male gender, can protect the person from being overwhelmed by shame, and hence the probability that he will resort to violence' (p. 67).

Our experience is that, within male youth culture, one which is dominated by shame, violence is often the only legitimate option as other skills have not been developed, practised or seen to work (Kivel, 1997). Furthermore, where aggressive behaviour is accepted as a socially influencing tool consequently no alternative behaviours are learned (Hong, cited in Crooks et al., 2007). Findings from a study carried out by YouthAction Northern Ireland (2002) found that, while the majority of young men spoke of having direct experience of violence, they felt powerless to change their circumstances or environment and despite their desire to avoid violence there were no realistic avenues for achieving this. This concurs with findings from the US where consultations with young men highlighted that 'without a dissenting voice...if someone threatens your dignity by calling you a name, you have to fight. If you don't, your safety will be threatened' (Kivel, 1997:232).

Reflecting upon shame as it may manifest itself in a young man's life helps us to understand better the complexities and subtleties that may lie at the root of feelings of embarrassment, incompetence, humiliation, disgrace and disapproval. These are crucial drivers that can have a seriously negative impact upon a young man's behaviour, self-esteem and self-efficacy. While shame can affect every individual, it is particularly useful within a context of understanding violence and masculinities. This does not mean, however, that we condone negative or aggressive male behaviour. Rather it can help practitioners to display empathy through understanding why certain types of young male behaviour may be instigated through boys and young men feeling ashamed.

Violence: 'Rackets' as a young male defence mechanism

Chapman (2000:186) has discussed how young men can develop 'rackets' as a form of resistance against oppression and negative labelling. Taken from transactional analysis, rackets are behaviours adopted because boys perceive they are being violated by those around them. The racket is a defensive mechanism for dealing with feelings of shame, fear, anger and loss. Chapman uses this metaphor to highlight why young people may present an outwardly aggressive identity that does not reflect who they really are. Rackets can be used by young men as a noise that distracts from what is actually going on beneath the noise. Alternatively, the metaphor of a tennis racket can be used by young men to defend against the judgements and insults that are directed towards them. In this context the racket is a tool whereby a young man metaphorically returns the insults back even harder. Chapman suggests it is important to distinguish between the young man and the racket. As the racket is used by him as a tool it can be *put down* which has the potential of helping boys and young men distinguish between their rackets and themselves. Chapman argues that, like a stereotype, a protection racket is a way of thinking and acting and, by creating protection rackets, young men create a sense of safety, esteem and control over their lives. However, while young men may develop these behaviours for good reasons in order to deal with their environment, Chapman concludes that rackets do not actually protect, but rather draw more trouble to themselves.

The stereotyping of young men also creates an assumption that their identities are fixed in stone. Dweck (2000) has argued that fixed identities can lead to the need to repeatedly prove yourself to others. Throughout our studies 'proving' was a consistent theme in young men's lives – particularly those who believe they do not match up to certain male stereotypes. Sukarieh and Tannock (2011) insightfully assert, however, that the challenge to critically understanding youth is 'not simply to replace negative stereotypes with positive ones, but to understand why particular kinds of stereotypes are mobilised by different groups in changing social and economic contexts over time' (pp. 688–689).

Violence and masculinity

This broad universal discussion on the literature in relation to violence, with specific reference to young males being influenced by their societal experiences, should not ignore the specific political connotation to young males and violence here in Northern Ireland, given that this may be an influential feature of the data collected in this study. The work of Harland (2009) about the construction of masculine identity has a distinct relation to this. He argues that 35 years of conflict, with the deaths of over 3,600 people, wherein young males have been the primary perpetrators and victims of the violence, has had a significant effect upon the construction of masculine identity. In previous studies of inner city Belfast youth, Harland (1997 and 2000) identified that young men clung desperately to narrow and contradictory interpretations of masculinity, believing that men should be powerful, strong, brave, intelligent, healthy and so forth so as to be in control of every aspect of their lives. In reality, however, their lives were full of contradictions as most young men felt powerless, feared the threat of daily violence, were labelled 'stupid' in school, did not pay attention to their health needs, particularly their mental health, had limited sexual education, rarely asked for support and felt they were perceived by adults as being 'immature'.

Whilst such findings may apply to young men the world over, they are distinctly exacerbated because of the political context of living and growing up in Northern Ireland. Young people's perceptions of violence, particularly in segregated urban areas such as Belfast and Derry/Londonderry, are well documented. For example, Hansson's (2005) study of the views of young people from these areas identified that they actively participated in violence at interfaces which was often initiated by them. However, unlike the youths in the past who were involved in violence for politically motivated purposes, the young people in this study acknowledged the violence was often 'recreational'. In addition, categories of violence perpetrated by young people of different ages, and from different communities, such as the prominence of violent assaults in Derry's city centre, created the perception of some young people being fearful for their safety. Hansson (2005:95) found 'their attitudes have been shaped by experiences of persistent sectarian and communal violence and many young people continue to experience intimidation and violence as part of their daily lives'.

Such situational forces have implications for any study of young men and violence. Harland (2009:2) highlights how young men present an avoidance to the world of emotions, believing that a demonstration by young males of showing emotion is 'perceived by others as inadequate or weak'. This, he goes on to argue, 'is central to why men keep intimate feelings to themselves and are more likely to display typically masculine emotions such as anger and aggression' (ibid.). The reluctance by young men to show their feelings has been a recurring theme in youth-work practice for many years (Lloyd, 1996, 1997; Harland, 1997; Harland and Morgan, 2003; Harland and McCready, 2012) and continues to have practice implications in relation to masculinity, becoming a man and perceptions of violence. This leads us on, before uncovering more voices of boys and young men, to examine the literature on masculinity. As stated earlier the connections between masculinity and violence are clear: 'masculinity is absolutely central to the question of violence' (Brown and Hogg, 1992).

4
Research with Boys and Young Men: Critical Reflections on the Theme of Masculinity

From the latter part of the 1980s masculinity, particularly within Western societies, has developed into an important area of global sociological interest. As a subject masculinity is also very much in vogue in the popular media and across academic disciplines. In the United States alone, for example, Bradley (2008) found that masculinity courses rose from 30 to over 300 from the 1980s. In 2015 the Centre for the Study of Men and Masculinity hosted an international conference entitled 'Masculinities: Engaging Men and Boys for Gender Equality' in New York, attracting over 400 abstracts from across the world. Part of this new-found interest and approach to studying men and masculinity, according to Flood (2007), has been rooted in the efforts of equality campaigners, intent on exploring how masculinity intersects with social discrimination movements such as feminism. Ashe (2007) contends that interest in the study of masculinity has been generated by a range of social, cultural, policy and political changes that led to claims that traditional forms of normative masculinities were being eroded by new social conditions. What has also became increasingly apparent is that masculinities as intersectional identities are being shaped not only by gender but also by factors such as ethnicity, social class, sexuality, age and disability (Ashe and Harland, 2014).

What appears to be less scrutinised is the extent to which boys and young men understand the broader forces that have contributed to the construction of their own masculine identities. Mac an Ghaill (1996:384) noted a paradox in the construction of masculinities, suggesting that, whilst we live in a male dominated society, we know very little about men, in particular young men. Crawford (2003) also argued that young men have problems in explaining and understanding how they become men and take for granted the journey from boy to man.

Crawford further argues that, whereas the topic of how boys become men features regularly in popular writings on masculinity, it is generally ignored in academic discourses. His reasoning for this is that academic writers tend to focus on the dominant hegemonic form of masculinity, male power and violence while popular works, which lean more towards the personal experiences of men, are aimed at a broader, more popular, reading audience.

In our studies over the past 18 years we have consistently found complexities and contradictions in regard to how boys and young men understand masculinity and what it means to be a man. We have also found that boys and young men are rarely given opportunities to discuss or critically reflect upon the way in which their understanding of masculinity shapes and informs their identities or impacts upon their behaviour. This does not mean that boys and young men are totally passive in how they construct their masculine identities. We have discovered that while boys and young men rarely consciously reflect upon notions of masculinity, subconsciously they are forming, or more precisely have already formed, concrete beliefs and expectations about becoming men. As we will demonstrate, boys in our studies construct their masculine identities according to a range of factors such as age, ethnicity, personal and family experiences, peer influences, school and community experiences, their individual thoughts and their levels of physical and mental maturity. It is within this multi-connected, micro- and macrosocial ecological context that localised masculinities are formed, understood, cemented and ultimately reinforced. This complexity helps us to understand better why, as a sociological area of interest, masculinity cannot be clumped as a homogeneous concept that can be applied and agreed across the world. We would argue therefore that, while masculine identities and expectations of men may be informed and influenced by global forces, they are nevertheless constructed locally through a multi-complex ecological framework that is determined according to the historical contours, culture and shared experiences of each society.

Traditional notions of masculinity

A century ago Northern Ireland led the world in regard to linen, rope-making and shipbuilding (the ill-fated Titanic was built in Belfast). During the mid-20th century around 50,000 men worked in some capacity in 'The Shipyard' at Harland and Wolff. Like coalminers leaving the coalmines in other parts of the world, local archives capture thousands of men in boiler suits with faces dirty from their labour pouring out of The Shipyard at the end of their working day. Such images of men as workers were firmly etched into the male psyche and poignantly captured an important aspect of what it meant to be a man, not only in Belfast, but throughout the Western world during the industrial era. While ships are no longer built at The Shipyard, the legacy of the industrial age is visible to everyone who comes to Belfast through two towering yellow cranes 'Samson and Goliath' which serve as a stark and proud reminder of the working-class history of Northern Ireland. The two cranes are an iconic representation of an industrial age where working-class men cemented and affirmed their masculine identity through the world of work. Therefore, like thousands of men in Western societies during the Industrial Revolution, the male breadwinning role in Northern Ireland was critically important in the creation of a typology of masculine identity that fulfilled men's patriarchal roles and expectations as providers and as fathers.

The end of the industrial era presented fundamental and unique challenges to both the construction of masculine identity and the traditional ways in which boys and young men from working-class communities acquire adult status.

An opening discussion on masculinity: Hegemonic masculinity

It is generally acknowledged that previous sociological enquiry in the arena of masculinity focused heavily on the position of men relative to that of women, with much emphasis placed on the subordinated position of the latter (Connell, 1995). However, research into men and masculinities that evolved over recent decades (e.g. Kimmel et al., 2005) developed a complex multi-faceted spectrum of masculinities with multiple ways of 'doing male' (Connell, 1995, 2000; Whitehead, 2002) and it is now accepted that there is no one singular way of being masculine within any given culture (Anderson, 2014). Rather, we consider a multiplicity of masculinities that are diverse and culturally determined and socially constructed from particular social groups, producing different types of masculinity as the result of their positioning in racial, class or sexual categories (Ashe, 2004).

Connell (1995) presents masculinity as a social construction that is achieved within a gender order that defines masculinity as an opposition to femininity. Crucially by doing so it sustains a power relationship between men and women as separate groups. For Connell there is no single definition that is masculinity. Rather, Connell argues that gender politics amongst men involves hegemonic struggles which she terms 'socially dominant masculinity'. Her approach opens up the possibility of examining subordinate masculinities and the ways in which certain categories of men may experience stigmatisation and marginalisation. It is difficult therefore to define precisely what we mean by masculinity. Interpretations of the term are undoubtedly culture specific and varied within a complex web of global traditions, myths and stereotypes. It is important to acknowledge, however, that whilst masculinity is a characteristic that can be found in men and women, its interpretation is solidly based on male stereotypes.

The work of Raewyn Connell has been seminal and extremely influential in critiquing contemporary studies of men and masculinities. In particular her concept of hegemonic masculinity[1] has been instrumental in informing the practices, attitudes and meanings of both masculinities and men (Moller, 2007). Connell and Messerschmidt (2005) speak about how hegemonic masculinity dominates what they term 'other marginalised and subordinate masculinities' whilst Gough (2007:3) summarises hegemonic masculinities as 'ideals and practices that oppress women and other men through a range of ideals and practices which privilege many men and actively subjugate subordinate masculinities'.

Connell furthers her argument by saying that men enact and embody different configurations of masculinity depending on their positions within a social hierarchy of power. Hegemonic masculinity is at the top of this, and is the type of gender practice that, given power, supports gender inequality. According to Connell (1995:77), hegemony, derived from Gramsci's class relations analysis, 'refers to the cultural dynamic by which a group claims and sustains a leading position in social life'. At any given time, one form of masculinity, rather than others, is culturally exalted. Rather than being determined as a set stable role or a biological instinct, the concept 'masculinity' associated with 'man' as a category is a myriad of discourses, ideologies, symbols and practices. As a concept hegemonic masculinity describes the processes of masculinity as 'embedded in the centrality of power and sustained by political, legal and social institutions' (Connell, 1995; Lorber, 1998). Hegemonic masculinity emphasises not only relationships of power between men and women, but also identifies a hierarchy of masculinities whereby hegemonic masculinity dominates and competes over other subordinate or marginalised masculinities, such as black and minority ethnic groups (Robertson, 2007), homosexual men or academic achievers (Lusher and

Robins, 2010). This helps explain why particular norms of masculinity become dominant and why specific contexts may encourage certain forms of behaviour (Lomas, 2014).

Anderson (2014) cautions against using hegemony as a categorical archetypal term as multiple masculinities exist amongst men. His preference is to use the term 'orthodox' masculinities. Others have criticised hegemonic masculinity as being too simple a model of understanding social relations in terms of a single power and the global dominance of men over women. Despite its contested nature, hegemonic masculinity has been widely used in recent years as a way of understanding the formation, practices and meanings of masculinity within a range of contexts (Moller, 2007). Connell and Messerschmidt (2005) strain to point out that, despite the contested nature of hegemonic masculinity, fundamental concepts such as the plurality and hierarchy of masculinities should remain. They contend that challenges to hegemonic masculinity also arise from the 'protest masculinities' of marginalised ethnic groups (p. 847).

Researchers have sometimes tended to treat masculinity as this single, one-dimensional concept of 'masculine hegemony' (the dominant masculine type), characterised by 'toxic traits' such as power, violence, emotional inexpressiveness, overt heterosexual behaviour, homophobic bullying and 'laddish' behaviour (e.g. Plummer, 2001; Jackson, 2002). Masculine hegemony is, in fact, a hierarchical concept which changes over time, within which can be found many expressions of masculinity including those that demonstrate positive[2] attributes such as earning a wage and being a father. However, a dearth of research in this field leaves certain questions unanswered, such as: How does masculinity vary with geographical location? What types and sub-types exist? What is the dynamic positioning and interaction of these masculinities within gender and society in general? And how does the construction of masculine identity play a role in mental health problems, especially suicide? (Savin-Williams, 2001; Connell and Messerschmidt, 2005).

Connell (1995:76) suggests the 'masculinity that occupies the hegemonic position on a given pattern of gender relations is always contested'. In contrast, working-class masculinity, ethnic minority and homosexual masculinity are subordinated or marginalised. Indeed, whilst it is recognised that men in general benefit materially, socially and politically from their position as the dominant gender, advantages described as the 'patriarchal dividend' (Connell, 1997), these benefits are not spread equitably amongst all males. As Connell (1997:64) maintains, other groups of men pay part of the price, alongside women, for the maintenance of an unequal gender order. Gay men are systematically made targets of prejudice and violence and effeminate and 'wimpish' men are constantly put down. Black men, in the United States (as in South Africa) suffer massively higher levels of lethal violence than white men.

The discussion on masculinity and hegemony reminds us that the same institutional and cultural settings can produce different masculinities. This is evident in the work of Willis (1977) with his research on schools in England, and also in Australian school studies (Kessler et al., 1985). However, once more we learn from Connell (1995:37) that the straight-forward recognition of diversity in masculinity is not sufficient. Instead, the gender politics within masculinity draws attention to the rela-tionships that are constructed through exclusion and inclusion, thus emphasising the relations between the different kinds of masculinity. This is true of sport, school, workplace, organisations and so forth or, in other words, of life in general, and we cannot understand the gen-der politics of masculinity without 'giving full weight to their class as well' (p. 75).

Masculinity and class

Donaldson (1991), in his work *Time of Our Lives*, observed how working-class masculinity is found in the toughness of hard labour, such as in coal mines and factories where work is controlled by management and economic pressure, in a subordinate destructive way. On the factory floor, the construction of working-class masculinity differs significantly from that of the middle class in the air-conditioned office. Such class differences are also found in the work of Tolson (1977) and his study of British working practices. This is also a theme of Messerschmidt (1993) who studied class difference in the United States and how the construc-tion of class-specific masculinities is linked to white-collar workers as well as street crime. However, as a causation of a socialisation model, we must not lose sight of the relationship integral to the construction of masculinities as being dialectical rather than singularly one-way. Whilst the institution or culture we have discussed can influence the formation of masculinity, equally so can these produce oppositional masculinity. This is again found in the work of Willis (1977) and the response of 'lads' to their school authority.

In this there are parallels with Westwood's (cited in Hearn and Morgan, 1990:56) assertion that 'certain currents within feminism have also promoted an essentialist account of men and women, masculinity and femininity, positing a polarity between the two which often belies the lived experiences of women and men in their everyday realities'. In subsequently discussing how masculinity has been made consistently problematic by feminist analysis, she maintains that 'this has provided an impetus to the current interest in masculinity and the development of men's studies'. Her discussion, in focusing on racism, black masculinity and space, attempts to de-essentialise the fixity of stereotypes whereby race, gender, motivation and behaviour are 'placed' as being natural and a substitute, rather than 'the complex realities they seek to describe' (p. 57). Her argument that it is fertile to attempt to replace one set of stereotypes with another emphasises that 'the point is to dismantle all stereotypes and to move to a much more shifting terrain in which identities are not seen as fixed and cannot, therefore, become stereotypical'. Westwood's discussion on de-essentialising black masculinity recognises that, in post-colonial Britain, in relation to the specificities of historical, cultural and class backgrounds, identities have been forged in recognition of commonalities with 'white working-class men because of their class position which generates both political and cultural overlaps related to them as men' (p. 57). This draws similarities to investigations within our own studies, because we recognise that we cannot separate identities, that they are simultaneously experienced and lived and that if constantly produced, unlike our models of socialisation would have us believe, they are not the finished product but rather part of a shifting terrain. However, in agreeing with Westwood, whilst identities may shift they are not free-floating. Instead, they are positioned within the family, the community, the school, culture, histories, class and language and, as such, 'there are contradictions and coalescences between the cultural and the social, identity and difference'.

Masculinity and the legacy of patriarchy

By its nature, the concept of patriarchal relations of power advocates and requires that men, and in particular the father, are attributed supreme status as head of the home and have dominance over women (Rahman, 2007). As noted by Baron (2013:92), 'this unequal and patriarchal state of affairs is based entirely on history, not on innate or biological differences between males and females'. Sobieraj (1998) argues that 'the social construction of gender must be acknowledged as something grander than masculinity and femininity; it is nothing less than the social construction of patriarchy' (p. 28). Under patriarchy, men have traditionally been exalted and privileged, and women relegated to a subordinate position. Patriarchy, as a sociological concept, may appear alien to young people growing up in modern Western societies. However, there can be no doubting the impact and influence that patriarchy has had in shaping masculine identities. In patriarchal societies boys grow up believing that, by virtue of being male, they are the rightful leaders while women are perceived as natural subordinates. This dominant form of masculine identity exists in patriarchal societies in terms of perceptions of inferiority and superiority whereby male dominance and female subordination is continually perpetuated and that, subsequently, boys become men believing that they are naturally superior to women. What became increasingly apparent, however, within the contemporary literature on men and masculinity is that patriarchal relations of power are harmful not only to women, but also to men (Morgan, 1992; Kaufman, 1993; Connell, 1995; Kimmel and Messner, 1995; Hearn, 2005). Outdated gender stereotypes formed and established within systems of patriarchy can be damaging for those men who struggle to measure up or fit within traditional masculine beliefs and ideals. This is an important observation in that young boys, in striving towards narrow and restrictive patriarchal notions of men and masculinity, will willingly reject or sacrifice certain aspects of their personality in order to match up to such stereotypes.

During the Industrial Revolution, boys were first and foremost prepared for the world of work, and working-class men affirmed their manhood primarily in and through the workplace. This factory age established a prototype of men and masculinity that not only produced, but legitimised, male domination over women. A woman's place was seen to be in the home looking after her husband and children, and this largely excluded them from public life. Importantly and ironically, however, whilst substantial social and economic changes have occurred, the patriarchal expectations of many men, and women, have not.

Within a patriarchal system boys become men by acting within a rigid set of masculine expectations and boundaries, otherwise they may potentially face a number of social sanctions. They are expected to refute any behaviour construed as feminine or that which contravenes traditional masculine hegemonic stereotypes. Moreover, some sociologists would argue that, in striving to achieve dominant hegemonic notions of masculinity, young men are compelled not only to check these unwelcome character traits in themselves, but also to actively police others.

This checking behaviour is very apparent in our studies with boys and young men. One example of this is demonstrated by Herek (2000), who maintains that vociferous expressions of homophobia serve to disprove conclusively that one is homosexual, thus proving heterosexuality; and this is one of the cultural expectations associated with the traditional male gender role. However, the effect of such demonstrations is two-fold: not only do displays of homophobia serve to reinforce group membership, but they also enforce the norms and values associated with hegemonic masculinity (Harland et al., 2005). The threat of homophobic verbal or physical violence results in many individuals changing or attempting to change their behaviour or the way in which they present themselves in order to fit in with this rigidly constructed gender stereotype. For those who claim not to follow gender stereotypes, they are faced with the challenge of either standing up for what they believe, or becoming complicit in the benefits to men through association with patriarchal values and beliefs.

Debates into masculinities have become intensely complex and hotly debated. The fact that patriarchal ideals have been increasingly scrutinised and dominant forms of masculinity challenged led some early theorists to identify what they termed a 'crisis of masculinity' (Brittain, 1989; Badinter, 1995; Mac an Ghaill, 1996; Macinnes, 1998:45). They argued that this crisis was an ideology produced by men as a result of the threat posed to 'the survival of the patriarchal sexual division of labour by the rise of modernity' and the fact that men could no longer hold the monopoly of power by virtue of their sex. Horrocks (1994) contended that the crisis in masculinity in Western societies was fuelled by the fact that men were increasingly haunted by feelings of emptiness, impotence and rage that were unrecognised by modern society during a period of rapid socio-economic change. Connell (1995), however, questioned the usefulness of the term 'crisis' and suggested that the questions being asked of men and masculinity at this time marked a decisive period in the development of critical thinking in regard to traditional understandings of masculinity.

In Northern Ireland, as in other parts of the world, significant socio-economic shifts weakened the organisational strength of working-class communities and eroded the vitality of community life. De-industrialisation, high levels of unemployment in Western societies during the latter part of the 20th century, the challenges of feminism to patriarchy and men, and new and sustained studies into men and masculinity were all important factors that have deeply challenged what it means to be a man in the 21st century. Growing up in violent societies that have experienced war and other forms of conflict can reinforce patriarchal ideals of men and masculinity. Men as soldiers, aggressors and defenders during conflict are expected, by necessity, to be brave, strong, leaders and even skilled killers. This was seen to be the case in Northern Ireland where protracted levels of conflict meant that lives were lived within an armed patriarchy which can produce a gendered ethnic order.

Throughout our studies boys and young men report that they are left to their own devices, typically without the support of adult men, to negotiate and understand the journey from boy to man. Shifting socio-economic trends and challenges to patriarchal relations of power have led to a re-examination of men and masculinity. What is perhaps less understood, and less scrutinised, is the impact upon the construction of masculine identities of boys and young men growing up in deeply divided and violent societies.

Protest masculinity

Contradictions between young men's perceived power and their sense of powerlessness capture Connell's (1995) notion of 'protest masculinity'. This has been defined as a 'gendered identity oriented towards a protest of the relations of production and the ideal type of hegemonic masculinity that has been conceived as a destructive, chaotic and alienating type of masculinity' (Walker, 2006:5). Talcott Parsons (1954) originally conceived the term 'masculine protest' as identifying adolescent boys raised by mothers and absent fathers. He claimed that these boys struggled with their gender identity and subsequently embodied masculinity in a reactionary 'bad boy' manner which was the complete opposite of stereotypical femininity (p. 305). Connell (1995) developed the concept further by connecting it to young men who make claims to power when there are no real resources for doing so. In his critique of protest masculinity Walker (2006) states that Connell importantly divides poor and working-class men from the rest of the working class (p. 7). Walker further suggests, however, that protest masculinity would be better described as 'anomic' according to Emile Durkheim's (1951, 1972) critique of how society is organized as this will help make language about working-class masculinity more precise (p. 7).

Masculinity and schools

Many studies have demonstrated how school has been instrumental in the formation of masculine identities and the place where masculinities are actively made, negotiated, regulated and renegotiated (e.g. Mac an Ghaill, 1994; Salisbury and Jackson, 1996; Frosh et al., 2002; Swain, 2006a). Over the past 30 years there has been a growing body of theoretical literature examining how interpretations of masculinity significantly impact upon mental health and well-being (Flood, 2007) with complex multi-faceted concepts of masculinities and what it means to be 'male' being developed (Kimmel et al., 2005). In *Learning to Labour*, Willis (1977) showed how the boys in his study were actively constructing social class relations during the last two years of schooling and doing so in terms of their gender and social class identities. Their anti-school behaviour as they moved towards the end of schooling was interpreted by Willis as preparation for the 'resistance within accommodation' that they would practice as workers within an industrial capitalist economy. Willis (1977) described 'lads' and Connell (1989) 'cool guys' as groupings that usually saw themselves as separate and often in conflict with teachers and the school. 'Laddish culture' and 'laddish behaviour' re-emerged in terms of drinking, anti-social behaviour and within schools as behaviour that impacted negatively on everyone within the classroom which became shorthand for a predominantly working-class masculine identity. Similar notions, but with different descriptions, cut across race and culture, with Majors (2001) coining the phrase 'cool pose'.

Research regarding how the concept of masculinity is defined within young males has asked if it is constructed by individuals themselves or imposed through normal social structures such as in the family or school. Swain (2004) argues that the school system imposes a dominant, heterosexual masculinity on young males that results in other emerging identities such as homosexuality as being subordinate (Flowers and Buston, 2002). Modern technology and those who control it provide increasingly overt sexual imagery and language and access to internet pornography.

Within our own 'Taking Boys Seriously' (TSB) longitudinal study with adolescent boys, as presented in chapter two we discovered complex and changing patterns of masculinity through the ways in which boys thought about what it means to be a man. The TSB study utilised a three-factor analysis of the ways in which boys thought about what it means to be a man during early to mid-adolescence. Findings revealed how masculine identity is heavily shaped by the localised context in which adolescent boys grow up and exist. Our study further showed how boys move from narrow male stereotypes in early adolescence, towards becoming more active in forming their own interpretation of masculinity during mid-adolescence and the extent to which masculinity is played out and rehearsed in school settings.

School occupies a powerful place, literally and metaphorically, in most young people's lives. For some, it is conducive of opportunity and mobility, yet for other young people it situates risk, exposure and danger as the varying territories and micro-spaces of inclusion and exclusion (the corridors, the playground, the classroom and the sports field) are incessantly produced and contested. Swain (2004, 2006a, 2006b) contests the standard notion that young men who engage in sports-related behaviour are simply living up to a stereotype that they learn from others around them. He accepts, through his literature reviews, that these stereotypes are often presented as negative and limiting to the development of young men. What he argues for is that this engagement with other young men in risk-taking behaviours relating to sports, such as competitiveness, aggression and horseplay, is not about the sport itself, but about their journey into manhood and their attempts at finding out who they are. He urges that this journey through the path of 'protest masculinity' (Connell, 1995) should not be stigmatised. Preventing them from exploring their identity in this way will only reinforce these as negative behaviours and stereotypes, thereby leading to unhealthy identities which are considered socially maligned. Swain's explorations of the young men's own perceptions of self and their interactions with their peers in different settings show that these young men themselves view their social interactions, and attempts at determining social status through any available means, as a way of claiming an identity which is being negated by the formal school environment.

Prior to the 1980s, masculinity researchers tended to assume that young people[3] passively accepted the dominant stereotypes imposed upon them by social norms and by school practices. However, it is increasingly accepted that adolescents are active agents in the meaningful construction of their own identities in such a way that it matters to them (e.g. Jordan, 1995; Walker, 2006). This active construction depends not only on the presence of quality-parental role models, but on good family communications, active negotiation and an acceptance of parental monitoring by the children with regard to their personal activities (Caprara et al., 2005; Fulkerson et al., 2006).

Masculinity and violence with particular reference to Northern Ireland

According to social learning theory (Bandura, 1977), people acquire aggressive responses the same way as other complex forms of behaviour, through observing others and meeting expectations. Bandura argued that it is through one's view of the world that one's world is created (Bandura, 2006). This supports the assertion of others such as Weisbach (1999) that very early on boys learn they are male and learn what it means to be a man and that it is this complex formation and entry into the world of men that ultimately leads to violence. Harland (2009) argued that while routes to adulthood are becoming more complex, perceptions about what it means to be a man are still bound up in historical memory. A report by Titley (2003) supported this assertion, suggesting that masculinity through industrialisation and urbanisation has faced its greatest challenge, specifically through a breakdown in traditional family roles. Biddulph (2003) argues that as industrialisation spread throughout the West and even more recently the marked reduction in apprenticeships and rites of passage for young men into adulthood where they can share and learn with other men and begin to take on an adult role within the safety and support of the community, has virtually disappeared. 'Men may experience considerable dissonance between the power that society has apparently bestowed upon them and their actual lived experience' (Crooks et al., 2007:220). Biddulph (2003) concurs, suggesting that the transition from boyhood to manhood presents a marked shift in role, responsibility and expectation and is dominated by more pitfalls, hurdles and ambiguity than in the past, the result of which is the creation of a race of boys who perpetually fear entering into the adult world, and in which the forming of adult relationships is one of a constant state of shame and anxiety. Violence linked with masculinity is a strategy to replace the dominant emotions, such as shame and sadness (Jakupcak et al., 2005), and those which are perceived as feminine, with more accepted emotions such as anger and aggression deemed more acceptable within the framework of masculinity (Richardson and Hammock, 2007).

In relation to Northern Ireland, Ashe and Harland (2014) contend that, while social and political changes weakened the traditional models of gender identities and fuelled interrogations of masculinities in other geopolitical contexts, mainstream analysis of the Troubles paid little attention to studies of masculinities and that the relationships between masculinities and men's violence remains under-theorised.

These authors note that, while masculinity did not cause the conflict in Northern Ireland, it has been an integral aspect of its contours and 'understanding dominant models of masculinity within particular societies is an important starting point for engaging with masculinities and political violence' (p. 751).

Research on masculinities indicates a relevance to interpersonal violence because 'defending a sense of self is fundamentally important to many men's use of violence' (Dragiewicz, 2008:435). Throughout the Troubles in Northern Ireland working-class young men often found status and a sense of belonging within their communities as defenders and protectors of that community. Men became defenders against any invasion from other communities or other *soldiers*. They were the protectors from unwanted intrusion. The aggression of these defenders often afforded young men status amongst peers and other community members (Harland and McCready, 2007). Men's localised violence in defence of community spaces served to reaffirm traditional roles in working-class areas (Ashe and Harland, 2014). Within a post-conflict society, underpinned by 20 years of paramilitary ceasefires, there has been a necessary and significant role change. The need for the defender and protector has become virtually redundant. Young men have now become the focus of aggression from within their own community. Their behaviour, once lauded and feted, has now become a focus for criticism, violent assault and/or expulsion from that community (Harland and McCready, 2007). This ambivalence may have always been there but it has become even more pronounced as the peace process evolves.

Throughout the Troubles, the most extreme forms of violence occurred in working class-areas and, as in many other areas across the world that have experienced war and conflict, it was young men who were both the perpetrators and victims of the violence. While women participated in all levels of the conflict, their activities were often hidden and tended to be overshadowed by the spectacles perpetrated by the 'men of violence' (Ashe and Harland, 2014). Extreme manifestations of a violent type of hyper-masculinity were evident throughout the Troubles by high profile paramilitaries such as Johnny Adair[4] (Ashe and Harland, 2014:749). Creary and Byrne (2014) argue that during the conflict joining paramilitary organisations offered certain young men a place of belonging as well as responsibility, respect and power, further carving into the male psyche the need for a defender. This may suggest why certain young men may be prone to radicalisation and justifying extreme acts of violent behaviour. Certainly, in Northern Ireland, extreme acts of violence were daily occurrences which to a certain extent appeared to almost become normalised amongst the population. Even as we write this book, 20 years after the ceasefires, pipe bombs and paramilitary shootings are regularly reported on the local news, but frequently not as the main headline. Kilpatrick (2013) reminds of us that violence remains an integral part of life in Northern Ireland by citing 2013 as 'a year of brutality' and listing a catalogue of paramilitary attacks across Northern Ireland carried out on young men:

November 29th: 15 year old boy is shot in the leg in his own house in Belfast.

November 18th: 15 year old boy is shot in both legs by a gang of three masked gunmen in Coleraine.

November 12th: masked men shoot a 21 year old man in both legs in Portrush.

October 19th: man is shot in both buttocks in broad daylight in west Belfast.

September 10th: man is beaten in his home by three masked men in Ballymoney.

July 9th: 20 year old man is shot twice in both legs in Newtownabbey.

June 27th: three young men are shot in Belfast 'by appointment' having been told to go to the venue beforehand.

May 16th: 18 year old man is shot in both legs in north Belfast.

This trend has continued into 2015 with headlines in the *Belfast Telegraph* such as 'Man Shot in Both Arms and Legs in Ballymoney' on 20 March and '26 Year Old Man Shot in Both Legs in West Belfast' on 1 April. Paramilitary justice through incidents such as 'knee-capping', 'shootings' and 'punishment beatings/paramilitary style attacks' have brutalised certain young men for over 40 years, leaving them scarred physically and emotionally for life. Their wounds served as a stark warning to other young men and members of the wider community of the unquestionable authority of paramilitaries. Typically this type of brutality was inflicted by young men wearing balaclava masks on the most marginalised young males in communities for antisocial and other forms of deviant behaviour.

Physical assault, in the form of paramilitary justice, was often expected, anticipated and routine and carried its own tariff. As one young man in our 2015 study commented:

If you steal or break into houses then the paramilitaries will come knocking. The first time you get warned and they take your cash and maybe give you a slap. The second time they would break your arms or your legs and tell you to get out of the area.

To date, however, not one paramilitary member has ever been charged with brutalising and violating children. Ironically, for some young men, these wounds became symbols which gave them status amongst their peers – a type of initiation which paradoxically served as proof of their masculinity. Mitchell's (2012) thesis of the biographical narratives of what he calls 'ordinary' young men who committed 'political murder' further emphasises the influence of strong situational and environmental factors. He argues that young men are both products and producers of the different environments they encounter. In certain social circumstances the rational norm of young men who behaved violently towards others perceived as 'different' had a significant cultural influence which was constructed politically, historically and symbolically and is a major causation of violently divided societies. The young men in Mitchell's study were living with this legacy and seeking to find meaning through factors associated with violence, masculinity and becoming a man. It is perhaps unsurprising that, for many, the conflict became normalised as people tried to live ordinary lives in the face of such adversity. Some say this is characteristic of the people of Northern Ireland who continued to show resilience and hope in the darkest of times. The point is that for many young men engaging in violence became an important tenet of their masculine identity and what it meant to be a man during a *war*. Not all young men actively engaged in the conflict. Nor did all young men support violence or indeed understand what the conflict was about. Therefore in discussing the construction of masculinities during periods of violence, consideration must also be given to how those who did not engage in the conflict constructed their masculine identities. This is an important observation, as to suggest that one type of masculinity captures the experiences of all young men is incorrect.

Shifting patterns of masculinity

Studying masculinity in Northern Ireland, as in other global contexts that have experienced violent conflict, is much more complex than questioning why certain young men engage in political violence, join paramilitary or other extremist groups, or support armed conflict. For example, as Horgan (2011) contests, Northern Ireland has a much higher proportion of children living in persistent poverty than is the case in Britain, with more than one in five (21 per cent) of children and young people, which is more than twice the proportion in Britain (9 per cent). Horgan further argues that the interaction of poverty with the legacy of the conflict means that young people in Northern Ireland continue to live in segregated areas with high levels of disability and chronic physical and mental ill-health. This is further confounded by the high number of young people with an undefined status that consists primarily of young males aged 16 and 17 who are not in education, training or employment (see for example, Horgan et al., 2014). Longitudinal research reveals that this trend has been a pattern in Northern Ireland over many years (e.g. Northern Ireland Economic Research Centre, 1996, 2001) and concurs with previous studies into working-class youth throughout the UK (e.g. Hall and Jefferson, 1976; Willis, 1977; Jenkins, 1982, 1983; Bell, 1990; Gillespie et al., 1992; Cohen, 2002).

We discussed in Chapter 1 how Harland's (2000) inner city Belfast study with adolescent males aged 14–16 found that young men increasingly felt alienated, powerless and disconnected from school and mainstream society and pessimistic about the future. They found it difficult to ask for emotional support and feared being 'shamed' amongst their peers by seeking help. They believed men showing vulnerability was a sign of weakness and that by withholding certain feelings and emotions they were expressing an important aspect of what it means to be a man – the need to be tough, which often led to them resorting to violence to sort out issues. Over a decade after Harland's study, evidence suggest that little has changed for marginalised young men in regard to their attitudes and experiences of everyday violence, conflict and safety (see Lloyd, 2009; Harland and McCready, 2010; Harland, 2011; Harland and McCready, 2012).

Reilly et al. (2004) after providing statistics showing that young men (aged 17–24) were over-represented amongst the victims of the 'Troubles', make the point that 'it would be naive to suggest that all of these male victims were bystanders to the conflict, thus reflecting the difficulty of distinguishing victim from perpetrator in situations of armed conflict'. They go on to suggest that thrill seeking, lack of parental supervision, aggressive male role models and the excitement attached to inter-community conflict all contribute to young men's active involvement in violence, both as victims and perpetrators. They also make the point that social class, age, religion and geography all play a part as well as gender.

We cannot ignore the importance of culture and historical context in defining how young males display and negotiate their masculinity. We highlighted how Connell (1995) provides a theoretical framework for this, leading to a hegemonic concept of masculinity. Such theorising has been instrumental in creating more nuanced analyses of young males' experiences, particularly with the documentation of the dynamics of masculinities in their lives. However, whilst we have asserted that there has been a significant number of studies into masculinity, Martino (2007:47) argues that this has 'been accompanied by what might best be termed a neo-liberal and neo-conservative political agenda that has impacted on and continues to impact significantly on social and educational policy'. This, he continues, has implications for establishing young males and men as the 'new disadvantaged', thus as those who suffer as a consequence of the feminising influences of women. We have previously drawn attention to how this is portrayed in the media in terms of a 'moral panic' and 'masculinity crises' which, according to Lingard and Douglas (1999), is driven by a recuperative 'masculinity politics'. Martino (2007:47) further argues that young males' rite of passage is being 'thwarted by the absent father and, more broadly, by men's absence as role models in boys' lives'. He supports this by citing Biddulph (1999) who claims that amongst other factors such as doing badly at school, joining gangs and getting into trouble, that young males with absent fathers are more likely to use violence.

In discussing the importance to the culture of manhood of boys wanting the guidance of fathers, Martino (2007:47). claims that 'to impugn his desire to become "one of the boys" is to deny that a boy's biology determines much of what he prefers and is attached to'. Education theorists, in denying the nature of boys, can, according to Flood (2000:4), cause them much misery. He claims that agendas of reform committed to defining sex-role expectations specific to girls to expand their skills beyond the limits imposed by traditional feminists have not been afforded to young males. This failure to address the impact of hegemonic masculinities on young men's lives within populist literature imposes a political framework wherein boys 'are still universally encouraged to purge themselves of any hint of femininity'. Part of this purging is underpinned by violence or its threat to the extent that 'violence is almost always a male practice' (Whitehead, quoted in Flood et al., 2007:469).

It is clear from reviewing the literature that there is a vast amount of material written from a theoretical and empirical perspective about men and masculinities from around the world. This is reflected in multi-disciplinary perspectives, drawn from the humanities, social sciences, popular culture, feminism and, to a lesser extent, the sciences. This demonstrates a wide-ranging, well-established scholarship which offers sophisticated theorisation and an increasing diversity of men and gender relations.

5
Critical Reflections on Education and Learning

Throughout our careers and studies we have become increasingly aware of the need to create appropriate learning environments for engaging boys and young men that take cognisance of the ecological context in which they live and exist. However, we have consistently found that some professionals do not necessarily take the context or actual lived experiences of boys and young men into consideration. We have found this particularly apparent in schools.

In this chapter we discuss education and approaches to learning, in particular experiential learning, and draw upon the work of theorists such as Dewey and Rogers. This chapter also critiques a youth work methodology with an emphasis on the importance of reflective practice through an approach that places young men and their issues at the heart of their education and learning.

A leading writer in this area, John Dewey (1938), believed that 'there is an intimate and necessary relation between the process of actual experience and education'. Before specifically addressing work with boys and young men we believe it is important to pause to reflect upon what we mean by education and learning within the context of work with boys and young men. Dewey (1910, 1938) argued that education comes about through experience and that learning takes place in both our social and personal worlds as well as from each other. He pointed out that a traditional approach concerned itself with delivering preordained knowledge and was not focused sufficiently on the individual students' own actual learning experiences. He insisted that education should be designed in a way that is earthed within a theory of experience.

Dewey's concept of education emphasised the importance of meaningful activity in learning and pupil participation. He was looking to ensure the individual was invested in what he or she was learning which he valued over a rote learning approach. Dewey argued that a curriculum should be relevant to learners' lives and that learning by doing, alongside the development of practical life skills, was crucial to children's education. Within Dewey's experiential learning theory, knowledge is socially constructed and should be based solely on real life experiences. This principle or value has been integral to our studies with boys and young men and underpins all aspects of our approach to practice. Dewey cautions that experiences only become educative when they connect with the real world and therefore 'everything depends on the quality of the experience which is had' (Dewey, 1938:27). Kolb and Fry (1975) argue that for learners to be effective they need four types of abilities which correspond to their learning cycle:

- concrete experience abilities;
- reflective observation abilities;
- abstract conceptualisation abilities;
- active experimentation abilities.

Kolb's (1984) model provides a holistic approach that combines experience, perception, cognition and behaviour. The core of the model is a simple description of how learning is translated into concepts which in turn are used as guides in the choice of new experiences (Boud et al., 2005:12).

Influenced by the work of Dewey, Kolb's learning model (1975) builds on this theory and identifies a four-stage learning cycle whereby learning comes from experience. While the cycle can commence at any point, stages must be followed in sequence. This experiential learning model has been criticised for being 'over individualistic' and not taking account of the influence of context (e.g. Ord, 2013) and it has also been criticised for being 'too mechanistic and lacking in strong empirical validation' (Skinner, 2010:61). Despite such criticisms the model is practical and relatively easy to understand. It encourages educators to reflect more critically upon their practice, their feelings, their thinking and action and challenges them to apply new approaches or techniques to learning.

Miettinen (2000:54) notes that Kolb acknowledges John Dewey, Kurt Lewin and Jean Piaget as the founding fathers who provided the conceptions and historical roots of experiential learning. Kolb states that the approach was further developed by therapeutic psychologies based on psychoanalysis theorists, such as Carl Jung and Erik Erikson, and on humanistic psychology, such as Carl Rogers and Abraham Maslow, as well as by radical educationists such as Paulo Freire and Ivan Illich (Jarvis, 2006:245). Ord (2012:56) points out that while 'Kolb himself refers to this model as Lewin's experiential learning model (1951) the cycle was drawn by Kolb to illustrate what he thought Lewin was trying to communicate' (Kolb, 1984:21) and that 'the common depiction of the experiential learning model is most often referred to as Kolb's four stage model'. Ord (2012:69) notes that according to Dewey 'experience is part of what it means to be in the world...and what it means to be alive'. Ord suggests that 'Dewey's theory of experiential education gives much needed support to many of the fundamental tenets of youth work, such as the importance of relationships, the role of conversation and why it is essential to "start where young people are at"' (Davies, 2005).

For Dewey the educator is important within the learning process and his or her role is to facilitate the actual experiences of learners based on their capabilities and readiness to learn (Grady, 2003). Dewey (1938:67) asserts 'there is no defect in traditional education greater than its failure to secure the active co-operation of the pupil in construction of the purposes involved in studying', whereby the educator 'loses the position of external boss or dictator but takes on that of leader of group activities' (Dewey, 1938:59). Piaget (1968) also rejected the idea that learning was the passive assimilation of given knowledge and presented it as a dynamic process during which learners actively construct knowledge by creating and testing their own theories of the world (p. 8). Moon (2002) notes that the educator will influence all aspects of the learning environment and therefore it is important that the educator 'understands the nature of reflection and how it relates to the qualities of learning and what they are trying to achieve in the learners' (p. 167).

Within education vocabulary, a tripartite categorisation of learning systems has emerged. That is: formal education, informal education and non-formal education. It is here that the work of Combs with Prosser and Ahmed (1973) is influential in offering a definition of each.

- **Formal education:** the hierarchically structured, chronologically graded 'education system', running from primary school through the university and including, in addition to general academic studies, a variety of specialised programmes and institutions for full-time technical and professional training.
- **Informal education:** the truly lifelong process whereby every individual acquires attitudes, values, skills and knowledge from daily experience and the educative influences and resources in his or her

environment – from family and neighbours, from work and play, from the market place, the library and the mass media.
- **Non-formal education:** any organised educational activity outside the established formal system – whether operating separately or as an important feature of some broader activity – that is intended to serve identifiable learning clienteles and learning objectives.

Within Northern Ireland, the home of the authors, the term 'non-formal education' is closely associated with youth work and therefore will be used in this context in this text.

Approaches to learning

Alexander (2008) identifies two main approaches to teaching and learning:

1. didactic, where the teacher controls the process;
2. exploratory, where the learner is central to the process.

Exploratory teaching encourages learners to be 'active agents in learning, with the classroom more like a workshop and the educator an experienced partner in learning' (Eaude, 2011:14). Coburn (2010:35) argues that 'formal education privileges the educator as knowing and powerful as they choose the content of programmes while learners have to learn content that may or may not be relevant to them'. In contrast non-formal educators adopt an approach that is driven by an exploratory relationship that is holistic, which puts the young person and their world and interests at the centre of the learning process. It is this emphasis which is fundamental to the pedagogy of non-formal education.

Deep and surface learning

Horgan (2003:77) claims that 'people learn better if they think about what they are learning and have an opportunity to engage with the material'. The idea that approaches to learning might influence the outcome of learning had its principal origins among researchers in Gothenburg, Sweden (Moon, 2002). Studies revealed that individuals either approached a task in order to elicit the meaning that was being conveyed, typifying a *deep approach* to learning, or to learn for simple recall purposes without the sense that they needed to understand everything, typifying a *surface approach* to learning.

Fry et al. (2009:10–11) assert that deep learning is typified as 'an intention to understand and seek meaning', leading learners to attempt to 'relate concepts to existing experience, distinguishing between new ideas and existing knowledge, and critically evaluating and determining key themes and concepts'. In contrast surface learning is defined as typifying 'an intention to complete the task, memorise information, make no distinction between new ideas and existing knowledge, and to treat the task as externally imposed'.

The educator at the heart of learning

Carl Rogers (1994) believed that there were certain qualities, attitudes or core values which, if present in an educator, would more effectively facilitate learning. Henry, Hammond and Morgan, (2010:30–32) critique how, within Roger's person-centred approach, 'three core conditions' are necessary and sufficient for growth and change to occur within the learner and how the *person-centred* goal of empowerment can be linked to the ethical principle of autonomy which involves 'respect for the young person's right to be self-governing' (British Association for Counselling and Psychotherapy, 2002). In presenting the three core conditions, Henry et al. highlight *realness* or *genuineness* as the first condition (Rogers, 1983:34–35), which features congruence and transparency of appropriate communication. Rogers and Freiberg (1994) argue that 'when the educator is a real person and enters into a relationship with the learner without presenting a front or façade the educator will be much more effective' (p. 154). The second core condition is 'unconditional positive regard' which emphasises the educator valuing the 'worth and significance of the person', which Rogers and Freiberg (1994:156) describe as 'a caring for the person, but a non-possessive caring and the acceptance of an individual as a separate person who has worth in their own right'. The third condition is the learner's perception of the educator's capacity for empathy (Rogers, 1980:149), which involves the person feeling fully understood, valued, cared for and accepted. In order to build meaningful relationships of trust and respect, Henry et al. suggest 'the educator must be a highly skilled communicator and be a confident, competent and self-aware individual' who is 'genuine and transparent in all interpersonal interventions and relationships with young people' (p. 29). Rogers and Freiberg (1994:157) posit that when an educator has the ability to understand the learner's 'reactions from the inside, has a sensitive awareness of the way the process of education and learning seems to the learner, the likelihood of significant learning is increased'. Smith (2007:2) adds that learners feel deeply appreciative and understood when they are not evaluated, not judged, but simply understood from their own point of view.

The reflective educator

We can see that the role of the educator and the relationship between the educator and learner is fundamental within experiential learning. This necessitates the need for educators to be reflective and self-aware. Being a reflective practitioner has been advocated as a core skill for all those individuals and professionals working with children and young people (Leverett and Rixon, 2011). However, as noted by Knott and Scragg (2010), it is also important to encourage and support reflection amongst young people as part of practice interventions. Dewey (1938) describes reflection as the kind of thinking that consists in turning a subject over in the mind and giving it serious thought – a chain of ideas that aim at a conclusion. Dewey believed that reflection involves complicated mental processing of issues and a mix of skill and attitude that can enhance the quality of learning. Race (2010) asserts that reflection deepens learning while, according to Postareff (2007:18), it is three dimensional and 'reflection can take place prior to (reflection for action), concurrent with (reflection in action) and retrospective to teaching (reflection on action)'. Olsson and Roxa (2013) speak of reflection being a key aspect of a 'scholarship of teaching and learning' and a useful tool for applying knowledge and discovering new aspects of everyday practice.

Moon (2002:10) presents reflection as 'a basic mental process with either a purpose or an outcome or both, that is applied in situations where material is ill-structured or uncertain or there is no obvious solution, but related to thinking and learning'. Moon further adds that 'for many, it appears the capacity to reflect purposefully needs to be fostered or coached. Those who can engage in such activity may promote it without appreciating the difficulties others have when trying to do this' (p. 9). Important to Dewey is the initiation of reflective thinking in a state of doubt, uncertainty or difficulty and the need to solve 'perplexity' – a sense of goal directedness and the notion of testing or evaluating that guides the process (Moon, 2002:12). Subsequently, reflection involves the complicated mental processing of issues. Dewey considers that a mix of skill and attitude govern the quality of the process, and that testing through action is necessary for reflective activity. Moon (2002) provides a comprehensive review of how reflection has been considered in the fields of professional education and concludes that it has a key role in experiential learning and that the outcome is 'action, learning or more learning' (p. 24).

Youth work, non-formal education and social education

In youth work social education has long been the associated underpinning theory. The roots of youth work has its origins in the mid-19th century (Milburn et al., 2003) when the Young Men's Christian Association (YMCA) was set up in 1844 as the first dedicated youth organisation (Jeffs and Smith, 2010). Other significant factors in the emergence of youth work was the increasing public interest in youth as a distinct category with specific needs, and a more scientific theorising of the term 'adolescence' by psychologists such as Stanley Hall (1904). The theory of youth work during the mid-19th and early 20th century was light and consisted of individual histories of organisations, such as the Boys' Brigade, the Girls' Brigade and the Scout movement, or was inspired by individuals and organised in, at times, an uncoordinated and, at other times, loosely linked parallel structures. However, we would be remiss not to give mention to social education as historically providing youth work with a theoretical underpinning. There have been a number of definitions of social education over the years that are associated with youth work writers:

> Social education is the conscious attempt to help people gain for themselves, the knowledge, feelings and skills necessary to meet their own and other's needs.
>
> (Smith, 1988)

> Social education curriculum is a specifically educational process that has existed in an identifiable form for a period of time … is generally non-vocational, non-academic, and (usually) non-compulsory and has aims to pursue certain principles held to be universally valid in democratic systems.
>
> (Booton, 1985)

Social education is the curriculum of youth work and is the interface between formal education and non-formal education. Social education gets a first mention specifically, or is identified as an underpinning theory of youth work, probably in the Albemarle Report (1960) into youth work in England and Wales and comes into Northern Ireland youth work literature around 1970. Since their inception youth organisations attempted to address the problems and needs of young people caused by industrialisation. However, the history of youth work has not been a simple tale of diversionary entertainment of young people. Underlying principles of *social change, social justice* and *education* have always been synonymous with youth work. Early pioneers may not have articulated their own particular methods in these terms but, rather, they could be said to have simply analysed a social need and responded accordingly, that is, a needs-response model of practice. Social education is not new and is not exclusive to youth work, but it has a close and important historical association with it. However, as noted by Booton (1986), youth workers 'have tended to study social education without an historical dimension and each successive generation of practitioners has virtually reinvented the concept for themselves'. Nevertheless, social education and youth work have had a special and distinct association through what Smith (1988) refers to as a 'conscious attempt to help people gain for themselves, the knowledge, feelings and skills necessary to meet their own and other's needs'.

According to Smith (2002) social education became the activity of a central organising idea within UK youth work. However, Smith (1982:55–56) cautioned that

> much social education has been uncritical of the society and time it has been born of. It has accepted the powerless position of those it is supposed to help and done little to change that situation, even though this would appear to be a direct contradiction of its core values. In an unjust society social education has to be critical.

Despite its history, we see that the concept of youth work can be difficult to define and has produced competing views as to its fundamental purposes and nature (Tucker, 1994; Harland et al., 2005; Spence et al., 2006). Jeffs and Smith (1999:48, 2010:3) identify several distinctive characteristics that have been present to differing degrees in youth work practice since the early 1900s. They suggest youth work:

- is directed towards young people;
- has an educational and welfare purpose;
- is a commitment to association, relationship and community.

Jeffs and Smith advocate working with young people in their own community so they may better relate to themselves, others and the world. They add that the personality or character of the youth worker is of fundamental importance, as is being friendly, accessible and responsive while acting with integrity. Importantly they note that the relationship needs to be voluntary whereby young people choose to participate in youth work programmes. It is this principle that differentiates youth work from almost all other services orientated towards young people. Unlike formal education where young people must attend school, in youth work young people choose to participate. One outcome of this is that young people have 'considerable control' over the process and can choose to withdraw at any time which, as argued by Davies (2010:3), shifts the power balance between the educator and the young person. McCready and Harland (2013:11) present youth work as non-formal education and highlight the key features of a youth work methodology which they say are effective in engaging young people in their own learning. They present youth work as a methodology that:

- looks to find *how education fits into* and contributes to the lives of learners;
- is characterised by a *specific value system* relating to social justice which helps to distinguish it from other approaches to learning;
- is about a *critical, relational-driven encounter* with young people;
- meets young people *on their own terms*;
- is an approach where the educator *extracts knowledge and meaning* from a young person's experiences and ideas;
- is about *creating environments* that engage, stimulate and motivate;
- is about *creating a safe place* where young people explore fears, complexities and aspirations in their lives;
- works with young people *individually and in groups*;
- views people as an asset not a problem;
- is concerned with how young people *feel*.

The role of the youth worker centres on the facilitation of young peoples' learning in the context of their real life experiences. Tolstoy wrote that 'the greater part of one's education is acquired, not at school, but in life' (Tolstoy, 1967:24) and this position is widely acknowledged. McCready and Harland discuss how a young person typically spends around 16 per cent of his or her time in school and note the fact that 70 per cent of learning actually occurs outside of school (p. 12). This sits in contrast with the fact that the majority of assessment processes within formal education are based solely on what is learned in school. Formal education typically centres on a taught curriculum, aimed at helping learners gain qualifications through achieving certain grades in examinations, whilst youth work and non-formal education is based around the conversation and dialogue between the young person and youth worker. Within the formal education approach there is less of a focus on the ecological context of a young person's *real life* experiences or on moral development or relational behaviour. This may mean that, within 12 years or possibly more of formal education, boys and young men are unlikely to be provided with the opportunity to reflect upon issues such as violence and masculinity. We acknowledge that, within formal education, there have been many innovative and inclusive developments in special needs provision and alternative education programmes (as well support services and educational advances in technology and internet learning), but youth work 'acknowledges the importance of education, learning and training which takes place outside recognised educational institutions' and works to enable young people to extract knowledge and meaning from their own experiences and ideas and help them to reflect on the way they feel about issues that affect their everyday experiences (Young, 2006). Youth work is 'rooted in respect for young people' and their individual richness and complexity (Davies, 2010:2). It is about creating a safe space where, through conversations, young people can explore their fears and aspirations (Jeffs and Smith, 2010). 'Youth workers seek to work in ways which encourage young people to use their experiences of everyday living as opportunities for learning about themselves and others' (Crosby, 2005:54). Spence et al. (2006) state that youth work practice is inextricably linked to the realities of young peoples' lives and is affected by local culture and the relationships that they have with other people and institutions such as the family, school and police. These authors suggest that 'these realities are given conceptual cohesion in the language of non-formal education, which encapsulates both the informal, relational aspects of the work and its intentions towards constructive learning and development' (Spence et al., 2006:134).

To illustrate the impact of this youth work approach within a youth justice context, the Youth Justice Review in Northern Ireland (Department of Justice NI, 2011:151–152) stated that young people, interviewed as part of the review, spoke of being motivated and inspired by youth workers who they described as 'supportive, non-judgemental and caring'. Young people also stated that the Youth Justice system would work much better if there were more youth workers and if other professionals adopted the same approach and way of working that they employ. The report specifically highlighted youth workers' skills and persistence in engaging and building relationships with the most isolated, marginalised and hard to reach young people. It also commended the way youth workers treated young people with respect but also checked and challenged negative behaviour and built support for law and order. A recommendation in the review stated: 'the success of youth and community work in Northern Ireland should be built upon by providing additional resources to support its expansion, allowing other agencies to draw on the skills and expertise of youth and community workers in engaging young people, especially those who offend'. Drawing on a qualitative study conducted in England, Kelly (2012:102) argues that targeted youth projects can benefit participants, but warns about over-stating their ability to prevent crime and anti-social behaviour.

We are not advocating that youth work, as non-formal education, is a panacea for all that happens in a young person's life, and we acknowledge the importance of formal education. However, we know that many young people can be labelled as failures within formal education from an early age – a label that is incongruent within the values and purpose of youth work. Fundamentally youth work, as non-formal education, is about a critical, relational-driven encounter with young people that is characterised by a specific value system relating to social justice which helps to distinguish it from other approaches to learning (see Spence et al., 2006; Blacker, 2010; McCready and Harland, 2013). It challenges 'policy rhetoric of young people as problematic to stressing the importance of young people for society as a positive resource' (European Commission for Youth, 2014). This is supported by Ledwith (2011) who suggests that youth work is founded on a process of empowerment and participation and a form of critical education that encourages young people to question their reality. Youth work's emphasis on personal, professional and skills development links to ideas of empowerment, social inclusion and progression that are best represented by an integrated approach (Freire, 1972), which is a key principle underpinning critical pedagogy (Santamaria and Santamaria, 2012:4).

In this chapter we have discussed education and learning and, in particular, the importance of a critical-driven relationship between the educator and the young person. We have presented a youth work methodology with a specific value system relating to social justice which helps distinguish it from other approaches to learning. It is an approach that views young people as an asset and not a problem. An approach that endeavours a young person to extract knowledge and meaning from their lived experiences and their ideas and it is concerned about how a young person feels.

6

The Voices of Boys and Young Men (1997–2015)

Talking to young men about violence and masculinity

From Harland's first ethnographic study in 1997 to the one-to-one and focus group interviews with young men in 2015, we have been provided with a wealth of commentary from boys and young men. Numerically this period of research represents over 1,000 different boys and young men talking and sharing their views on violence and masculinity (and other things).

The freshest data comes from a series of focus groups with young men carried out specifically for writing this book. Between October 2013 and January 2015, the Centre for Young Men's Studies engaged with 180 young men aged 14–23 from across Northern Ireland with the aim of understanding their experiences and perceptions of violence, masculinity and the broader issues that affected them in their everyday lives. In conducting this research the Centre used a qualitative methodology through a series of semi-structured focus group interviews and in-depth one-to-one interviews. A total of 24 focus groups and 25 individual interviews were carried out by three male interviewers and one female interviewer. The average focus group consisted of six young men. They included those in custodial establishments, those linked to LGBT organisations, those with experience of being in care, those in youth and community centres, and those in vocational training establishments. Access was gained through gatekeepers currently working with young men in these settings. Interviews were carried out by experienced researchers within the Centre – all of who had previous experience of interviewing boys and young men. All interviews were digitally recorded and specific themes were identified that emerged from informants and pieced together to form a comprehensive picture of the collective experience. The next step was to build a valid argument for choosing the themes for analysis and comparing these with previous studies carried out by the Centre and existing literature. Ethical approval was sought for and approved by Ulster's Research Ethics and Governance procedures. The specific objectives of the project were to increase our understanding of:

- young male experiences of, and attitudes towards, violence and violence related issues;
- how boys learn about violence;
- why certain boys engage in violence (and why other boys do not);
- how traditional interpretations of masculinity impact upon male behaviour development;
- how boys learn about masculinity;
- the 'blur' between perceived acceptable and unacceptable levels of violence;
- ways for educators and practitioners to engage boys and young men in addressing the themes of violence and masculinity.

Our approach is to present the voices of young men gathered not just from this latest data collection, but from across a number of years. Particular attention is paid to the freshest data (2015), though our experience has shown that a number of points remain the same, whether it is from 1997 or 2015. We present the data with minimum commentary and analysis from the authors in order that it will not deflect from the power of their voices. The first theme examined is violence.

The early years

When the boys and young men searched their earliest memories what became clear to us was that, for many, the violence between their parents featured prominently.

Early observations in the home

Family structure, parental practices and parenting styles are empirically proven to be important risk factors for serious crimes including violence. In terms of family risk, stability, abuse, domestic violence and parenting have been seen to impact upon the behavioural outcomes of young people (Olate et al., 2012:397). Whilst poverty and social status has long been cited as a risk factor associated with violence, and numerous studies have found a high correlation between violence and inequality (Fajnzylber et al., 2002; van Wilsem et al., 2003), this may be partly explained by the pressure on parenting that is experienced by people living in poverty (James, 1995; Weatherburn and Lind, 2001).

'It is argued that the frustration and exhaustion of life in poverty render parents more likely to be irritable, conflictual and to use harsh and inconsistent parenting. This produces violence in the sons who are exposed to it' (Fitzgerald et al., 2004:14).

What the boys and young men said

The first time I saw violence was when I was seven or eight with my ma and da' taking drink and drugs. My ma and da use to beat the f*** out of each other. My ma stabbed my da' once. As I got a bit older I use to try and stop them fighting but **they were usually drunk** and wouldn't stop. In the end the drink and drugs killed my da'.

My da' would come home drunk and start **beating my mum up**. I wouldn't stay in the same room as my da'. We all dreaded him coming home at night because we never knew how he would treat us. One night he would be joking and messing about and the next night he would become angry and start hitting my mum and threatening us. I think this really affected me. I feel sometimes that I should have stopped him. But we were all scared of him. We were always frightened and didn't know what to expect. **My da' was an angry man.** I hated the pain my mum suffered at his hands and I couldn't do anything about this. It's hard when you're young to watch violence in the home – especially watching a man hit a woman – it's not right for a man to hit a woman. I hated watching it. If I had been older I may have been able to stop him. But we were all scared of my da' – everybody was. He had a big reputation for being a hard man and just lived up to that. They split up when I was about ten.

I remember when I was about nine hitting my sister over the head once with a plank of wood and my da' hitting me a dig on the mouth – like he's right you shouldn't hit a girl. But he hit my mum. **I hated it when my dad hit my mum. I never spoke to anyone about it.** You just accepted it and thought it was normal, but deep down you knew it wasn't. My dad seemed to have a selective memory. The next day he seemed to forget about what he did. **Maybe it was because he was drunk** when he did it. But it destroyed our family. I know now that it's not normal for kids to see their dad's hitting their mum.

In our house there was always fighting and arguing. I don't see myself as a bad person and I don't like fighting. Seeing **violence in the home was just part of the way I grew up**. I guess when you see a lot of violence you become violent yourself.

Regardless of age, race, religion, geographical location, sexual orientation or family composition, young men, over the years of collecting data, could recall their early experiences of violence. For a minority of young men, violence was first perceived to have been experienced within the home. For them, their father was the main perpetrator. Alcohol, anger and violence between spouses featured a lot.

But then there was violence easily available on TV, and over the years the boys and young men described how watching TV was a regular part of their day and much of it accessed from their own room and probably without restrictions.

> The first time I can remember seeing violence was on television when I was about five. There was lots of shooting and killing but my parents didn't stop me from watching. They were very easy going about what I watched.

In conversations about their early years young men talked of the discipline they experienced in the home: who was responsible for carrying it out, how it was administered and what it taught them.

'My dad disciplined me – but it didn't do us any harm'

Yea I was smacked. I think **it's okay for parents to smack children** – you've gotta let them know right from wrong – you've gotta hit them a smack on the head 'cause shouting at them is not gonna make a difference – I don't mean giving them a beating – **just a smack.**

I used to get beat with a slipper until I was about 10 [laughs]. My da' says he wouldn't do it now 'cause I'd knock the head off him.

I got smacked with a **belt.**

My da' smacked with a belt. It didn't do me any harm – **it teaches you right from wrong.**

Everyone gets slapped when they were young when they do something wrong but that's not violent.

My step dad would hit me when I was younger when he was drunk – **but only a smack.**

My da' would smack me but he didn't smack my sisters. He would shout at them but he just **smacked me around the head.**

My da' went too far with punishment. He would lose control and make us all afraid. He used to get angry and beat us around the head.

Everyone got slapped when they were young when they did something wrong but that's not violent.

Loyalty to their fathers, despite their disciplinary measures and approaches, was noticeable:

> If anyone said anything about my ma or da', I'd swing for them.

A *little* violence was expected, necessary and it seemed the best way to keep children under control. The sense of reluctance to be overly critical of the parent, and in this case the father, comes through and the consistency of the language that refers to a 'smack' implies a hierarchy in their thinking as to what is acceptable to them and what may not. The message coming through is that it was not unexpected to be *smacked* by your father but occasionally the use of force in behaviour management extended to instilling fear in the recipient.

Whilst the forms of punishment varied from family to family and indeed parent to parent, the common thread was that many had experienced this. In many cases within the focus groups there was a broad consensus that the punishment was justified as a socially and cultural acceptable form of parents gaining and maintaining control of the children, particularly the boys. The tone of the boys comments was very 'matter of fact' and there was a legitimacy given to 'the little smack'. It was acceptable.

For some young men, they even went as far as to state that they were grateful for this as without it there was a perception they would have 'gone off the rails'. There was greater disagreement, however, for when a physical punishment is acceptable and when it becomes unacceptable and could be more easily defined for them as 'violent'. For some it became unacceptable if there was bruising left on the body, for others it was based upon the justification for the punishment in the first place, that is, if the smacking or beating outweighed the seriousness of the offence then it was unwarranted and was unacceptable. For others it was still unacceptable if there was no explanation for the punishment and no closure following its application. In general terms, physical chastisement became 'violent' when it was harsh, inconsistent and 'overly aggressive'. It is not surprising that there was no consensus amongst these young men interviewed, given there is little coherent or conclusive arguments for this nationally and internationally contentious and subjective issue. The key message, however, was that most young men regarded justifiable forms of physical punishment in the home as valid, accepted and appropriate, which conveyed an understanding that there was such a thing as justifiable violence.

We were interested in young men's feelings around discipline and violence in the home, but also how violence was represented in their street or town and the Troubles in general.

How did all this make you feel?

Revenge and family solidarity comes to the fore in our conversations with young men as they recalled some of the more horrific incidents in their lives and homes. Whilst there were only a few such incidents they were not unfamiliar to many of the boys. If such incidents were not in their own home, they were talked about in the school playground, in the street, in the town or on the news.

> [On his father being shot in front of him by the paramilitaries] This makes me think about violence every day and want **revenge**. I think one day I would love to kill the person who did it. I know who did it – everybody knows who did it but nobody will stand up to him. You're told to f*** up or your family will get shot. Seeing this messed me up a lot and that's why I got involved in drugs and stealing and fighting from the age of ten. When I got older about 13 I was always fighting. I would not know when to stop. That was the problem. Others would say that's enough but I just kept going. I wouldn't let them get away with anything. If they thought I would back down they were wrong. I have **a lot of anger in me and** it just comes out.

> But then when I think of the b******* that killed my da' – I think the Troubles haven't even started yet – nobody's getting away with killing my da'. My older brothers know who did it– but they are married now and have wee children, but **I haven't forgot**.

But then views get formed out of these experiences and young boys rationalise their experiences and some find there is value in using *some* violence on maybe their own children:

> Children – you've gotta let them know right from wrong – you've gotta hit them a smack on the head – not give them a beating – shouting at them is not gonna make a difference – **you have to smack children for them to learn**.

What emerged for us was the significance of the father in these young men's lives. The relationship between young men and their father was a consistent and profound factor in regard to how these young men reflected upon their formative years within the family home. Interestingly in the focus group with gay young men the father was not perceived as the male archetype. In contrast to the father who was perceived as an authority figure, these young men were more inclined to speak of their mother as a matrifocal figure who held the family together – often in difficult circumstances. Fathers were perceived as authority figures, the disciplinarians who were typically emotionally distant, whereas these young men were more inclined to speak of their mother in a loving and protective manner. In almost every conversation, the mother was consistently perceived as the rock and the strength behind the family home – even when she was being victimised. In contrast the vocabulary from young men, when talking about their father, did not contain the same personal and loving language as they used when talking about their mother. This does not mean, however, that they do not love their fathers. Rather, they did not appear to have a vocabulary to articulate how they felt about their fathers. It was not a feature of our discussions that the boys gave examples of having previously spoken to their fathers about their feelings and emotions. When probed it was apparent that fathers did not appear to have spoken to their sons on an emotional level, nor did this appear to be expected. The expectation was that their emotional needs would be met by their mother. But a key feature of these conversations, about their early years, was the inevitability that violence would be part of their lives when growing up: the expectation that, at some time, you have to defend yourself, defend your family or defend your community. There was also a sense of duty and responsibility for younger members of the family.

> Growing up here he's [his young brother]
> going to be in a fight – it's that simple.

The sense of the inevitability that a *wee smack* or a *fight* would be part of a young boy's growing up experience came through consistently. It was just what happened, it was just part of the transition from boy to man. You could expect it and you would need to deal with it. That's just the way it is.

Primary school years

In Northern Ireland there is early year's provision for children in the form of nursery schools and playgroups but around the age of five a child will enter primary school. Primary school was seen as playful as opposed to violent by the young men. However, the seeds of violence and prejudice were clearly being sown as some of their earliest memories referred to experience of bullying from an early age.

> I was always behind in school. It didn't really bother me that I couldn't do the work. I don't have good concentration. When I was eight or nine **I was bullied** at school. It went on and on probably for about three years. They were bigger than me so I couldn't do much about it. They would hit me or just verbally bully me and say 'you're nothing but a wee rat'. Sometimes it stopped for a while but it would start again. People made me do things I didn't want to do and if you didn't do it **they would beat you up**. I felt really **lonely and scared**.

> I was bullied throughout my days at school from when I was six. **I knew I was different and so did others.** I was called 'gay boy' all day long. I guess because I wasn't manly. I didn't like things the other boys liked. I didn't like sports either. I didn't like to fight and I didn't do anything about the bullying. I just tried to get on with my life. It hurts and you just keep it to yourself.

When talking about primary school their stories did not really involve the recollection of academic pursuits and success but centred more around their social experience and recollections about their early teachers and some of their interactions with them. For most, their time in primary school was positive but the transition from primary to secondary school evoked memories of anxiety and some fear as they faced the challenge of integrating into a new social circle and meeting the expectations of their new school which they found very different from their experience in primary education.

Secondary school years

The primary school years are traditionally from 5 to 11 and children progress from primary 7 (the final year) to post-primary school by completing a transfer form from the Department of Education (NI) listing the choice of secondary schools. There is also a voluntary transfer test children can complete if a grammar school is preferred.

On the subject of violence and secondary school and teenage years the boys and young men easily recalled their experiences.

> I became a violent person about the age of 11 – when I went to secondary school. I probably carried some of the things I seen at home into school.

It's like you are either **bully or get bullied** – there's no in-between.

In school boys are **always hitting each other**. In the playground and corridors but this was never seen as violence – so when others hit me, because they thought I was gay, I just seen this as **normal**.

You sort of learn about different types of violence in school but you don't realise it at the time – it's only when you look back that you think that maybe **it was violence. But no one ever spoke about** it in that way. It was supposed to be just a bit of fun. You're supposed to be able to take it – but it's not funny – **it hurts deeply**. It messed my head up and made me hate school.

I started fighting when I was about 13. I got into fights all the time. I don't know why – it just happened. I knew I was a good fighter. But **you don't know when to stop** – you think will I hit him again or not? It depended on what age they were or what height they were. I didn't like picking on small boys but sometimes they act hard 'cause they're with their mates. So you fight harder to show everyone that you don't back down. That's the problem with fighting, you don't know when to stop. In school somebody usually stops it. But when you're outside of school nobody steps in to stop it and **things can get out of control** – especially if there is a crowd watching.

I remember in secondary school someone called me for a fight – they thought I wouldn't turn up because they knew me from primary school – but I did – **I gave him one punch** and he fell to the ground and wouldn't get up – **this stopped the bullying and no one would bother me after that**. There was another boy who said something about me in the class but I got him outside school and kicked his bollocks in as well. You get a reputation – I guess people in school began to **respect** me for this – they knew I wouldn't take anyone messing me about – no one messes me about now.

I was getting jumped every week and because I wasn't hitting back **I was an easy target**. One of the ones who did it must have felt bad one time and said 'Here mate, everyone gets picked every week, you're just the one they picked this week.'

In these recollections there is a connection made between the violence observed in the home being played out in the school. There was the casual *normality* of violence as what was expected in school and the early signs of boys having to show they could defend themselves or act like a man in order to fit in. They stressed the importance of *not backing down*. In the voices there is evidence of reflection and a hint that many wished for things to be different.

Our conversations with the boys and young men, and talk of violence in their lives, did not confine itself within the school gates. Yet again their comments were about the fact that *violence remains all around you in your home, in your community*. In fact 'it's just the way it is'; and the invasion of violence into the home featured once again.

> Four hooded men came into our house one morning about 8.30 a.m. and beat me with baseball bats. I got this scar at the side of my head from that. Another time a couple of older men gave me a bit of a kicking because they said I had been fighting with one of their sons and heard that I was talking about somebody they knew.

Boys were beginning to connect with the threats that existed in their communities if you *stepped out of line* or didn't do as you were told. Just like a local corner shop may have been conveniently at the end of a street boys talked of violence being conveniently on hand.

> You walk to the end of the street and there's rioting or someone's getting a beating. Violence is everywhere so it's hard to avoid it and hard not to do it.

> Yes, when you're about 12 you can go different places and you know there's different gangs there. Up here the TCH [Tullycarnet hoods] and the Ballybeen ones always meet up on the Comber Greenway and have a brawl. The TCL [[Tullycarnet Loyalists] and the Comber ones, the 'onion rings', just meet up and beat the heads off each other. The other ones are from 'six toe city' Ards 'cause they're inbred.

There is a sense that violence is unavoidable. If you are not looking for it, it will find you. If you are looking for violence there are other will-ing players to join you. But inevitably their thoughts turn to their own safety and protection and paramilitaries feature prominently in their recollections.

> There is no authority in my area, it's crazy, people drinking and no-one does anything about it. The police don't do anything. If the crowd's drinking and there is a cat up a tree, the police go after the cat.

No-one protects the community now. You felt safer with the paramilitaries. They would sort things out.

Violence – it's just the way it is. You don't go looking for it, but you have to watch your back all the time.

Violence is all around you. It's just part of everyday life.

Because this social–ecological context was seldom addressed in the class-room, boys perceived school as being disconnected from the reality of their everyday lives and experiences. Despite the changing political context of peace-building, boys voiced ongoing concerns about their personal safety and reported various forms of violence as simply 'nor-mal'. As these boys progressed through adolescence their perceptions of violence, law and order became more complex, and more consid-ered thought was given to the place of violence in their lives. However, they found nothing in school or their community, or indeed the family, which helped them to cope with the threat of violence or conflict.

Growing up in Northern Ireland, in what is euphemistically known as the Troubles, meant it was virtually inescapable that paramilitary elements would not feature at some point in your life when growing up. Whether it was the murals on the gable walls, the occasional dis-plays of men (and women) dressed in balaclavas on the streets or on the TV or in your house, street, town centre or estate, the role of the paramilitaries has a prominence and association with violence.

Paramilitary organisations

What was it like sharing this place with the paramilitaries?

Given these boys and young men were living in Northern Ireland through the early days of new and ground-breaking political agreements and paramilitary ceasefires, violence was an ongoing part of their lives. The violence on the streets and towns also came into their homes.

My da' got shot by paramilitaries. **He was shot in front of me.** They busted into our house and shot him dead.

This single quote is illustrative of an experience understood, if not directly experienced, by many of the young men. The home, for so many of them, did not provide security or immunity from the paramilitaries. In the close-knit communities where these boys and young men lived the impact of such an incident, as described in this quotation, extended beyond the doors of the invaded home. But when they talked of discipline and violence in the home it was clear that there was something outside their doors that entered that private space.

'It wasn't just in the house it was all around us'

Living in Northern Ireland can mean it is hard to escape the violent backdrop of the Troubles. Young men, living in communities steeped in over 40 years of violent struggle and endeavour, meant it was hard for them to feel immune from what was going on outside the front door.

> It was when we were young like eight or nine. I'll tell you how young we were, we were out playing 'cribby' [a ball game] and our ma's grabbed us in and we were lying on the floor in the living room and you could hear all sorts going on outside and then you realised your da' wasn't there and you were pure shitting yourself thinking he's out there.

> Growing up I saw a lot of violence in the area where I lived. There was always fighting. They were older people. I never really knew what was going on. But when you think about things now you realise how it all affects you.

> My area was very violent, especially for kids growing up. My Mum tried to keep me away from it and shelter me. I would have seen riots on TV and recognise the area up the street, thinking I'm not 20 feet away sort of thing. I wasn't involved in violence and it wasn't towards me, but I could see it a lot. I couldn't understand it, I didn't know why. It was something my mum wanted to keep me away from.

The community offered security and also posed a threat. Their street or town was, for many, a contested space and what they described was the occasional random outburst or violent incident that necessitated either getting to a point or place of safety. As they were to grow older there was even an anticipation that you could hang around and observe what was going on, or perhaps even participate. In this way there was often a rite of passage in the community thrust upon the young men. The early years of observing what was going on was not a passive experience but one that required some form of participation.

> If you join them [the paramilitaries] then it's going to be pretty hard to get back out of it. There's only two ways out of it, you either pay or you get a beating. If you become a Christian you can get out of the paramilitaries because you're not allowed to be in it.

This latter comment offers an interesting twist on tactical youthful conversion to Christianity. The sense that a 'turn to God' was perceived to be accepted by the paramilitaries as reasonable and would allow exemption from joining them implies an understood and agreed moral code that extended into the apparent lawless ranks of these organisations.

And then there are *double standards* about law and order that can install a sense of confusion in the minds of young people:

> It's okay if they [the paramilitaries] do something wrong, it's justified, but if we do anything we get punished. This is how it is and nobody can do anything about it – you just have to live with this.

But then there has to be *consequences when you do the 'odd thing wrong'*. Many of the young men had processed their experiences in a way that left them trying to form an understanding of why the paramilitary personnel exercised control over them. They rationalised it in such a way as to accept that, if you take risks or did something that many might refer to as normal juvenile behaviour, there would be consequences. The problem was that for many of these young men what was constituted as a *risk* was defined, not by the police, but by the paramilitaries.

'They [the paramilitaries] are the law around here'

> The paramilitaries put you in the boot of the car and drive you about and then kick you out. They do this to scare you – warn you that if you do anything bad again it will be worse next time.

Then there is punishment by appointment:

> The first time was when I was 15. I was hit with steel batons by three masked men. They told me if I didn't stop anti-social behaviour they would shoot me. The second time was when I was 16. I was ordered by paramilitaries to attend a meeting. I was not given a reason why but I knew it was because of my behaviour. You get word from somebody that you have to be at a certain place for a certain time. I just said who the f*** are they to tell me what to do. But you know that these b******* mean what they say. You know if you don't go it could be worse. They threaten to shoot anyone who doesn't do what they were told. Some of my mates were shot by them. They think they are the law. So I went to a place near a park. When I got there three men in masks came over to me. They just said that I had been warned about anti-social behaviour and held me down. I was shot in the knee. They

tried to shoot the other knee but the gun jammed. They say it's for anti-social behaviour, but they do the same things. They take drugs and sell drugs. But nobody else is allowed to do that. Nothing gets said when they cause trouble or break the law. But they shoot us for doing the same thing.

There was a sense of relief when the beating was over:

A few years ago I got my arm broken by four boys. They [the paramilitaries] jumped out of a car and put me up against a wall and beat me with clubs for selling drugs. I'm not saying I didn't do it but they had no proof. Funny thing was that after that nothing was ever spoke of it by anyone – it was just forgotten about after this.

They don't frighten me:

These guys who burst into our house to do me tried to make me afraid of them. I knew they were paramilitaries but I don't give a shit about these ones. They think they are hard men because they are in the paramilitaries. But they don't know that I don't give a f*** how hard they are.

But they do frighten me:

It scares you [getting beaten up by paramilitaries] – you feel frightened 'cause you know what they could do to you. You feel angry but there's nothing you can do. But it eats away at you. You feel scared when you are out 'cause you never know what could happen to you.

I remember growing up, my family were afraid of the paramilitaries. Paramilitaries ran the show in our community and we were always frightened of what they would do. Some of our neighbours were in the paramilitaries and some neighbours were shot by paramilitaries. Lots of families in my community have had hassle with paramilitaries. They've hassled me for years wanting me to join or get involved. They try to tell you what to do – get you to take drugs. Some of them are the same age as me. But I just tell them who the f*** are you to tell me what to do. They have double standards. They commit crimes but threaten others if they do the same things. But you have to take warnings seriously – I know others who have been victims of paramilitaries. Why are they allowed to do things and we're not? Once they grabbed me and threw me on the ground – but a man I knew came by who was in the paramilitaries and told them to leave me alone. I think he sorted things out 'cause I don't get as much hassle now but I still try to stay out of their way.

The stories all refer to the way in which violence was used as a form or control and punishment. Locally this form of paramilitary action is known as 'punishment beatings'. We read earlier of Kilpatrick (2013) referring to 'a year of brutality', with young men statistically being the highest proportion of victims of these 'beatings'. The fact that the term 'punishment beatings' is the way these attacks are described implies there is guilt on behalf of the victim who is in receipt of the beating. By describing these incidents in this way can contribute to legitimising the perpetrators and demonising the victims. They are *not punishment beatings* they are *paramilitary style attacks*.

The consistency and regularity of experiences of these paramilitary style attacks on boys and young men from all parts of Northern Ireland across the 18 years of our research cannot be ignored and our attention is drawn to their pain, their trauma and their hurt. For many the scars are visible in the form of broken limbs (or even kneecaps that have been replaced by plastic ones as their own had been shot off) and there are also psychological scars. A lot of the young men were victims of this violence and many were perpetrators, but their stories are harrowing. A mention of paramilitaries means an immediate association with violence and quite obviously – *men*. This leads on to the matter of role models for young men. If we accept that a role model is someone who can offer you support and guidance at a critical moment in your life, the story, so far, is of the significance of the mother, father, perhaps the teacher and the paramilitary member as the significant adults who are in the lives of these boys and young men. The picture emerging is that the main acts of violence in their lives are carried out by men.

> Furthermore, youth may be exposed to a substantial degree of chronic community violence that is either non-sectarian or sectarian in nature. Studies in both Northern Ireland and Palestine have shown that in the context of political conflict and community violence, the family environment is often high in stress and conflict (Cummings et al., 2010; Dubow et al., 2010) and parenting may be compromised.
>
> (Goeke-Morey et al., 2013:244)

Whether from Catholic or Protestant backgrounds, the presence and control of paramilitaries in working-class communities was a recurring theme. Many of the boys recalled the injustice of paramilitaries inflicting *punishment* on them and their friends for so-called anti-social behaviour, while those inflicting this punishment were not being held to account for their own actions in drug dealing and other crimes. They believed that while paramilitary members were often the main administrators of justice within their communities, they set double standards by carrying out the same types of anti-social behaviour for which other young men received punishment. Similar types of 'rough justice' that shape how young people in Northern Ireland construct their understanding of law and order has been argued by others (see McAlister et al., 2009). Young men spoke of 'unwritten rules' whereby they cannot go to the police to report any crime for fear of being seen as a 'tout/grass' [informer]. The fact that young men and other community members do not go to the police for fear of reprimand undoubtedly makes it much easier for paramilitaries to exert fear and control. Young people not reporting victimisation to the police concurs with other research (e.g. Zaykowski, 2013). However, unlike the young people who may not report to the police because they can seek help from others in authority roles such as parents, teachers, principals and child protection services, the young men in this Northern Ireland study felt there was no one they could talk to about victimisation (for similar findings see Haydon et al., 2012).

Our studies have shown that during early adolescence (age 11–13), of those who experienced being a victim of violence, 48.8 per cent did not talk to anyone about it. This increased significantly to 68 per cent during mid-adolescence (age 14–16), showing that as these boys got older they were less likely to report victimisation to the police or seek support from others. Zaykowski (2013:54) similarly found that 'violent behaviour and witnessing violence were significant and negatively related to adolescents reporting to the police'. There was a notable decrease in the number of boys getting into trouble as they progressed through adolescence (74.9 per cent in early adolescence down to 42.6 per cent in mid-adolescence). However, the fact that so many adolescent boys felt there was no one they would talk to about being a victim of violence, including paramilitary victimisation, is extremely concerning.

Hurt people, hurt people

Talking to boys and young men brings us into their world and experiences of violence in their lives and we are left wondering how it impacts on them and how it will manifest itself as they grow up. For some they turned it inwards and upon themselves, and for some they turned it towards others.

> I used violence against myself because I couldn't handle my anger. I was physically abused by my father at a time when my mother was really ill. He used to throw things at me. He got really angry and he reacted by being violent. I would cry and take a blade to the back of my legs and cut myself. I didn't want to kill myself; it was a punishment I think. This went on for about two years during the time of their divorce. I never really talked to anyone about it before. I use to try and protect my sister – be strong for her. It wasn't direct physical violence on us, it was usually throwing things near us. I was about 13. When my father left I had to be the man of the house. About that time I used violence against a boy at school who slapped me. He said it was just a bit of craic [Irish word for fun and enjoyment] but I gave him a bad beating. Another time a girl at school was messing around and hit me in the stomach with a pipe and I picked up a table and threw it at her. I have to be aware now all the time when things happen – like when something triggers me off. You don't like fighting with girls but you can't let anyone feel they are stronger than you are – especially a girl. I try to think now before I act, but it's hard. You feel pressure to do something. I don't know where the pressure comes from. It's something inside you. I don't like violence but it's all around you – every day you get into situations where the outcome could be violence. As you get older you think more about how to respond, but when you are young you are left to yourself – some people try to tell you what to do but you don't know how you will respond – like there's no script to follow when violence happens.

> Sometimes I get angry with myself for fighting. I think about the other person and the way I used to feel about being bullied. I also feel bad thinking about how my mum feels when I get into trouble.

> Anyone messes me about and I knock their f*** in. I am not afraid of anybody. Getting bullied when I was young taught me that you need to stand up for yourself – 'cause nobody else will.

The voices portray bravado as well as young men wrestling with their own emotions about being violent towards others. For some it is connected to what they witnessed and experienced when they were younger. For others they reveal a lonely place and a search to understand what is causing their actions. There is evidence of young men being reflective and considered when describing being hurt or hurting others.

> For me it's because I have been through it – I have been attacked and I wouldn't want to do that to someone else. I wouldn't want to put someone else in a position where they felt that vulnerable or that scared.

> I remember as a boy of ten getting involved in smashing windows and throwing bricks at people for fun. I liked the buzz – it made your mates look up to you – got you respect. But you think about things afterwards and realise you could have hurt other children.

> I'm a bit of a loner [laughs]. I've always kept my feelings inside. But at times I just feel full of anger. I need to get it out – I don't know why.

> One time I ended up fighting with someone for no reason. I just picked on him and I ended up with a broken nose and a cracked rib. He was very tall so I bit his face. Fights start over anything; you look at someone the wrong way and a fight starts. You don't back down and if you have taken drugs you don't even think about what you do until the next day when someone tells you what happened and then you feel shit about it.

> I think it was being bullied that made me rebellious when I got older. I just don't let it happen anymore – I don't care who it would be, I stand up for myself now. But life in school was hell.... I used to set off small fire alarms in school. I only did this because I was frustrated. It was probably a call for help.

Their talk is of *anger, fear, being fearless, hurting people, hurting themselves and being hurt*. In our conversations we were able to be patient and draw out emotions behind the commentary. If you have been hurt through violence it was not unusual to fight back or take it out on yourself or someone else. The violence they experienced was, for some, internalised, for others there was a need to hit back and hit out. But what was it all about and how did they explain and rationalise it?

What is violence about?

Over the years our conversations with young men went beyond listening passively to their stories and experiences. We began to get much deeper into dialogue with them in an attempt to get a better understanding of the place of violence in their lives. Patterns emerged as they disclosed their thoughts and beliefs. The first things they typically touched upon were the normality of violence, the fight for *territory*, the defence of their community or turf, and the combination of emotions such as *excitement* and the fear that violence generates.

> Violence has been part of all our history and even globally you hear of violence all the time.

> Fighting is all about territory. Like in football you fight with other supporters. It's just normal. You don't wanna see anybody from another territory coming into your area. It's important that they know who runs the area. Like in some communities you hear about people selling drugs and stealing cars and mobile phones. We don't want any people like that in our area.

> Fighting makes you feel like you're part of the estate and when you walk about the next day people look at you. It's a good feeling, people look up to you. They think you're a hard man – it's the best feeling.

> The six of us, have all been involved in riots. Every single one of us. It's absolutely mad but great fun. There's no fighting like it. When you're about 13 or 14 and you have a crowd behind you and a crowd against you, it's just brilliant. The adrenalin flows. You chant a bit of abuse at others and then get stuck in. It's about defending your community. So you have no remorse, you're doing something for your community. You're doing something for what you believe in. You go out to do proper damage and harm. You get respect for standing up for your community and then we watch it on the news the next day.

In a way this defence of community and territory may come from the Troubles and the way paramilitary groups were formed to protect communities and fight for either a retention of the Union or a United Ireland. With the various peace processes and paramilitary ceasefires came a reduction in paramilitary activity and, in some cases, disarmament by some groups, but, with over 40 years of Troubles, it is hard to expect that they will just simply go away. This is not the case. For these young men it was an easy step for them to explain their involvement in violence as a way of protecting their community, their own territory and, of course, *backing up your mates*.

> You're doing something for what you believe in.

You sometimes don't want to get into a fight but you have to back up your mates. It's hard to say no.

It's not just our area, the tunnel beside the church and the VG shop, none of us were looking for anything, but a bunch of under-age drinkers hit one of our mates with a bottle. We were just sitting there and he got bottled and a big massive fight broke out. So we had to back him up and it was nuts just because of one person. But we have to protect each other.

When fights start you always try to phone your mates to come round.

But it was not all about protecting territory; for some it was the long memory of past experiences and a drive for revenge that was their explanation for violence:

A while ago I was walking along the street when this older boy who had always bullied me in school came walking by. He had left school now. But I was much taller than him now. I looked at him and said to myself he will never do that again to me. As he walked passed I asked him if he remembered who I was. He didn't answer but I 'laid him out' and gave him a kicking. It was a great feeling. I knew from that point no one else would ever bully me again.

So, how is all this making you feel now?

It's a laugh when the police are chasing you – it gives you an adrenalin rush. It's the same when you are fighting, your adrenalin is flowing and you can't feel the punches, but you have to know when to stop 'cause the rush can make you feel like killing them.

Once you cross the line it's easier next time – once you stand up to teachers or fight with them or get chased by the police or steal a car – you are hooked. You think this is cool. You don't think of the consequences. This is where people are wrong. They think oh he'll feel bad about that but you don't. You think this is OK and so you do it again.

I like talking about fights I've been in before – then you get all wound up and go into town looking for a fight.

The adrenaline makes you want to get involved. You don't go looking for them. But sometimes wee girls you're with start the fights and you have to get stuck in. It's just the way it is.

> I like fighting. I don't know why. I just do it if I'm bored I knock some c*** out. I don't really think about it.

The excitement, the buzz, the fun and the adrenaline were frequently the primary drivers for being involved in violence. It provided them with something that was physical and bordered on an addiction and the need to keep doing it. But how do they process these experiences?

Do you talk to anyone about violence?

> Nah you don't talk about violence, it's just something you do or get done to you.

> As I grew up I learned to do things for myself. I didn't really talk much to my mum or dad – definitely not my dad. I didn't talk to anybody about the way I felt about things especially about things like violence. I used to just sit on my own and think about things and get angry.

> In school people made me do things I didn't want to do and if you didn't do it they would beat you up. I felt really lonely and scared but I wouldn't tell my da' 'cause he would look down at me and I wouldn't tell my ma 'cause I didn't want to upset her or make her feel she had to go to school to stand up for me. I wouldn't tell the teacher either 'cause if the bullies found out you would just get bullied more.

This learnt response around self-discipline and manliness was taken mostly from their relationship with their father. For many, it was the father that did not open up opportunities for these young men to discuss feelings and emotions. A man who kept things to himself provided the model for growing up and being a man.

Young men's reluctance to seek emotional support has been a key and consistent finding in the Centre for Young Men's research over the past 18 years (Harland, 2000, 2001, 2011; McCready et al., 2006; Beattie et al., 2006a, 2006b; Lloyd, 2009; Harland and McCready, 2010, 2012, 2014).

As the conversations developed around how and why violence was so much a part of their lives the role of alcohol, especially in relation to incidents of violence, became a key point.

The influence of alcohol and drugs

In terms of individual factors, strong and convincing arguments have been made on the correlation of alcohol and violence, particularly in

nightlife settings (Hughes et al., 2008). Sociological, as well as neurological, investigations have found that alcohol and drug use directly
affects cognitive as well as physical functioning and reduces self-control
and the ability to process information rationally and respond logically
(Peterson et al., 1990; Graham, 2003). As a consequence, this combination of deteriorated responses and cognitive understandings can lead to
antisocial or impulsive behaviour, including violence (Schnitzer et al.,
2010:1096). National survey data from England and Wales show that
nearly half of victims of violence believe the perpetrator to have been
drinking alcohol at the time of assault (Kershaw et al., 2008). For young
men here in Northern Ireland they were very clear about the role alcohol
and drugs played in violence.

> When you're out drunk at the weekend it's easy to get into a fight.
> When you are out with other guys you always have to be careful.
> If anyone says anything to you when you're drunk you take it the
> wrong way – you don't care if it's a joke, you just want to fight and
> usually can't even remember the next day what it was about. Drink-
> ing is supposed to make you feel good but it usually ends up in fights.

> When you're out drunk at the weekend, you always want to fight. If
> anyone says anything to you, it's easy to get into a fight.

> When you're drunk you take everything the wrong way and when
> you're hammered you don't know what happened that night.

> If you're drunk and somebody messes you about you don't care if it's
> a joke, you just want to fight.

> Fights start over anything especially when you are drinking; you look
> at someone the wrong way, and the next thing you know there's a
> gang kicking you. You go to the toilet and you have to watch your
> back. You have to be careful if you are outside your own commu-
> nity, some fellas go out just to start a fight. You never know when it's
> gonna happen but you watch all the time. You have to be with mates
> otherwise you could get done over easily.

> I like being stopped by the police [laughs] especially at the weekends
> when I have been drinking with my mates. You just keep drinking
> cider until you're out of your head and then you get into fights.
> Sometimes older boys attack you when you're drunk. I've had a few
> beatings – once with batons – and was so drunk I couldn't even
> remember who did it. Drinking and fighting is just the way I deal
> with issues.

There's always violence when there is drinking and drugs. Sometimes when girls are there there's also fighting.

My two mates were going to stab each other once. They had been drinking and taking drugs. I don't know where they got the knives from, but they were swinging them at each other.

Over-drinking gets you into stuff that you don't really want to do. Like when I used to be blocked [local expression for being drunk] and get into fights. I know 100 per cent I did things I wouldn't have done if I wasn't blocked.

There's better ways to deal with this. Stop under-age drinking and this might stop so many fights, but when I was 16 it's all I wanted to do – I've grown up a bit now but...

Most fighting I was involved in was when I was drunk or on drugs. Most people in here [Young Offender's Centre] got into trouble because of drink or drugs.

This range of comments relating to alcohol and violence extended across all our age ranges of boys from 11 up to 25. Violence simply became synonymous with alcohol and to a lesser extent drugs. It provided the bravery and the excuse before, during and after the violent incidents. It dulled any pain and excused any action. It fooled and deceived the memory of the events and enabled the story teller just simply to explain it all away as if, for many, it didn't really matter "cause drink was involved'.

There is no alternative

We asked if there was an alternative for these young men to violence and probed as to whether or not violence was just as inevitable in their lives as they have made it out to be.

You have to make the call. Do you become aggressive or do you stay calm? You have to think on your feet. You have to decide, do I hit this guy or do I try and talk to him? So it depends where you are. It depends if the person is drunk or with mates or if you are alone or with mates or you think he is carrying a weapon. Should I just turn away or take him on? You weigh this all up and then you act. In school, fights used to be arranged so you knew you had to fight. But when you get older you don't know where the trouble will come from. This is just something boys have to learn for themselves.

You're not really told how to approach things or think of alternatives. When you're young you're told if someone hits you, you need to hit them back.

It appeared to these young men it was about 'learning on the job'. You need to learn from your experiences, it was the experience that taught you what to do.

Violence is definitely the wrong way to go about it, but I'm telling you now if someone punched the head off you, you've nothing else to do but fight back – there are no alternatives.

OK you're walking home and you're on your own and you see someone and you're thinking like 'they're going to hit me' and you just need to be ready for it but you keep walking and if there is any movement you need to get in there first. This is the way it is – you just learn what to do.

You don't go looking for violence, but you have to watch your back all the time.

One day I punched my stepdad. He has never hit me again.

Young men spoke of passing their knowledge and experience on to other male siblings:

I don't want my wee brother to get beat up so I want to teach him how to fight but on the other hand I don't want him to get into fights and if I teach him I'm scared that he'll get into more fights – it's hard to explain – it's complicated.

The challenge of being young and male and living with violence and the threat of violence required these young men to make at times 'instant decisions' in regard to either fight or take flight. Decisions needed to be made quickly and therefore consequences, or alternatives, do not always get thought through. For these young men there was a perceived need to be aware at all times. The need to save face, the need to be alert and the need to watch out for yourself were *calculations* that were regularly in the forefront of these young men's minds when contemplating issues associated with violence.

If you hear someone calling your name you have to see if they may be picking a fight with you. You have to turn round or they'll think you're a dick and talk about you and all.

You look for things like someone moving their hand or arm or touching their nose – if you see anything like that you better 'get in' there first. You get it wrong sometimes but better that than getting it right and not doing anything about it.

No matter now who I walk past or what age they are or gender they are, I'll keep an eye on them in case they move at me.

Walking on by to avoid conflict was an option for some young men. However, this required a stronger character than standing up for yourself and getting into the altercation:

To avoid violence **you have to keep yourself to yourself.** If you are outside your area, you just don't look at anybody, make sure your phone is fully charged so you can ring your mates if you get into trouble. If someone is giving you trouble, just keep walking, and if they come after you then you still keep walking. No one feels safe – especially on your own.

I come out of my house, get in the car, go to school and I get the bus home. I go straight indoors and I am on the computer most nights. Weekends are the same. If you pass them and they are in a crowd they shout at you, if you stop they would even take your trainers off you. **I keep walking.**

What is described here is the loneliness of the young man who walks on by. Keeping yourself to yourself may deprive you of the camaraderie and security of belonging to a group described earlier that comes from backing up your mates.

Many young men opened up their understanding of the *rituals* that come in this sub-culture of violence: a world of 'mood', 'runners' and 'honour':

If you are walking past a group and they are slabbering at you, the biggest one in your group will walk over and the biggest from their group will come forward, and they will start fighting and everyone will join in. **If you are the biggest, it is your decision,** depends what mood you are in.

If it is a sober fight and you draw blood you walk away; especially if it's over something stupid, if you have been drinking or on coke then you just can't stop until you can't lift your arms.

There's **a runner** who will go between two groups. These are the ones **who make the trouble**. They will come over to you and say 'he's been saying this about you' and runs back and forward telling stories, until it breaks out in to a fight.

Within the *rituals* are *rules and boundaries* that are learnt and understood by the protagonists. Here the talk was of knowing how far you should go in a fight and the reputations that can accrue from fighting:

It's not how violent you are, but how far you are prepared to go.

When I am fighting I have to be pulled off – I don't know when to stop. If you want to fight – do it yourself – don't get others to do it for you. I guess I like to feel in control and that is why I often start a fight. I used to look for people to fight my battles – but not now.

When it's fair dig it's about reputation – you're not really doing it for revenge or anything or because your pissed off. If you want to do serious damage you bring a weapon like a bar or bat or something. The story changes from wanting to fight to wanting to seriously damage someone.

I don't plan to be violent it just happens. One minute I am cool and the next thing I know I am in a fight or wrecking something.

Once you use violence you'll do it again.

Talk of 'weapons', 'fair fights' and 'fighting your own battles' helped construct their fighting world with its own language built on ritual and boundaries. It was as if those that took part knew and agreed to the rules.

We asked young men if sexuality played a part in their world of violence. It is here their language changed and there were strong comments about young people being gay. However, at the same time there was an appreciation of people who were gay and the language was not always homophobic. A sensitivity and understanding of sexuality was apparent.

Only fruits back down.

I don't like gays. But I **wouldn't hit someone just because they're gay**.

Gay just means wee lads that are more girly if you get me. Look, I've got no problems with gays. I know gay people who you wouldn't mess with.

I know people who don't like gays. But I don't have a problem with someone just because of their sexuality.

When asked about the role of girls and fighting this revealed a chivalry that had echoes of respect for women that perhaps went back to their childhood and the revered way in which they held the motherly role. When it came to hitting a girl or young woman there were some lines that a boy or young man must not cross. In this they were emphatic.

You can't hit a wee girl. Especially if you are a boy. You're mates would look down on you. Even if you have a reputation for being hard, there's no excuse for hitting a girl – that breaks all the rules.

Boys can't hit girls, that's the worst thing you can do. I saw my da' hitting my ma and that taught me never to hit a girl or a woman.

No you never hit a girl, that's terrible.

If a girl hits you, you feel so annoyed but you can't hit them back.

When you're growing up, you always learn that you don't hit girls – that's totally unacceptable.

They're not as big as you so they're probably going to be weaker so you don't hit them.

It's knight's chivalry, like in medieval times, the knight's code not to attack women.

You'd never hit a woman, that's terrible.

I guess by the age of 14 I decided I needed to fight back. But one thing I do know – I won't hit any woman or a child – if you hit a child eventually they will get used to it – it should be discipline not violence.

You don't like fighting with girls but you can't let anyone feel they are stronger than you are – especially a girl.

This section of the voices of young men talking about violence commenced with experiences of domestic violence whereby fathers were witnessed as being violent to the mother. In the above passage it was clear that hitting a girl or woman was a step that should not be considered. This was not part of being a man. It was not in the equation. The fighting code did not extend to hitting a woman or a girl.

The rules associated with violence were presented as standard ethical codes of conduct, a moral compass and guide by which young men could enjoy a sense of 'doing the right thing'. These rules were voiced frequently and included comments like: 'you have to stand up for yourself'; 'you never hit a girl'; 'you shouldn't hit a child' (a distinction was made between hitting and smacking); 'you shouldn't hit anyone for nothing'; 'you can't gang up on people – it has to be a fair dig'; 'you're a fruit if you use a weapon especially if the other person doesn't have one'.

Listening to the young men, their codes seem reasonable, logical and indeed verging on the noble. The complexity of these views became apparent with further reflection. Many young men described physical chastisement not only as normal but as culturally acceptable. Broadly they agreed with this. However, with further discussion around the distinction between hitting and smacking, the objectivity and accountability appeared fragile. It appeared there was no real consensus around where (if any) the defining line between physical discipline crossed over to become what young men perceived as violent. Indeed there was regular contradiction within and between groups. Within each of the focus groups, the most commonly cited rule for the application of violence was that a young man could not hit a girl.

It was notable when speaking to gay young men that their rules towards violence were much more considered and less stereotypical. There was also less tolerance of violence and its place within society or the use of violence as a justifiable method of conflict resolution. While these young men spoke of experiencing potential threats to themselves because of their sexuality, they could not conceive of a time when they would ever become violent. They were more likely to refer to human rights and equality as being their main issues than speak of codes or rituals. These young men in particular spoke highly of their mothers being a major influence in forming their attitudes towards violence and, while some spoke of witnessing violence in the home from their fathers, they abhorred this violence.

The story so far is one of violence emerging early in boys' lives within the home and carrying on through their school days and teenage years. Living in Northern Ireland through the Troubles meant the inevitably for so many of these boys and young men to encounter, join, know, be aware of and hear about paramilitaries and their association with violence. From their experience of violent encounters they described the value of friendships and fighting for what you believe in. There was talk of struggling with the consequences of violent encounters, with alcohol being consistently part of the conversation and linked to violent incidents occurring. We heard about the rituals surrounding this fighting and the codes associated with it that had echoes of chivalry towards women. When talking to young men about violence it became clear that it was all around them from an early age and for many they negotiated this world on their own without formal instruction or opportunity for facilitated reflection. Our second theme was young men and masculinity.

Boys and young men talking about masculinity

What is masculinity?

When the word 'masculinity' was introduced into the conversation, for many it was not a word with which they were familiar. The tendency was to focus on 'masculine' and to associate it with being a 'man'. For many, masculinity was about how you talked, looked and behaved.

> Being a man is all about taking responsibility and **standing up for what's right**.

> It probably is about being manly – but I don't think about being manly – I just am who I am.

> I think the manly thing is an old-fashioned way of looking at things – don't get me wrong there are many gay men who camp it up a bit but you're always aware of how you're presenting yourself to others.

> As a gay man I find it funny if you're in a taxi or the barbers they usually talk about football – even though I've no interest in them things – like say you're in a taxi on a Friday night and you pass young women in shorts skirts – the taxi driver says – 'Hey check them out' – what am I supposed to say?

There were considered views on 'masculinity' that did not automatically associate the term with being violent:

> I don't think it is necessarily a masculine thing to be violent. I've grown up in a good area and none of my family has ever been violent. People that get into fights I look on them as scum. I was brought up to understand **that anger can be controlled**, like you should have more

self-control and if you express your anger as violence to someone else you are just as bad as them. There's nothing that can't be talked out. These are the values I've grown up with.

But then, inevitably, there were those who presented stereotypical views by associating 'masculinity' with being loyal, tough and fighting:

Anyone who **squeals to the police are touts**. That's something you don't do at any cost. You learn that as you grow up. Touts need put in a shallow grave and die slowly.

You **want to be the man, the guy** so you can't let anyone talk down to you or disrespect you.

You think the girls all want the bigger lads the ones who are the best fighters.

There were times I've went into a fight knowing that I'm going to get a beating. **But it's better to fight than walk away.** You have to stand up for what you believe in if you're a man. Other people will respect it. If you don't stand up, other people will walk all over you and no one will give you any respect in life. It's what you do when you're younger that makes you a man when you're older.

Over the years of introducing the word 'masculinity' into a conversation with boys and young men we found that many had not thought about defining it or explaining it to others or themselves. It was not a conversation they had very often, if at all.

What does it mean to be a man?

Instinctively many started with their fathers as the template for being a man:

I remember my da' was a hard man. He taught me that if you're gonna get hit – stand up for yourself. He would say to me '**I'll hit you if you don't hit back.**'

My dad used to say to me '**you've got no balls**' [laughs]. I'm not like that now 'cause I would stand up for myself even if there was a 100 wanted to fight me.

My father's **a typical manly type** who thinks his son should be a certain way. I guess he would rather I was not gay. Even though

I was raised in a typical stereotypical male environment, I have never warmed to the stereotype male. I guess I was always a mummy's boy.

They were also very clear about gender roles within the family set up:

Your **dad does the disciplining** and your **mum shows you the love.**

For others their *older* brothers, and sisters, had an important role in this process of growing up:

I had two older brothers so I got a bit of a hard time growing up from them. I didn't see this as violence and in some ways I thought it was just part of me being prepared for life as a man. When I was young my **dad would have disciplined me** – usually a smack or a kick in the ass. But as I got older around ten or eleven **my brothers would smack me about** – sometimes for nothing and other times because of something I did they thought was wrong. I suppose they thought this was OK. They probably wanted to show me my position in the 'pecking order' of males in the family [laughs]. But like my dad they thought the best way to deal with me was through a slap around the head or talking down to me. I don't think **they ever meant to hurt me – more a kind of initiation** – the way males show each other how to act like a man. **I guess this teaches you that you become a man through knowing your place and respecting your elders.**

I don't get on at all with my big brother but I look up to him 'cause he doesn't take shit off anyone. He wouldn't let anyone hurt me. I wouldn't want to be like him but it's good to know someone is looking out for you.

The early influence of the father in the family home was important for many. It was only when reflecting upon the answers they gave to interview questions that young men appeared to appreciate the significance of their father in shaping their own attitudes and behaviour. For some this meant defending their father. For others speaking about their father stirred feelings of anger as they reflected upon how he had treated their mother or instilled strict discipline within the family home. It was uncommon for young men to criticise or question their father's role and behaviour. Even those whose father had been absent as they were growing up spoke of having wanted to get to know him better.

The key issue again is the significance of the father in young men's lives. While present, physically absent or emotionally absent, the relationship between young men and their father was a consistent and profound factor in regard to how they reflected upon their formative years within the family home. In almost every conversation, however, the mother was consistently perceived as 'the rock' and the strength behind the family home.

Violence as part of becoming a man

Violence is an integral and complex aspect of male identity (Harland, 2011:428) and also 'serves to maintain group solidarity, reinforce kinship ties, affirm allegiances and enhance status within the group' (Burman et al., 2001).

We were struck by those who believed there was a *rite of passage* to being a man, though they retreated to the safety of defining being a man and associating it with violent behaviour. The talk was of 'reputations'; 'showing others you are not afraid'; 'gaining respect for standing up for yourself'; 'having balls'. It seemed the comfortable place to go, particularly for those young men who found themselves in a juvenile detention centre or prison.

> That's why I am doing time now – fighting and getting into trouble with the police. I have a **reputation** now of being a fighter. I have been suspended from school many times for fighting, sometimes even with teachers. Teachers would talk down to me and get in my face so I would swear at them and tell them to f*** off. They use to tell me to get out of the class – but I just told them to get the f*** out of the class. When I was 13 a teacher threw me against the wall but I just stood there and told him to get the f*** out of my face. You think about others in the class. **You know they are watching.** You say to yourself I'm not going to back down. I guess once you stand up to a teacher you have to always do it **or those who are watching will think you're afraid.**

> I think it's important for a man to stand up for himself – but also to show people respect, know your place, not let people tell you what to do, working and getting paid for what you do – able to keep yourself together.

> 'If you do the crime – do the time.' I don't mean this in a macho way. But it is part of being a man. You can't say I'll take risks and then cry about being caught. That's the way it is in here [prison].

> Growing up violence was everywhere – in the streets, amongst neighbours, paramilitaries, in school. You have to learn how to deal with

this. This is part of becoming a man. As you get older you stop accepting some things. You become a man and you need to look at things differently. Like for me there were no adults I could trust so I just worked things out for myself. But it's hard 'cause you can make bad decisions.

For these young men, to be a man meant it was important to fight back and avoid becoming a victim or being labelled in a way that threatened their manhood. This was particularly apparent in the teenage years in the school playground or in the street or town where you lived. Showing fear was not really an option and the importance of having pride and an identity gained from *fighting back* and standing up for yourself was associated with being strong.

To be a man you need to be tough, you need to be able to take it.

I never set out to be violent. But you learn that if you don't stand up for yourself you will always be bullied or seen as someone who has no balls. You have to weigh things up – this is part of growing up. You ask yourself, do you accept being victimised or do you become violent yourself. I guess by the age of 14 I decided I needed to fight back.

I think it was the bullying that made me rebellious when I got older. I just don't let it happen anymore and I don't care who I take on – I stand up for myself now – you've gotta do that when you become a man no matter how it makes you feel or whatever the consequences.

If someone slabbers about you, you've got to fight back – otherwise they call you a poof and people would think they could say whatever they want to you in the future to you if you didn't fight. If you're in front of all your mates, they will laugh at you if you don't do anything and don't stand up for yourself. You have to fight or you lose respect.

There were times when you could only take so much:

It's like when I was in first year in school I got threatened a lot, people would say they were going to beat me up after school and there was this one time when some boys followed me after school. They punched me but I didn't fight back at all. I kind of feel that that's the type of person I am. I'm not someone who would fight back. I would walk away as much as I can. But then there's times when someone forces me into a position where I become angry because someone has said something to me. I hold it all in but when I go to my bedroom I throw things about and get mad. It makes you feel like you're a nobody – you feel like you're not a real man.

If you don't stand up, other people will walk all over it and no one will give you any respect in life. So it's what you do when you're younger makes you a man when you're older.

Whenever you're walking past a crowd you tend to turn your head but you can't cross over you have to walk past them otherwise they'll think you're scared.

The progression from boy to man was marked by not being the coward and the need to stand up for beliefs and make sure you are not pushed around:

If someone has a go at you, and you walk away, people think you are a coward.

If you sit in the corner of the classroom quiet no one's going to know what you've done and everyone's gonna think you're a wee 'gay' boy, so they're gonna start to push you about. It's not gonna happen if you stick up for your own guns and start standing for what you believe in. Other people will respect it. If you don't stand up, other people will walk all over it and no one will give you any respect in life. So it's what you do when you're younger makes you a man when you're older.

As the discussions unfolded around the theme of how boys become men we took them into the area of how boys and young men talk to others about their feeling of growing up and about becoming a man. Unsurprisingly, this revealed that for many they were trapped in the belief that talking about how you felt or your emotions was not something that boys did.

You think nobody would listen or your mates would laugh at you or tell you to wise up. So **you let on you can cope.** Boys never talk about how they feel. It just doesn't happen. They just mess around and nobody takes you seriously even if you say you're feeling bad. So you **learn just to get on with things and keep things to yourself.**

Sometimes you need to talk to someone but **there is nobody** you feel you can to talk about how you feel. You hold things in and then you lash out. You explode. The feelings build up 'cause **you can't talk about how you feel**. You think **nobody would listen** or your mates would laugh at you or tell you to wise up so you let on you can cope and just keep your emotions to yourself. Girls seem to be able to talk to each other about how they feel but boys pretend everything is ok.

There were echoes here of how many had viewed the way in which their fathers had probably behaved in this way in front of them. It seemed as if it was learnt behaviour from fathers and other men. Talking about emotions and feelings was not something that men did. But then there were those who were searching for somewhere and someone to talk to who would understand and listen to what is going on.

You need to get your anger out – it's better than keeping it in – it helps calm down rather than bottle it all up – you don't want to hear 'hey that's wrong.' **You want someone to listen** and say what you're doing is wrong. **Adults talk down to you** – but they don't listen to what you've got to say. No point them saying 'don't be angry' – that's what you are.

I think it would be easier in school to put people in a room and talk out stuff instead of just kicking you out 'cause 90 per cent of the time if you have the space to talk it's like 'OK fair enough' and that's the end of it but **there is nowhere to talk about these things**.

It would be good to have a class like just to talk about this sort of thing. If you're not talking about it you're thinking about it, like even us talking about it now is making me think about it more.

But overall the story came through that growing up could be a lonely journey and one, as a boy, you might be expected to make on your own:

As I grew up I learned to do things for myself – I didn't really talk much to my mum and dad – definitely not my dad. In a way this makes you more independent – like trusting in yourself.

What emerges from the Centre for Young Men's conversations with young men is that violence is consistently perceived by them as an accepted and normal part of their lives and experiences – 'It's just the way it is.' Their emphasis, when talking about violence, tended towards men's violence to other men. Sexual violence to children and boys'/mens' violence to women did not receive the same focus or attention. In fact, there was often reluctance for young men to be critical of those fathers who were observed as having been violent towards their spouse.

This study into the lives of young men in Northern Ireland draws parallels with other studies from across the world, such as Cameron (2000) in Australia, Adler (2000) in America, Moser and McIlwaine (2000) in Columbia, Crownover (2007) in the Balkans and Swartz and Scott (2013) in South Africa. What becomes apparent from these studies and is underpinned by our own research over the past 18 years is that violence permeates the lives of boys and young men in a variety of forms and settings and is closely associated with their expectations and perceptions of men and masculinity.

Over the past 18 years we have asked young men, in particular, to share their beliefs and experiences of violence – how they learn about and experience violence – and we discover that, for many, it is perceived as an accepted part of young male culture and sub-culture. Violence is another area of male development that must be negotiated, once again without guidance. We speak to boys and young men about their experiences of family, school and community and find that these established social structures are often perceived as places of threat or danger. We find that as adolescent boys get older they feel more distant from adults whom they believe treat them with increasing levels of suspicion. We also find a disconnect between young men and their communities and a lack of participation in decision-making processes, whether it is in the school, the care home, the detention centre or their community. For many, school subjects were disconnected from the realities of their everyday lives and experiences that make them question the value of education in preparing them for their future lives. We see how the journey from boy to man is full of complexities and contradictions of masculinity and that this journey is often negotiated without the support or guidance from adults.

In a society emerging from 40 years of political conflict in Northern Ireland we learn how paramilitary members remain an everyday threat to the majority of young men, particularly, but not exclusively, within inner city areas. We see how this has resulted in a form of child abuse through what is known locally as 'punishment shootings or beatings'. These are inflicted typically upon young men, by other young and older men, as an informal, yet terrifying, administering of community justice. Within their voices we find many contradictions as to how boys and young men construct their masculine identities in a society emerging from years of political conflict and extreme forms of community violence. We hear how they become more active in creating new representations of men and masculinity that contrast with the traditional working-class masculinity that was so apparent during the Industrial Revolution. Despite this, however, we also hear of the struggle of some boys and young men to let go of traditional notions of men and masculinity within working-class communities where patriarchal notions are still reflected and reinforced in the attitudes and behaviour of many men. This is most obvious within paramilitary groups. For over 40 years, images of paramilitary men in balaclavas brandishing guns and painted on the gables walls of streets has been the norm in many working-class communities throughout Northern Ireland. Therefore, while young men may seek to express new representations of men and masculinity, the legacy of the Troubles and the industrial heritage of Northern Ireland are powerful reminders that have moulded their working-class history and fixed working-class masculinities.

Yet, we see, there is no one type of masculinity that captures the experiences of all boys and young men. We know that they are not a homogeneous group that can easily be clumped together for the sake of sociological study. Yet this is sometimes the way they are portrayed in the media and other popular representations of them. In our conversations with them we have learned that the way they construct their masculine identities shifts according to age and experience. We have also learned the importance of local contexts and how this influences their thinking, behaviour and expectations.

Findings also reveal the extent to which these boys and young men are struggling at every level of their experience while feeling totally unprepared for the future. They appear to exist without support from others or the necessary resources to match their masculine expectations. In their attempt to 'squeeze' into these increasingly tight gender roles ascribed to them and by them, and exhibit the type of power they believed men should possess, they feel compelled to demonstrate certain ways of proving their masculinity. Yet talking to these young men reveals the extent of powerlessness that they actually experience either in school, at home or in the community.

What has consistently stood out for us is the apparent lack of opportunity for boys and young men to engage in conversations with adults, and other boys and young men, about issues such as violence and masculinity and becoming a man. For so many it was the first time these subjects had been introduced to them.

We began our journey into the world of over 1,000 boys and young men living in Northern Ireland with the intention of sharing insights and lessons we have gleaned over the past 18 years. Therefore in the final chapter we turn our focus to practice issues and considerations for working more effectively with boys and young men.

7
Critical Reflections on Practice

This chapter presents insights and learning from our studies and practice with boys and young men around the themes of violence and masculinity that have been raised in this book. The chapter emphasises the importance and value of building critical and meaningful relationships with boys and young men that are underpinned by the skills, knowledge and qualities of the educator. These include empathy, respect and appreciation of contextual issues that impact upon young male development and behaviour. We present an integrated model to working with boys and young men that takes cognisance of the social ecological context in which they live. Finally this chapter presents some of the practical lessons from our evidence based research over the past 18 years that we believe will be of value to educators and practitioners aiming to engage and work more effectively with boys and young men.

Practice informed by research

In previous chapters we have discussed the importance of the social ecology in the lives, development, experiences and attitudes of boys and young men. We have presented how growing up in difficult socioeconomic conditions, in family circumstances that can be problematic and the exposure to violence and role modelling are crucial factors in a boy's development. We have heard their voices and experiences and how in the home:

- domestic violence was common;
- many witnessed their father hitting their mother, an action typically fuelled by alcohol;
- the father is the key person that provides a template for being a man.

Their experiences of being disciplined within the family home left many with conflicting paradoxes and ambiguities. Many were left confused about what actually constituted acceptable and unacceptable levels of physical punishment upon a child.

In the school and community:

- fighting with other boys was common;
- those who spoke of being bullied in school felt powerless to change their circumstances and were reluctant to seek support as the feared being seen as a 'tout';
- these boys and young men believed they had either to accept the bullying or learn to fight back;
- boys felt particular internal pressures to be seen to 'stand up' to teachers and other adults;
- they felt the need to demonstrate that they would not back down from conflict situations;
- they had a fear of being shamed amongst their peers;
- there was pressure on them to prove to others that they were no longer children;
- it was important to them that they should not be treated as children.

In their voices we also identified complexities and inconsistencies in what they perceived as actual acts of violence and when they were just 'messing around'. Within these experiences it is in the home, the school and community where boys learn *the rules of the game* and develop their moral codes and rituals. Yet within these voices we hear consistently their expressions of feeling disconnected from the world of adults and alienated from decision-making processes within their communities and wider society.

Our study of boys and young men has been in Northern Ireland and as such this local context is important in understanding these voices. Over the past 20 years Northern Ireland has been a society in transition moving away from political and community violence towards peace-building. This has necessitated engaging in post-conflict transformation work to ensure lasting peace and attempting to find ways to deal with the legacy of the past. The peace process has included addressing complex issues such as reconciliation, justice for victims, reintegration, decommissioning of paramilitary weapons, police reform, security, paramilitary prisoner release and an end to paramilitarism. It has meant economic investment and the administration of a Local (power sharing) Assembly. It is clear that resolving these issues is not, and will not be, straightforward. Young men continue to grow up in segregated and polarised communities, particularly in the interface areas where peace walls serve as a lasting reminder of the physical, as well as mental, barriers of a divided and contested society. We have heard how segregation affects the way in which young men move and interact and how it directly impacts upon daily activities such as going to school, to work, meeting friends and building relationships with people from different communities. We have heard how boys and young men did not only feel isolated from decision-making and peace-building processes, but did not even understand the concept, the language, vocabulary and terminology of the 'peace process', in particular because this was not addressed directly in school or the community.

We also heard how the outworking of peace-building is confusing for young men who see violent men being *glorified* as the defenders of their communities. Twenty years after the paramilitary ceasefires boys and young men talked of:

- knowing violent young men who were in a paramilitary organisation, who not only inflicted pain on other young men, but actively tried to recruit them to join a paramilitary organisation;
- their experiences of being threatened in their own communities by paramilitaries;
- the double standards of paramilitaries;
- their distrust and suspicions of the police;
- their confusion around law and order.

It is clear from these voices that boys and young men are not being prepared for living in a peaceful society or actively encouraged to participate in shaping its future. The long shadow of the Troubles with its haunting reminders and inherited memories were present in many voices as they talked of:

- heinous and harrowing experiences, like witnessing their father being shot dead in front of them;
- the need to revenge the death of a loved one;
- their feeling of powerlessness about not being able to do anything about it;

- feelings of being angry all the time and unable to control their temper;
- being beaten with sticks and batons in so-called 'punishment beatings'.

We have discussed how violence is a disturbing and concerning aspect of modern societies and we are particularly horrified when we hear of young people suffering as victims of violence and we know that, in war zones across the world, children have been victims of atrocities that can make our world appear an extremely dangerous, unjust and intimidating place to live. However, we are similarly horrified when we hear of young people as perpetrators of violence. We have discussed how being male is a key risk factor in the likelihood of a person becoming a victim of violence. Yet we have also heard that, while some young men spoke of being fearful of violence and concerned about their personal safety, other young men spoke of being drawn to, and excited by, certain types of violence. Despite violence being perceived as part of their everyday life, boys spoke of rarely being given time or space to reflect upon it or related issues within school, in their community or by their parents or other significant adults. It is this *separation* that can make a boy's education and learning seem so irrelevant and disconnected from the reality of their everyday lives.

Hegemony, duty and dissonance, and constructing masculinities

We have also presented how boys' everyday experiences of violence, particularly in divided and contested societies, can perpetuate and exalt a certain type of normative masculinity. In our *Taking Boys Seriously* study (Harland and McCready, 2012) we identified three factors associated with masculinity: hegemony, duty and dissonance. We discussed how boys spoke of the types of behaviour they believe is expected from them as they attempt to 'match up' to their preconceived notions of what it means to be a man. For example, during early adolescence these boys appear to accept willingly and aspire to hegemonic masculine types. They also believed that men, for example, should be dominant, aggressive, a good fighter, competitive, powerful, heterosexual and able to stand up for themselves, which separates them from the world of feelings and emotions. At this age boys appear to readily accept and reinforce stereotypical notions of men and openly display homophobic attitudes. Our studies found that higher levels of hegemony in boys were closely associated with lower levels of academic motivation and performance and higher levels of misbehaviour. Boys with higher levels of hegemony also spoke of the need to 'act tough', believing that by doing so they were fulfilling an important part of their masculinity – namely that men do not need the support of others. Yet contradictorily we found that many believed they did not *match up* to this masculine expectation and believed this to be a key reason why they were bullied or singled out for ridicule.

Our findings further showed that during mid-adolescence boys became increasingly active, as opposed to passive, in constructing their own localised notions of men and masculinity. Boys at his age were more likely to contemplate other aspects and characteristics of being a man that they believe are important, such as duty and being responsible, caring and kind. Whereas hegemony reduced across the five years of the longitudinal study, duty was a consistent finding. We also found that as boys mature they experienced higher levels of dissonance in response to questions, for example, about whether or not it is appropriate for a man to hug another man or have a boyfriend, or should shout at his children. This experience of dissonance around these issues, in our view, did not necessarily represent accepting the hegemony or representing homophobic views on their part, but rather it represented a move from certainty to uncertainty and evidence of reflection. Importantly, evidence from this longitudinal study suggests that from early to mid-adolescence, boys are capable of at least beginning to consider the kinds of issues, values and beliefs that are important to their future development as responsible young men who have begun to process complex and emotionally challenging issues. Findings further suggest that perceptions of masculinity shifted over time and the nature of becoming a man became more complex during mid- to late adolescence as boys begin to form their own, rather than stereotypical predefined, masculine identities. These are important areas for educators and practitioners to consider when working with boys and young men, particularly as throughout our studies we have observed that there are few opportunities for them to reflect upon their notions of masculinity or their thoughts on becoming a man. Once again it would appear that boys are left to their own devices, or the potentially negative influences of others, to make sense of their world and day to day experiences. It is within this complex localised social ecological context that we now switch our attention to thinking about engaging and working effectively with boys and young men.

Starting points for working with boys and young men

Often the focus of work with boys and young men is concerned with addressing issues such as behaviour, motivation, school performance, academic achievement and under-achievement, social justice, anti-social behaviour, crime, sexism, violence and discrimination. Essentially the focus of practice will depend on the context in which you work. For example, if you are working with boys in school your primary focus will likely be on academic attainment and preparing boys for the future. In a youth justice context your primary focus may be on managing behaviour and issues concerning law and order. If you are a health worker your focus may be on a young man's mental health and well-being or physical health. As a youth worker your focus may be on personal and social development. If you are involved in sport your focus may be on participation, competition, success and winning. If you are a parent your focus on your son may be on personal safety, education, health, moral development, social relationships, peer relations, growth and personality development and overall general well-being. The point we make is that starting points are important in developing practice with boys and young men as this will determine the purpose of your work.

Working with boys and young men

Many educators, professionals and practitioners work with boys and young men. While some gain fulfilment from this work, others find them difficult to engage and are discouraged by the outcomes (Geldard and Geldard, 2010). Lloyd (1997:53) has previously identified two problems when developing practice with boys and young men. Firstly, 'many young men have difficulties in communicating and expressing themselves' and, secondly, 'many professional workers have difficulties in developing their relationships and work with young men'. We acknowledge that many reading this chapter may be highly experienced educators or practitioners with many years' experience of working with boys and young men in various contexts. Our intention therefore is not to tell educators and practitioners what to do. Rather we aim to share how our experience, knowledge and understanding of boys and young men has informed and shaped the way in which our practice has developed. As with all our work, we have been led by the voices, thoughts and opinions of the boys and young men we have worked with and remain grounded within the reality and social ecological context of their everyday lives and experiences.

While our work has been located in Northern Ireland, we believe the principles and learning presented throughout this book can be usefully applied in other contexts across the world. From the outset we acknowledge that working with boys and young men can be a demanding and challenging undertaking that necessitates certain skills and knowledge on behalf of the educator. We use the terms 'educator' and 'practitioner' to cover all those whose practice involves working with boys and young men in a professional, community or organisational context, or what Rogers (1983) calls 'the facilitator of learning'. It is also important to note that when we refer to working with boys and young men our intention is to be inclusive. We are not suggesting that this work should only be carried out with boys and young men who may be presenting themselves as 'challenging' or 'hard to engage'. However, we acknowledge that the focus of practice is often, but not always, directed at those who may be perceived as disenfranchised, on the margins of society, or known, for example, to social services or youth justice bodies. These may be boys who have been identified as 'not fitting in' or 'turned off' by formal education systems and structures and who are struggling academically or falling behind with school work.

Towards an integrated model of practice

We have previously discussed how successful programmes have been developed with an appreciation of the lives and experiences of young men who have been included as integral members of the community, been long term and have had a mixture of reflective and skills based approaches (Mattaini and Maguire, 2006). Data from our longitudinal study highlighted the value of finding new and more creative ways to engage and work with boys and young men by addressing real life situations that connected more directly with their everyday lives and experiences. It has been one of the more concerning findings from our studies that young men feel so disconnected from adults and their communities and have little involvement in decision-making processes. In light of all that we have discussed in this book we present the following model as a more coordinated and integrated way to address the perceived disconnect between them and their education and learning (see Figure 7.1).

Our integrated ecological model aims to bring about desired changes for boys and young men as individuals, members of their communities and wider society. The model provides a balanced and inclusive approach that supports young men yet challenges broader societal structures such as patriarchal relations of power, inequality, injustice and oppression. Whilst the model encourages the educator to appreciate 'context' in addressing issues such as violence through an exploration of masculinities, it positions the young people at the centre of the intervention and emphasises a more holistic approach to education and learning. Importantly the model promotes stronger and more direct links between formal, non-formal and informal education. Illich (1971) has previously argued that most learning is not the result of instruction but the result of 'unhampered participation in a meaningful society'. The model acknowledges that much of a young person's learning occurs beyond the school gates and therefore necessitates healthy partnerships and interdisciplinary working to harness and foster that learning. The model also takes cognisance of the importance of gender, class and ethnicity and a strengths-based approach (Barwick, 2004) whereby skills and knowledge are found in individuals, families, schools, peer groups, communities and local people in local contexts (Figure 7.1).

Core to the model are four areas that we believe can be useful for educators and practitioners to consider when working with boys and young men in a social ecological context. In doing this we place emphasis on the educator's skills, knowledge and self-awareness as opposed to their gender. These areas are not meant to determine what an educator should do, or how to do it, or what issues they should address with boys and young men. Rather they are offered as part of an overall ecological framework for supporting an educator and practitioner in their

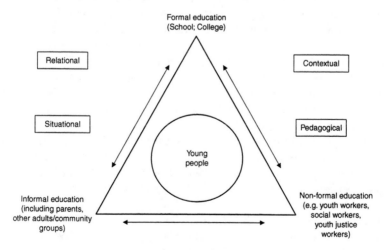

Figure 7.1 Integrated social ecological model

work. While we regard youth work as non-formal education, the model is applicable within any educational setting or context. The areas are presented under four interconnected headings: relational, contextual, situational and pedagogical.

Relational considerations for working with boys and young men

The centrality and importance of 'relationship' is core to many approaches to working with children and young people (Spence et al., 2006; Petrie, 2011; Dugmore, 2012). Within a youth work methodology the educator is committed to building critical, meaningful relationships with boys and young men and is aware of the qualities that young men look for in an educator. These are respect, trust, genuineness, humour, empathy, support and acceptance. The educator sees young men as an asset and not a problem and has a concern for how they feel and express emotions. The educator is reflective and a highly skilled communicator who is a confident, competent and self-aware individual who is genuine and transparent. The educator's focus is on developing boys and young men by helping them acquire new skills and confidence through promoting their voice and extracting knowledge and meaning from their experiences and ideas. The nature of the relationship enables the educator to challenge stereotypes and behaviour that is discriminatory, offensive, sexist or potentially harmful towards others.

Contextual considerations for working with boys and young men

The local and global social contexts of young men's lives has a strong bearing upon their thoughts, attitudes, beliefs and behaviour, yet this is rarely addressed within many educational settings. The educator will be aware that factors that impact upon boys' and young men's lives must be considered within a wider context of socio-economic issues such as poverty, class, race, ethnicity, social disadvantage and the decline in traditional industries. The educator will encourage boys and young men to explore ways in which masculinities are constructed and how this can influence behaviour. The educator can also explore why certain types of masculinities are dominant while others may be perceived as subordinate. This focus can support the educator to explore issues of violence, gendered violence and other violence related issues, and how this is experienced by boys and young men as victims, perpetrators and witnesses of violence. By addressing issues that they do not typically discuss, for example within formal education, will encourage discussion and dialogue that is driven by their voices and therefore issues that are important to them. This approach requires active listening on behalf of the educator and facilitation skills that enable boys to talk. In all of our work we have consistently found that boys and young men have plenty to say when a supportive environment is created. Educators do not see their work in isolation but understand that work with boys and young men often necessitates a multi-disciplinary and multi-agency approach involving schools, teachers, parents, youth services, youth justice, social and health services, the police, community safety initiatives and local community groups. The role of the educator is to support boys and young men to reflect on how communities and societies work; it encourages and promotes their ideas and solutions to the issues facing them, their community or wider society. This focus will help boys to feel better connected to other aspects of community life and increase their understanding of how their own education and learning is connected to the wider community. In our model, for example, the youth worker as a non-formal educator could be the bridge between school and the local community, thus providing a connection between the formal and non-formal and informal. The interface between all of these is social education.

Situational considerations for working with boys and young men

The educator supports young men to evaluate and reflect upon the contexts and circumstances of their everyday lives and to find creative ways to address the specific issues which affect them. This involves the exploration of their sense of alienation within their communities and their absence from decision-making processes. The educator will be aware that the environment, rather than the young men, may be a problem. This will involve exploring how geographical areas can be made safer for them, and others, and examining why older adults may be suspicious and distrusting towards certain of them. The educator will support young men to develop critiques of economic, political and cultural structures to help them to match better their expectations with reality. The educator also explores why certain boys and young men may not seek emotional support. By encouraging them to talk about themselves and their lives, and by linking this to emotional intelligence, will increase their self-awareness of their internal world of feelings and emotions and how these can impact positively upon their behaviour and well-being. This complex area of male experience is integral to working effectively with boys and young men, particularly when addressing their experiences of violence (or the threat of violence) or exploring alternative ways to respond to potential incidents of conflict.

Methods employed to help young men develop skills to deal with issues around violence have included community safety techniques, relaxation techniques, self-defence, storytelling (Leonard, 2006), forum theatre and role play (McKenna et al., 2006). Our experience is that role play is an effective method of working and involves physical and participative activity that combines movement and creativity which enables young men to see and experience tangible and realistic alternatives to everyday scenarios they face (Mattaini and Maguire, 2006). Role play can provide an opportunity to explore feasible alternatives to existing problematic situations and enable exploration of appropriate social responses. In our experience the use of role playing in the *Taking Boys Seriously* research in schools was very effective in engaging boys in their learning and encouraging them to talk about real life situations. Whereas many boys found some school subjects boring, they found the youth work interventions through the role plays excited their curiosity through addressing, in a different way, potentially controversial and sensitive issues not typically covered in the school curriculum. Boys reported learning new skills and thinking more about conflict situations rather than just reacting to them. Through using a story telling approach that referred to 'other boys' this meant that controversial issues (e.g. violence against the person, alcohol and drug misuse) were less personal, yet enabled boys to identify readily with the issues being raised. This methodology was highly effective and fully engaged their participation and captured their imagination which unlocked their creativity. They very quickly connected this to their own lives and experiences and were able to add their own personal story to each scenario. This gave them a sense of control over content and increased their confidence to participate in discussions. What was particularly striking was the way in which they listened attentively to the stories. For example, there was total silence as the storyteller outlined a scenario where young men were confronted with a potentially violent situation. Each time the story reached a possible threatening point, the story was 'frozen' and the boys broke out into small groups and asked what they would do in that particular situation. They were then encouraged to think of the types of skills and strategies they could use to try and alleviate potentially violent situations. Skills development was a key outcome of the interventions. This methodology led to intense facilitated discussions amongst the boys.

Through such activities school was perceived as connecting more directly to their everyday lives, experiences and their learning. The sessions increased the boys' knowledge and helped them rehearse new skills in regard to resolving potential conflict and violent situations.

They appreciated being asked about what they were thinking and responded to being encouraged to share their experiences and feelings. They reported feeling positive about being listened to and experiencing that their opinions were being valued. They also appreciated learning in a way that established trust and mutual respect. The interventions challenged the notion held by these boys that school was a place that was boring and repetitive, and often irrelevant to their everyday lives. In contrast the interventions enabled the educators to penetrate deeper into aspects of the inner world of these boys and young men.

When working within a classroom environment in this way it was seen to be an advantage that teachers were present to observe the sessions. In our experience comments from teachers revealed that they discovered parts of the boys' lives they had not previously understood or known about: 'I can see how much these boys have to cope with external issues that have nothing to do with school' and 'I can't believe how much they had to say about their experiences, beliefs and their communities'.

The focus on violence also enabled the educator to explore other complexities and paradoxes within young male experiences. Our research revealed that many referred to having a *blur* between what actually constituted a violent act. Was it violence or was it simply an act of bravado or were boys simply 'messing around'? Exploring this area enables a discussion to progress into an examination of young men's subcultures. It opens up conversations about the effects and consequences of bullying and broadens their understanding of violence on others. In our case it led on to examining alternative ways to resolving conflict such as restorative approaches. Benefits can also be found in organising opportunities for young men to meet and discuss violence-related issues with those who respond to it (e.g. the police, fire brigade, army, door personnel/bouncers) and those who were previously involved in violence (e.g. ex-paramilitaries, ex-prisoners).

A key feature of our sessions was encouraging boys and young men to examine hegemonic beliefs that emphasised men's use of 'power' and 'control' over others. We saw this as the foundation for addressing other challenging work around their attitudes and behaviour in regard to violence-related issues such as crime, sectarianism, sexism, racism, homophobia, cyber bullying and recreational violence.

Pedagogical considerations for working with boys and young men

Keddie (2006:99) argues that quality pedagogy is central to improving educational outcomes and in particular suggests that, for disengaged boys, there is a need to facilitate a broadening of their narrow constructions of gender identity through productive teaching informed by understandings of masculinity. This has important training implications for a range of professions that work with young men as it suggests that working with boys should be underpinned by knowledge and understanding of the complexities and contradictions in the construction of masculinity and how boys become men. This is particularly necessary in the formal education sector.

Harland and McCready (2012) note that in a year the average time spent in school is just 16 per cent which leaves a lot of time for learning to occur elsewhere. Our model acknowledges the value of non-formal and informal education in supporting and complementing a boy's formal education and learning. Youth work is process driven and concerned with a young person's personal and social development through an empowering practice approach emphasising their participation. It aims to bring about agreed and desired changes in individuals, communities and society. Our model supports boys and young men to identify and accept their responsibilities as individuals, citizens and group members. Youth work respects and values young people for who they are (now) and views them as a resource/asset for society. It is founded upon, and wedded to, establishing critical meaningful relationships with young people based upon the value set of respect, openness, trust and choice. It aims to provide a safe space for them to explore issues, fears, behaviours and aspirations through a combination of reflective and participatory activity.

Creating effective learning environments are necessary to engage boys and young men fully. This is not to suggest that one learning style fits all. Educators in formal and non-formal education have many opportunities to connect learning and the curriculum to the reality of young men's lives outside of school. Learning methods should aim to engage, motivate, stimulate and excite them. The use of movement, energy and creating a sense of adventure significantly reduces boredom and enhances their learning. Our classroom sessions were intentionally designed to encourage boys to discuss their feelings and emotions within a climate where their opinions were valued. A further positive aspect of these sessions was that this process enabled participating teachers to identify and demonstrate a greater appreciation and empathy towards young males who may be at risk or susceptible to contextual factors outside of school.

An underpinning theme of our longitudinal study was reflecting upon masculinity. This was important as quantitative data had highlighted shifting complexities within the formation of masculine identities particularly throughout early to mid-adolescence. The sessions in the classrooms were designed to enable boys to reflect upon male attitudes and their behaviour, whilst challenging their hegemonic beliefs about men, women and masculinity. Themes addressed in sessions were: masculinity and becoming a man; boys and young men and emotions; boys and young men's conflict and violence; personal safety and anger; risk taking; education and learning; health; and male transitions and life skills. These had not been topics addressed during their time at school.

As part of creating an effective learning environment tables and chairs were moved around to suit the non-formal aspects of the sessions and to allow for movement while using role play techniques and icebreakers and energisers. Sessions were interactive and used small group work, large circles and work in pairs. When in the classroom set-up these different techniques enabled available teaching staff to take part in the smaller working groups. Regardless of the setting, consideration was given to making the physical environment conducive to learning.

The sessions took cognisance of the fact that boys were often restless and nervous in new situations. They believed the interactive style broke up the intensity of sessions and liked the fact that icebreaker games were used to orientate them to the subject matter. They also enjoyed learning by visualising situations rather than memorising information, which gave them a strong sense of personal achievement. Boys who reported 'not being good at school work' often displayed other qualities during sessions which made them feel good about themselves. On occasions when this did happen the facilitators reinforced the value of the boys' input.

Our research revealed that, for most boys, the school was, in general, a relatively safe and preferred space where they could reflect upon difficult and controversial issues such as violence. They perceived that this would be much more difficult outside of school. For the boys it was also important who delivered these sessions. It needed to be an adult with whom they had some trust. Other boys believed it was useful to talk to youth workers as they would have found it difficult to discuss certain issues in front of a teacher, particularly with someone with whom they may have had some previous conflict. This was the view of the majority of boys, although there was a small minority who initially resisted getting involved in some of the exercises. Participation was not compulsory and no boy was forced to engage, but all were encouraged to get involved.

Our model does not necessarily require additional resources. Rather the focus is on finding more creative ways of engaging and responding to the needs and issues that are important to boys and young men in environments where they feel safe and are conducive to learning, whether in the classroom or in other settings, for example, care homes, juvenile justice centres or youth clubs. It requires more collaboration amongst the professions in order to provide added value and support that can complement formal education. Implementing these suggestions will necessitate a commitment from schools, teachers, parents, other organisations working with boys and young men, and local community groups to *take boys seriously*. It will require an educational experience that puts the needs of individual boys and young men at the heart of the learning process.

Our model firmly does this. It encourages expression of thoughts, feelings and expectations. The ecological model is underpinned by principles of empowerment, participation and accountability that aim to bring about desired changes in individuals, communities, institutions and wider society.

Some final thoughts on working with boys and young men

We have presented our social ecological model as a framework for engaging and working more effectively with boys and young men within a context that is grounded within the reality of their everyday lives and experiences. We complete our chapter on practice, and indeed this book, with a summary of some practical reflections from our work over the past 18 years. Once again these considerations are not meant to tell an educator or practitioner what to do. Rather our intention is to offer suggestions that educators and practitioners may, or may not, find useful in their own practice, whatever the context, when engaging boys and young men about their lives, their experiences and their aspirations.

Talking to young men about their experiences of violence

If we are to understand how and why some people engage with the world in an aggressive way, we must first come to understand how they understand the world they inhabit (Gilligan, 1996; Harland, 1997; Lloyd, 2001; Anderson and Bushman, 2002; Forrest, 2004; Gibson, 2004; Crooks et al., 2007). As the majority of boys progressed through adolescence there was evidence of their growing awareness and how they gave more considered thought to violence and its place in their lives. Yet they reported that they were rarely provided with opportunities to reflect upon or discuss violence or violence-related issues. Throughout our studies boys appeared resigned to the reality of violence as part of young male experience. For them concerns about their personal safety had become a daily consideration – 'it's just the way it is' – and violence was something that was part of 'growing up'. Subsequently, key practice elements encouraged individual reflection on issues, attitudes and behaviour associated with violence through open discussion and various group activities and boys were also encouraged to express and respect differences of opinion and to request clarity on particular issues throughout the education and learning process.

Community

While boys spoke consistently of feeling part of their school, they also perceived school as separate from the wider community. Their thoughts on their community, as in the home and in school, were determined primarily by the ways in which they believed they were perceived by other adults. They thought that, as they got older, adults increasingly treated them with suspicion and distrust. This was consistent regardless of which school type or community they belonged to. Throughout our studies boys spoke of wanting acceptance and wanting to be part of the community and the adult world, but were unaware of any processes to enable this to happen. The community, for many, was an unpredictable and, at times, an unsafe place where they felt vulnerable and exposed to the influences of paramilitary and other negative role models.

Space and territory

As boys got older, there was a welcoming sense that their recreational space had significantly changed and widened. For example, they used public transport on their own and worked in part-time jobs which meant they could participate in a range of recreational activities. However, changing spaces exposed them to more sinister aspects of youth culture such as drugs and alcohol. Having their own space and territory was important for these boys. They liked to go to places where they could be themselves and potentially escape local labels of 'hoods' and 'trouble makers'. With growing older came opportunities to go outside of your own community with new places and spaces to explore and new identities to create. But, for many, there was a gap in their educational experiences that could have provided a preparation and foundation to take advantage of these opportunities.

Shifting patterns of masculinity

Throughout our studies, boys consistently spoke about the pressures, complexities and confusion of moving away from childhood behaviours to becoming, and being accepted, as a young man. As they matured they felt increasing frustration when they attempted to engage with adults, as they felt they were still treated as children. For these boys becoming a man was not defined by age or experiencing a rite of passage. Rather it represented a time when adults would treat them as adults and show them respect and accept them into the community in which they belonged. Receiving support during the transition from dependence to independence was strongly welcomed by the majority of boys. As we have discussed throughout this book, issues surrounding masculinity and what it means to be a man are increasingly complex, contradictory and confusing. Appreciating how masculinity affects male behaviour and development is integral to working effectively with boys and young men. Educators should therefore take cognisance of approaches that reinforce stereotypical and restrictive expressions of masculinity. Crucially, however, this is no easy task as there is much in our world that continues to promote, reward and perpetuate unhealthy aspects of masculinity that can be so detrimental to young men's health and self-esteem.

Communication and emotional expression

In our *Taking Boys Seriously* study, experienced teachers were concerned about boys' general lower ability to communicate with others and show and articulate their emotions in an intelligent way. Schools tended to describe their poor communication skills and their lack of emotional expression as cutting across many of the other reasons why they disengaged from their education and learning. Teachers identified that boys were more likely to get into trouble in school because of a lack of talk-based strategies for resolving conflict or violent situations. Teachers spoke of boys being less willing to participate in classroom discussions, to ask questions and to participate in lessons generally. They suggested this was because boys feared that they might look inadequate in front of their peers. Boys were also reluctant to use the pastoral and support services as much as girls. This was, in part, down to boys feeling less confident of a process that was an emotion-led form and also because 'it wasn't cool' for boys to be seen in counselling. Enabling boys to feel comfortable with using support services and developing their communication and emotional skills to take advantage of such services are important issues.

The public and private worlds of young men

Male gender roles can force boys and young men to reject as *feminine* a wide range of characteristics that are simply part of normal human behaviour. This means that boys can grow up believing they should not, indeed cannot, display certain emotions in public, forcing them to keep their emotions private. In public spheres boys and young men can feel enormous pressure to appear confident often to the point of display-ing their masculinity to others in a forceful way. This can mean that they are willingly dismissive of the pain in their lives and experience a separation from their internal world of feelings and emotions. In pub-lic spheres they are more prone to communicate aggressively through 'slagging' and banter which can be perceived as threatening and deroga-tory to others. Conversely, in private spheres, they are more likely to internalise their feelings and keep their emotions to themselves, believ-ing that showing certain feelings in public will be perceived by others as a sign of weakness. According to Lloyd (1997) understanding these *two worlds* are important for developing practice with boys and young men. Lloyd notes that 'in public environments boys and young men are less likely to talk openly and honestly or appear vulnerable, whereas when young men think they are in private environments they are much more likely to talk honestly and openly and are more prepared to be vulnerable' (p. 63). Seidler (2007) posits that, for many boys and young men, there are 'no emotional spaces' in which they can become con-scious of their emotions. In order to redress this absence of emotional spaces, boys and young men must overcome their fear of intimacy, vul-nerability and stigma. This presents a huge challenge not only to them but also to those educators and practitioners who support them, as it can fundamentally challenge deeply accepted, entrenched, stereotypi-cal interpretations of men and masculinity. Understanding how boys and young men communicate within public and private spheres can support educators to understand the complex way in which boys inter-nalise complex mental processes and how this can impact upon their subsequent behaviour.

Appreciation of the 3 Rs: Respect, recognition and responsibility

As boys matured they desired and expected to be treated with more respect, recognition and increased opportunities to be given more responsibility. They perceived that teachers, other professionals and adults did not appreciate the complexities and realities of male youth culture and perceived these people as being 'out of touch'. While these boys acknowledged that they were not quite adults, they appreciated times when teachers and other adults treated them as if they were. They found it extremely patronising and disempowering when educators and other adults did not consult with them or involve them in decision-making processes and believed more recognition should be given to other qualities and abilities they possess. Boys felt strongly that teachers and other significant adults should make more efforts to let them know they are valued within school for who they are and treat their views, opinions and ideas with respect. They asked for respect, recognition and believed with these would come responsibility.

Our own attitudes

Educators and practitioners often report finding it difficult to engage certain boys and young men with their overt displays of machoism, often admitting to feeling intimidated and lacking the confidence and skills to develop a meaningful practice with them. Working with young men can bring to the surface a range of powerful emotions that as educators and practitioners we may have previously suppressed. Reflecting upon the key influences and people who shaped our lives as we grew up enables us to have more empathy towards young men and their issues. In the media, and in the minds of many adults, boys and young men are often demonised as part of a deviant youth culture that has lost all of its morals and values. They are this 'problem' that requires to be 'sorted out'. As educators we need to be aware of the attitudes and perceptions that we may have of young men, particularly as the reason many educators and practitioners are required to work with them is because they have been perceived by others as 'difficult or troublesome'. Such negative generalisations may provide a barrier and make it difficult for educators to engage certain young men in a positive way and is therefore not a good starting point for meaningful practice to begin.

Environments within which to engage

It is important for educators to appreciate the internal pressures that boys and young men may experience in order to behave in a particular way. For example, in front of peers they can feel enormous pressure to appear confident and in control – and therefore they often display their masculinity in a forceful way. As we have discussed, many believe that it is only by 'acting tough' that they will get status and respect from others, and the fear of being shamed or put down will seriously inhibit their potential to talk about what they think and feel or engage with the subject in a meaningful way. Creating environments that are safe from threat and non-judgemental attitudes helps free young men from the pressures they feel to prove themselves to others. This in itself helps build trust and encourages them to talk, think and consider other viewpoints. This can be challenging work, however, as for many communicating at a feelings level is not seen as 'cool'.

The importance of listening

Listening to the things that boys and young men have to say may seem an obvious skill for educators. However, if we are to engage effectively we must learn to listen actively to what boys and young men are saying. The use of banter and 'slagging off' amongst young men can make it difficult to carry out effective group work. Too often the focus of the educator is on disruptive behaviour which so easily deflects from understanding the things they are trying to tell us through their non-verbal communication. It is important therefore for educators and practitioners to work at building relationships that move them *beyond macho behaviour* to where listening is respected and valued.

Positive use of energy

Anyone working with boys and young men will be undoubtedly aware of the large amounts of energy and untapped potential they possess. The use of movement and fun are valuable tools for harnessing young men's natural energy and enabling them to enjoy their education and learning. Sitting in a classroom for six hours a day while your testosterone is popping up all over the place is not easy for any male, never mind boys and young men. This is perhaps why so many young males struggle within formal education settings. Examples of facilitating movement include outdoor activities and role plays which encourage creativity. Such active approaches enable young men to engage in risk-taking behaviour within a climate of safety and trust. Within this exciting and appealing approach young men can be facilitated to reflect, and it provides a solid foundation for more challenging work around attitudes and behaviour, masculinity and violence.

Skills development

An important factor contributing to young men's involvement in violence is that they do not know how to avoid violence or minimise the potential for conflict in certain situations. This can be attributed to a lack of skills in this area or an inability to choose alternative courses of action. In order to improve knowledge of alternatives, skills based sessions should be part of the repertoire of educators and practitioners in order to support and encourage boys to make better informed choices in relation to violence and conflict resolution.

Being clear about purpose

Boys and young men often report that they are unclear as to why they are on programmes or what educators expect from them. It is important therefore that educators consult with them throughout programmes to ensure that, for everyone involved, there is clarity of purpose (Lloyd, 1997) and a structure for evaluation.

Challenging problematic behaviour and attitudes while being supportive

Working with boys and young men, whilst they are searching for their identity amid a form of role confusion (Erikson, 1950), is an opportune time for educators and practitioners to more fully understand their behaviour. Within normative interpretations of men and masculinity boys may believe that they become men by acting in aggressive, oppressive and potentially threatening ways and that this is the best way to resolve conflict. As we have discussed previously, not all boys feel this way. However, most boys will be affected, or influenced to some extent, by aggressive behaviour and acts of violence but, as we have also discussed, this socialisation process can be embedded and fostered in the family home, in school, in the community and the wider world of which they are a part. Findings throughout our studies have consistently demonstrated the extent to which violence, and violence-related behaviour, is perceived by boys and young men as 'part of their everyday lives'. One outcome of this can be that they may become desensitised to certain manifestations of violence. Challenging long established traditional beliefs and attitudes with boys and young men can be an onerous, yet rewarding, task. Building relationships through which they can reflect, think, talk, have fun and explore complex and potentially controversial issues necessitates skilful facilitation of learning by an educator or practitioner. This approach, however, can help free them from the pressure of needing to appear *macho* or display other forms of normative masculinity that *masks* who they really are. Breaking these patterns of behaviour will begin to unlock the skills, creativity, individuality and potential that each undoubtedly possesses.

Reflecting on shame

We have discussed how some boys will stand up to adults in authority rather than experience being shamed in front of their peers. In conflict situations boys spoke of being motivated towards aggression and violence by a need to prove to themselves and others that they are not afraid. Otherwise they perceive they will be humiliated by those around them. This behaviour can transfer itself onto the streets and, as we have also heard from boys, that violence can be intensified by alcohol and drugs. Conversely boys can experience shame because they feel they do not 'match up' to hegemonic notions of masculinity or feel fearful in the presence of 'hard men'. Repeatedly in our studies boys and young men have spoken of how the fear of 'losing face' or 'being rejected' strongly influences their response to potential conflict or violence situations. They may also fear being rejected, or bullied, because of their identity, ethnicity, appearance or sexuality through being perceived as a 'sissy' or 'gay'. We have also heard how feelings of rejection lie at the root of why they may hide certain emotions from others and choose to *mask* the way they truly feel. When working with boys and young men it is important that the educator responds to the *person* and not the *mask* and refuses to label a young man solely through his behaviour. This approach can help free them from their perceived need to hide behind masks that prevent them from recognising and accepting that they can be sensitive, caring and at times vulnerable, without believing that they are somehow compromising what it means to be a man. Our inference is that the construction of such a mask may be related to the influences on them in understanding and performing their masculinity. Zimbardo (2007:447) argues that 'individual differences should be celebrated, but in the face of strong, common situational forces, individual differences shrink and are compressed'. He proposes that resisting undesirable social influences should include practice strategies which would provide simple, effective methods to deal with them. He identifies the three Ss of 'self-awareness, situational sensitivity and being street smart' as potentially an effective way to inform practice (p. 452).

'Rackets'

By the time educators or practitioners intervene, boys and young men may have already built up a very tough 'racket', a tight combination of internalised stereotypes requiring them to be tough, in control and aggressive towards perceived external threats to their security. When we judge the racket negatively, the young men receive a shaming message that they themselves are bad. If we say to them 'You shouldn't be violent' then they have every right to respond with 'You don't live in my street'. Our question could instead be 'How is what you are doing now working for you?'. If they say 'Not well' then you will have a better chance of success than forcing them to change. Your role then becomes one that offers young men a better alternative than the racket they are using.

Concluding thoughts

Throughout this book we have presented the findings from our research and practice during the past 18 years with over 1,000 boys and young men. During this time we have been privileged to talk to boys and young men about issues they say they rarely discuss with other adults. Boys spoke of how they are struggling not only to find their place, but also their value, in a world that has changed significantly from that of their forefathers. Public expectations demand that families, schools and local communities are safe environments where young people are supported, encouraged, valued, mentored and loved. In reality, however, our studies reveal that these settings are often hostile environments where young men feel marginalised, fearful, unsupported and exist without mentors (Harland, 2001, 2011; Lloyd, 2009; Harland and McCready, 2012, 2014). Boys spoke of being left to their own devices, or the influences of their peers or other more sinister means to negotiate their way through the journey of life. We heard how issues associated with violence are an everyday experience for boys and young men and how issues surrounding masculinity are complex, shifting, contradictory, outdated and, for some, unattainable. Yet we also heard how these subjects are seldom addressed in the family home or in school. This in itself is quite revealing, and concerning.

We have discussed the importance of understanding the local ecological context in which boys grow up and become men and how this is affected by wider socio-economic issues such as poverty, class, ethnicity and social disadvantage. In particular we have presented how in Northern Ireland a declining industrial base with less demand for traditional male jobs, high levels of youth unemployment and a re-examination of men and masculinities over the past 40 years have run parallel with 40 years of political and community violence known as the Troubles. All these factors have significantly impacted upon young men's lives and powerfully shaped their experiences and expectations of masculinity and what it means to be a man. Each society will have its own local ecological context in which boys grow up and become men and, as we have discussed, each society will have its own unique history and experiences of violence and youth violence.

Globally we see disturbing male trends in drug dependency and alcohol abuse, male suicide, mental illness and poor academic attainment. In Northern Ireland we have also seen how paramilitary influence and an unstable peace process remains a constant threat that makes young men feel intimidated, vulnerable and confused in regard to issues surrounding the police and law and order.

Understanding this local ecological context was fundamental in how we set up the research design and also our responses to the issues that emerged from all of our data. It was this growing knowledge base that informed our research methodology and rationale for an experiential learning approach to boys' education and learning. The model we have presented in this chapter acknowledges the importance of formal, informal and non-formal education as all having a place in the education of boys and young men. The model places young men and their issues at the centre of their learning and focusing on appreciation of relational, contextual, situational and pedagogical factors.

With the decline of traditional industry in Western societies and the shift in favour of new knowledge economies, the value of education is arguably greater than it ever has been. Yet we have heard how school is perceived by many boys and young men as simply part of a system that perpetually denounces and reinforces them as failures. Failure to address effectively the developmental, educational and social needs of boys and young men will have serious implications for their emotional and mental health and well-being.

As a final point we would emphasise that education policy and practice should be more directly informed by the reality of young men's lives and experiences; neither should we underestimate the value of research for informing practice.

Appendices

Appendix 1: Being a man questionnaire

We would like to know your views and experience about being a man

Which of the following things do you disagree or agree describes what a man is? (Please tick one box only per question)

A man...	Strongly disagree	Disagree	Not sure	Agree	Strongly agree	Don't know
Is caring	☐	☐	☐	☐	☐	☐
Is responsible	☐	☐	☐	☐	☐	☐
Stands up for himself	☐	☐	☐	☐	☐	☐
Stands up for his family	☐	☐	☐	☐	☐	☐
Has a girlfriend or wife	☐	☐	☐	☐	☐	☐
Is a good father	☐	☐	☐	☐	☐	☐
Accepts people who are different from him	☐	☐	☐	☐	☐	☐
Is good at sports	☐	☐	☐	☐	☐	☐
Is tough	☐	☐	☐	☐	☐	☐
Is rich	☐	☐	☐	☐	☐	☐
Is smart/intelligent	☐	☐	☐	☐	☐	☐
Keeps his feelings to himself	☐	☐	☐	☐	☐	☐
Is a good fighter	☐	☐	☐	☐	☐	☐
Has a boyfriend	☐	☐	☐	☐	☐	☐
Earns money to keep his family	☐	☐	☐	☐	☐	☐
Is someone who shouts	☐	☐	☐	☐	☐	☐
Is not afraid to cry	☐	☐	☐	☐	☐	☐
Will walk away from a fight	☐	☐	☐	☐	☐	☐
Will hug another man	☐	☐	☐	☐	☐	☐
Is aggressive	☐	☐	☐	☐	☐	☐

Appendix 2: Violence questionnaire

(1) How violent do you think the following acts are? (Please tick one box per question)

	Not at all violent	A bit violent	Not sure	Violent	Extremely violent	Don't know
Punching someone is...	☐	☐	☐	☐	☐	☐
Calling someone rude names is...	☐	☐	☐	☐	☐	☐
Hitting someone is...	☐	☐	☐	☐	☐	☐
Smacking a child is...	☐	☐	☐	☐	☐	☐
Deliberately ignoring someone is...	☐	☐	☐	☐	☐	☐
Bullying someone is...	☐	☐	☐	☐	☐	☐
Being mentioned on the internet in a bad way is...	☐	☐	☐	☐	☐	☐
Hitting someone with a weapon is...	☐	☐	☐	☐	☐	☐
Spreading rumours about someone is...	☐	☐	☐	☐	☐	☐
Stabbing someone is...	☐	☐	☐	☐	☐	☐
Shouting at someone is...	☐	☐	☐	☐	☐	☐
Kicking someone is...	☐	☐	☐	☐	☐	☐
Pushing/shoving someone is...	☐	☐	☐	☐	☐	☐
Spitting at someone is...	☐	☐	☐	☐	☐	☐
Sending bullying text messages to a mobile phone is...	☐	☐	☐	☐	☐	☐
Threatening someone is...	☐	☐	☐	☐	☐	☐
Damaging someone's belongings is...	☐	☐	☐	☐	☐	☐

(2) Since starting school last September, has anyone been violent to you? (Please tick all that apply)

I was punched	☐
I was called rude names	☐
I was hit	☐
I was smacked by an adult	☐
I was deliberately ignored by others	☐
I was bullied	☐
I was mentioned on the internet in a bad way	☐
I was hit with a weapon	☐
Rumours were spread about me	☐
I was stabbed	☐
I was shouted at	☐
I was kicked	☐
I was pushed/shoved hard	☐
I was spat at	☐
Bullying text messages were sent to my mobile phone	☐
I was threatened	☐
My belongings were damaged	☐
Other (please say) _____	☐
None of these happened to me	☐

If you ticked any of the above, please complete parts (a) to (d) on the next page.

If you ticked 'None of these happened to me' then please go to question 3.

(a) Where did this incident or incidents happen? (Please tick all that apply)

In school	☐
Somewhere else	☐

(b) How seriously were you hurt? (Please tick one only)

Not hurt at all	Hurt a bit	Not sure	Hurt	Very badly hurt
☐	☐	☐	☐	☐

(c) Has the incident affected you in the last seven days?

In the last seven days ...	Not at all	Rarely	Sometimes	Often
I could still see pictures of it in my mind, even when I didn't mean to think about it	☐	☐	☐	☐
I had strong feelings about it	☐	☐	☐	☐
I remember it when sleeping or trying to sleep	☐	☐	☐	☐

(d) Did you talk to anyone about what happened?

☐ Yes   ☐ No

(3) (a) Since September, have you bullied other boys or girls? Please circle the number of times.

0 times   1   2   3   4   5   6 or more times

(b) Since September, have you sent a text message to someone where you wanted to upset them. If yes, how many times?

0 times   1   2   3   4   5   6 or more times

(c) Since September, have you started any fights? If yes, how many times?

0 times   1   2   3   4   5   6 or more times

(4) (A) Since September, have you been in trouble at this school?

☐ YES – now please answer below OR ☐ NO – you have finished!

How did being in trouble make you feel? (Please tick the ones you agree with)

I didn't care	☐
I felt sad	☐
I felt angry with myself	☐
I felt there was no-one to talk to	☐
I felt stupid	☐
I felt sorry	☐
I felt scared	☐
I just wanted to get it sorted	☐
I felt ashamed	☐
I felt angry with someone else	☐
I felt good	☐

(Continued)

Don't know how I felt	☐
I don't remember	☐
Other (please say)	
_____	☐

(B) Who were you in trouble with?

A school teacher	☐
A parent or guardian	☐
The police	☐
Other (please say)	
_____	☐

Thank you for completing this questionnaire

Notes

1 Context for Our Research Work with Boys and Young Men

1. The Good Friday (Belfast) Agreement (April 1998) addressed relationships within Northern Ireland, between Northern Ireland and the Republic of Ireland, and England, Scotland and Wales.
2. 'A paramilitary group denotes or relates to a force with military structure conducting armed operations for or against a ruling or occupying power' (*Collins English Dictionary*).
3. 'Bollocks' is a slang term for testicles.
4. An interface area is the name given to areas where segregated nationalist and unionist residential areas meet in Northern Ireland. They have been defined as 'the intersection of segregated and polarised working class residential zones, in areas with a strong link between territory and ethno-political identity' (Jarman, 2004).

2 Taking Boys Seriously (2006–2012): A Longitudinal Study

1. The 'gapper' was a young man who was given work experience during a one-year break between his academic studies as part of the Rank Foundation Gap Scheme. The gapper volunteered for nine months, dividing his time between the Centre for Young Men's Studies and YouthAction Northern Ireland. During this time he was trained in certain aspects of youth work and in research methodology and research design, while helping with the research project itself.

4 Research with Boys and Young Men: Critical Reflections on the Theme of Masculinity

1. For a fuller discussion on understanding the formation, practices and meanings of hegemonic masculinity, see Connell and Messerschmidt (2005).
2. Connell and Messerschmidt (2005) have criticised the trait model as a means of classifying features of masculinity exclusively on measures of personality. To avoid confusion, in this book the term 'construct' (with an emphasis on *con*) is used (e.g. Kelly, 2012) to denote any type of attribute that can be used to define masculinity. Within Kelly's theory of personal constructs, constructs are the building blocks that any individual uses to create a construct system, which is how they represent any issue or object in their mind.
3. It is interesting that passivity was assumed, since theories of cognitive learning, such as those of Jean Piaget, Jerome Bruner, Lem Vygotsky and George

Kelly, have generally accepted learning as an active, constructive process since the 1930s.

4. An Ulster Loyalist and former leader of the 'C Company', 2nd Battalion Shankill Road, Belfast of the 'Ulster Freedom Fighters' (UFF) which was a cover name used by the loyalist paramilitary organisation the Ulster Defence Association (UDA).

Bibliography

Adler, J. S. (2000) Young Men and Violence. *Journal of Urban History*, 26:657–668.

Aebi, M. and Linde, A. (2012) Conviction Statistics as an Indicator of Crime Trends in Europe from 1990 to 1996. *European Journal on Criminal Policy and Research*, 18:103–144.

Africa Check (2013) FACTSHEET South Africa: Official Crime Statistics for 2012/13. Available at: http://africacheck.org/factsheets/factsheet-south-africas-official-crime-statistics-for-201213/ Accessed 17 April 2015.

Agnew, R. (1992) Foundations for a General Strain Theory of Crime and Delinquency. *Criminology*, 30 (1):47–87.

Alegre, A. (2011) Parenting Styles and Children's Emotional Intelligence: What Do We Know? *The Family Journal*, 19 (1):56–62.

Allansson, M., Baumann, J., Taub, S., Themner, L. and Wallensteen, P. (2012) The First Year of the Arab Spring. In *SIPRI Yearbook 2012*. Oxford: Oxford University Press.

Alexander, R. (2008) *Essays on Pedagogy*. Abingdon: Routledge.

Anderson, C. and Bushman, B. (2002) Human Aggression. *Annual Psychological Review*, 53:27–51.

Anderson, T. (2014) *Understanding Deviance: Connecting Classical and Contemporary Perspectives*. New York: Routledge.

Ashe, A. (2004) Deconstructing the Experiential Bar: Male Experience and Feminist Resistance. *Men and Masculinities*, 7 (2):187–204.

Ashe, F. (2007) *The New Politics of Masculinities*. London and New York: Routledge.

Ashe, F. and Harland, K. (2014) Troubling Masculinities: Changing Patterns of Violent Masculinities in a Society Emerging from Political Conflict. *Studies in Conflict and Terrorism*, 37:747–762.

Aughey, A. (2014) Northern Ireland: 20 Years On. *Studies in Conflict and Terrorism*, 37:815–823.

Badinter, E. (1995) *XY: On Masculine Identity*. New York: Columbia University Press.

Bandura, A. (1977) *Social Learning Theory*. Facsimile Ed. Paperback. London: Prentice Hall.

Bandura, A. (2006) Toward a Psychology of Human Agency. *Association for Psychological Science*, 1 (2):164–180.

Barber, B. (2008) Contrasting Portraits of War: Youth's Varied Experiences with Political Violence in Bosnia and Palestine. *International Journal of Behavioral Development*, 32 (4):298–309.

Baron, R. and Byrne, D. (Eds.) (2003) *Social Psychology*. (10th Ed) Boston, MA: Allyn and Bacon.

Baron, L. (2013) *Social Theory in Popular Culture*. London: Palgrave MacMillan.

Barter, C., McCarry, M. and Evans, K. (2009) Partner Exploitation and Violence in Teenage Intimate Relationships. NSPCC. Available at: http://www.nspcc.org.uk/globalassets/documents/research-reports/partner-exploitation-violence-teenage-intimate-relationships-report.pdf

Barwick, B. (2004) *Young Males: Strengths-Based Male-Focused Approaches.* New Zealand: Ministry of Youth Development.

Bateman, T. (2005) Youth Justice News. *Youth Justice,* 5 (3):204–211.

Beattie, K. and Harland, K. and McCready, S. (2006a) Boys and Violence: Reflections on Some Boys' Lives, Experiences and Attitudes in Northern Ireland. Centre for Young Men's Studies, University of Ulster.

Beattie, K., Harland, H. and McCready, S. (2006b) Mental Health and Young Men: Suicide and Self Harm. Centre for Young Men's Studies, Research Update Number 2, University of Ulster.

Becker, H. S. (1963) *The Outsiders: Studies in the Sociology of Deviance.* New York: Free Press.

Belfast Telegraph (5 February 2008) Majority Want End to Barriers. Report by Vargo, T. US-Ireland Alliance.

Bell, D. (1990) *Acts of Union: Youth Culture and Sectarianism in N. Ireland.* London: Macmillan Education Ltd.

Bernard van Leer Foundation (2014) Responsive Parenting: A Strategy to Prevent Violence. *Every Childhood Matters Journal.* The Hague, The Netherlands. Available at: file:///C:/Users/Ken/Downloads/Responsive-parenting-a-strategy-to-prevent-violence%20(1).pdf Accessed 27/7/2015.

Biddulph, S. (1999) *Manhood: An Action Plan for Changing Men's Lives.* London: Hawthorne Press.

Biddulph, S. (2003) *Raising Boys: Why Boys Are Different – And How to Help Them Become Happy and Well-Balanced Men.* London: Harper Collins Publishers Ltd; New Ed Edition.

Blacker, H. (2010) Relationships, Friendship and Youth. In Jeffs, T. and Smith, M. K. (Eds.) *Youth Work Practice.* Basingstok: Palgrave. pp. 15–30.

Blades, R., Hart, D., Lea, J. and Willmott, N. (2011) *Care — A Stepping Stone to Custody?* London: Prison Reform Trust.

Blakemore, S. and Choudhury, S. (2006) Development of the Adolescent Brain: Implications for Executive Function and Social Cognition. *Journal of Child Psychology and Psychiatry,* 47 (3):296–312.

Booton, F. (1985) *Studies in Social Education: 1860–1890.* Hove: Benfield Press.

Boud, D., Keogh, R. and Walker, D. (2005) *Reflection: Turning Experience into Learning.* Milton Park, Ablington, Oxon: Routledge.

Bradley, R. M. (2008) *Masculinity and Self Perception of Men Identified as Informal Leaders.* USA: ProQuest LLC.

Brittain, A. (1989) *Masculinity and Power.* Oxford: Blackwell Press.

Bronfenbrenner (1979) *The Ecology of Human Development.* Cambridge, MA: Harvard University Press.

Brown, D. B. and Hogg, R. (1992) Policing Patriarchy. *Australian Left Review,* October 8–9.

Browne, B. and Dwyer, C. (2014) Navigating Risk: Understanding the Impact of the Conflict on Children and Young People in Northern Ireland. *Studies in Conflict & Terrorism,* 37 (9):792–805.

Burman, M., Tisdall, K. and Brown, J. (1997) Unpublished Report to the Gulbenkian Foundation.

Burman, M. J., Batchelor, S. A. and Brown, J. A. (2001) Researching Girls and Violence: Facing the Dilemmas of Fieldwork. *British Journal of Criminology,* 41 (3):443–459.

Byrne, J., Gormley-Heenan, C. and Robinson, G. (2012) Peace Walls: Public Attitudes and Impact on Policy. Policy Briefing University of Ulster/Institute for Research in Social Sciences.

Cairns, E. and Cairns, T. (1995) Children and Conflict: A Psychological Perspective. In Dunn, S. (Ed.) *Facets of the Conflict in Northern Ireland*. London: Macmillan Press Ltd. 97–113.

Cameron, M. (2000) Young Men and Violence Prevention. *Australian Institute of Criminology*, ISSN: 0817–8542.

Caprara, G. V., Pastorelli, C., Regalia, C., Scabini, E. and Bandura, A. (2005) Impact of Adolescents' Filial Self-Efficacy on Quality of Family Functioning and Satisfaction. *Journal of Research on Adolescence*, 15:71–97.

Carlson, N., Buskist, W. and Martin, G. (1992) *Psychology: The Science of Behaviour*. Boston MA: Allyn Bacon Publishing UK.

Carr, A. (2005) Contributions to the Study of Violence and Trauma: Multisystemic Therapy, Exposure Therapy, Attachment Styles and Therapy Process Research. *Journal of Interpersonal Violence*, 20 (4):426–435.

Cary, M., Butler, S., Baruch, N. and N. Byford, S. (2013) Economic Evaluation of Multisystemic Therapy for Young People at Risk for Continuing Criminal Activity in the UK. *PLoS ONE*, 8 (4) e6070 DOI:10.1371/journal.pone.wo61070

Catalano, R. F. and Hawkins, J. D. (1996) Social Development Model: A Theory of Anti-Social Behaviour. In *Delinquents and Crime: Current Theories*. New York: Cambridge University Press. pp. 149–197.

Centre for Social Justice (2009) *Dying to Belong: An In-Depth Review of Street Gangs in Britain*. London: Centre for Social Justice.

Chaffin, M. (2006) The Changing Focus of Child Maltreatment Research and Practice within Psychology. *Journal of Social Issues*, 62 (4):663–864.

Chapman, T. (2000) *Time to Grow. A Comprehensive Programme for People Working with Young Offenders and Young people at Risk*. Lyme Regis: Russell House Publishing.

Chapman and McCready (2002) *Young Men and Violence – A Programme to Reduce Violence and Engender Peace*. EU Special Support Programme for Peace and Reconciliation. Belfast:Youthnet

Child Exploitation and Online Protection Centre (June, 2013) Threat Assessment of Child Sexual Exploitation and Abuse. Available at: http://ceop.police. uk/Documents/ceopdocs/CEOP_TACSEA2013_240613%20FINAL.pdf Accessed 15 March 2015.

Clarke, J. (1976) The Skinheads and the Magical Recovery of Community. In Hall, S. and Jefferson, T. (Eds.) (1996) *Resistance Through Rituals*. London: Routledge. p. 99.

Coburn, A. (2010) Youth Work and Border Pedagogy. In Batsleer, J. and Davies, B. (Eds.) *What Is Youth Work?*. Exeter: Learning Matters. 33–46.

Cohen, S. (2002) *Folk Devils and Moral Panics*. (3rd Ed) London: Routledge.

Cock, J. (2001) Gun Violence and Masculinity in Contemporary South Africa. In Morrell, R. (Ed.) *Changing Men in South Africa*. Pietermaritzburg: University Natal Press. pp. 43–56.

Coie, J., Watt, F., West, S., Hawkins, J., Asarnow, J., Marman, H. and Long, B. (1993) The Science of Prevention: A Conceptual Framework and Some Directions for a National Research Program. *American Psychologist*, 48:1013–1022.

Cohen, S. (1972) *Folk Devils and Moral Panics: The Creation of the Mods and Rockers*. (3rd Ed). Oxford: Martin Robertson.

Cohen, L., Manion, L. and Morrison, K. (2011) *Research Methods in Education.* London: Routledge.

Coleman, K., Hird, C. and Povey, D. (2006) *Violent Crime Overview, Homicide and Gun Crime 2004/2005.* London: Home Office.

Connell, R. (1997) *Gender and Power.* Berkeley: University of California Press.

Connell, R. W. (1989) Cool Guys, Swots and Wimps: The Interplay of Masculinity and Education. *Oxford Review of Education,* 15 (3):291–303.

Connell, R. W. (1995) *Masculinities.* Cambridge: Polity Press.

Connell, R.W. (2000) *The Men and the Boys.* Sydney: Allen and Umwin; Cambridge: Polity Press; Berkeley: University of California Press.

Connell, R. W. and Messerschmidt, J. W. (2005) Hegemonic Masculinity: Rethinking the Concept. *Gender and Society,* 19 (6):829–859.

Connolly, P. (2002) *Race and Racism in Northern Ireland: A Review of the Research Evidence.* Belfast: Office of the First and Deputy First Minister.

Coombs, P. and Ahmed, M. (1974) *Attacking Rural Poverty.* Baltimore: The John Hopkins University Press.

Convery, U., Haydon, D., Moore, L. and Scraton, P. (2008) Children, Rights and Justice in Northern Ireland: Community and Custody. *Youth Justice Review,* 8 (3): 245–263.

Cottrell-Boyce, J. (2013) Ending Gang and Youth Violence: A Critique. *Youth Justice,* 13 (3):193–206.

Criminal Justice Inspectorate. (2006) *Handling Volume Crime and Use of Bail.* Belfast: CJINI.

Crooks, C. V., Goodall, G. R., Hughes, R. Jaffe, P. G. and Baker, L. L. (2007) Engaging Men and Boys in Preventing Violence against Women. *Violence Against Women,* 13 (3):217–239.

Crawford, D. (2003) Becoming a Man: The Views and Experiences of Some Second-Generation Males. *Electronic Journal of Sociology,* ISSN: 11983655.

Creary, P. and Byrne, S. (2014) Youth Violence as Accidental Spoiling?: Civil Society Perceptions of the Role of Sectarian Youth Violence and the Effect of the Peace Dividend in Northern Ireland. *Nationalism and Ethnic Politics,* 20 (2):221–243.

Crime Survey of England and Wales (2014) Recorded Crime. Available at: http://www.ons.gov.uk/ons/rel/crime-stats/crime-statistics/period-ending-september-2013/sum-crime-stats.html Accessed 11 March 2015.

Crosby, M. (2005) Working with People as an Informal Educator. In Richardson, L. D. and Wolfe, M. (Eds.) *Principles and Practice of Informal Education: Learning through Life.* New York: Routledge. 53–60.

Crownover, J. (2007) *Exploring Dimensions of Masculinity and Violence: Western Balkan Gender-Based Violence Prevention Initiative.* Washington: ICRW.

Dahlberg, L. and Potter, L. (2001) Youth Violence: Developmental Pathways and Prevention Challenges. *American Journal of Preventative Medicine,* 20: 3–21.

Daiute, C. and Fine, M. (2003) Youth Perspectives on Violence and Injustice. *Journal of Social Issues,* 59 (1):1–14.

Darker, I., Ward, H. and Caulfield, L. (2008) An Analysis of Offending by Young People Looked after by Local Authorities. *Youth Justice,* 8 (2):134–148.

David, D. S. and Brannon, R. (1976) *The Forty Nine Percent Majority: The Male Sex Role.* Reading Massachusetts: McGraw Hill Education.

Davies, B. (2005) Youth Work: A Manifesto for Our Times. *Youth & Policy*, 88 Summer:5–27.

Davies, B. (2010) What Do We Mean by Youth Work. In Batsleer, J. and Davies, B. (Eds.) *What Is Youth Work?* Exeter: Learning Matters Publications. 153–165.

Day, D. M. and Hunt, A. C. (1996) A Multivariate Assessment of a Risk Model for Juvenile Delinquency with an under 12 Offender Sample. *Journal of Emotional and Behavioural Disorders*, 4 (2):66–72.

Department of Justice NI (2011) *A Review of the Youth Justice System in Northern Ireland*. Youth Justice for Northern Ireland. Available at: http://www.dojni.gov.uk/index/publications/publication-categories/pubs-criminal-justice/report-of-the-review-of-the-youth-justice-system-in-ni.pdf

Dewey, J. (1910) *How We Think*. Boston: Heath.

Dewey, J. (1938), (1997 Ed) *Experience and Education*. New York: Touchstone.

Donaldson, M. (1991) *Time of Our Lives: Labour and Love in the Working Class*. Sydney: Allen and Unwin.

Dragiewicz, M. (2008) Masculinities and Violence. In Renzetti, C. and Edleson, J. (Eds.) *Encyclopedia of Interpersonal Violence*. Thousand Oaks, CA: Sage. pp. 436–437.

Dubow, E. F., Boxer, P., Rowell Huesmann, L., Khalil Shikaki., Simha Landau., Shira Dvir Gvirsman and Ginges, J. (2010) Exposure to Conflict and Violence across Contexts: Relations to Adjustment among Palestinian Children. *Journal of Clinical Child Adolescent Psychology*, 39 (1):103–116.

Dugmore, P. (2012) Working with Young People. In Pickford, J. and Dugmore, P. (Eds.) *Youth Justice and Social Work*. London: Sage. pp. 169–190.

Durkheim, Emile (1951) *Division of Labor in Society*. New York: Free Press (originally published in 1893). New York: Free Press.

Durkheim, E. (1972) *Emile Durkheim: Selected Writings*. Translated by Anthony Giddens. New York: Cambridge University Press.

Dweck, C. (2000) *Self Theories: Their Role in Motivation, Personality and Development*. Philadelphia, PA: Essays in Psychology Press.

Eaude, T. (2011) *Thinking through Pedagogy for Primary and Early Years*. Exeter: Learning Matters.

Elliott, D. S. (1994) Serious Violent Offenders: Onset, Developmental Course, and Termination – The American Society of Criminology 1993 Presidential Address. *Criminology*, 32:1–21.

Erikson, E. H. (1950) *Childhood and Society*. New York: Norton.

Erikson, E. H. (1994) *Identity and the Life Cycle*. W.W. Norton & Co Ltd; Rev Ed edition.

European Commission for Youth (2014) *Working with Young People: The Value of Youth Work in the European Union European*. Prepared by Allison Dunne, Daniela Ulicna, Ilona Murphy, Maria Golubeva Checked by Daniela Ulicna, Margaret James Commission and the Education, Audiovisual and Culture Executive Agency. Brussels.

European Union Agency for Fundamental Human Rights (2014) Violence AGAINST Women: An EU-wide Survey. Belgium.

Fagan, A. (2005) Civil Society in Bosnia Ten Years after Dayton. *International Peacekeeping*, 12 (3):406–419.

Fagan, A. and Catalano, R. (2013) What Works in Youth Violence Prevention: A Review of the Literature. *Research on Social Work Practice*, 23 (2):141–156.

Fajnzylber, P., Lederman D. and Loayza, N. (2002) Inequality and Violent Crime. *Law and Economy*, 45:1.

Farrington, D. P., Gallagher, B., Morley, L., St. Ledger, R. and West, D. J. (1990) Minimizing Attrition in Longitudinal Research: Methods of Tracing and Securing Cooperation in a 24-Year Follow-Up Study. In Magnusson, D. and Bergman, L. (Eds.) *Data Quality in Longitudinal Research.* Cambridge: Cambridge University Press. pp. 122–147.

Farrington, D. P. (1995) Key issues in the Integration of Motivational and Ppportunity Reducing Crime Prevention Strategies. In Wikström, P. O. H., Clarke, R. V., McCord, J. and Stockholm, J. (Eds.) *Integrating Crime Prevention Strategies: Propensity and Opportunity.* Sweden: National Council for Crime Prevention. pp. 333–357.

Farrington, D. P. (1999) Cambridge Study in Delinquent Development (Great Britain), 1961–1981. Inter-university Consortium for Political and Social Research. ICPSR 8488.

Farrington, D. P. (2003a) Key Results from the First 40 years of the Cambridge Study in Delinquent Development. In Thornberry, T. P. and Krohn, M. D. (Eds.) *Taking Stock of Delinquency: An Overview of Findings from Contemporary Longitudinal Studies.* New York: Kluwer/Plenum. pp. 137–183.

Farrington, D. P. (2003b). Developmental and Life-Course Criminology: Key Theoretical and Empirical Issues-the 2002 Sutherland Award Address. *Criminology*, 41:221–255.

Federal Ministry for Family Affairs (2004) *Violence against Men: Men's Experiences of Interpersonal Violence in Germany.* Project team: Ludger Jungnitz, Hans-Joachim Lenz, Dr. Ralf Puchert, Dr. Henry Puhe, Willi Walter. Berlin.

FitzGerald, M., Stevens, A. and Hale, C. (2004) *Review of Knowledge on Juvenile Violence: Trends, Policies and Responses in Europe.* (Final Report to the EU). University of Kent.

Flood, C. (2000) Safe Boys – Safe Schools. *WEEA Digest*, November: 4–7.

Flood, M. (2007) Suicide. In Flood, M., Kegan Gardiner, J., Pease, B., Pringle, K. (Eds.) *International Encyclopedia of Men and Masculinities.* London: Routledge.

Flood, M. and Pease, B. (2009) Factors Influencing Attitude to Violence Against Women. *Trauma, Violence & Abuse*, 10 (2):125–142.

Flowers, P. and Buston, K. (2001) 'I Was Terrified of Being Different': Exploring Gay Men's Accounts of Growing-Up in a Heterosexist Society. *Journal of Adolescence* 2001, 24:51–65.

Forrest, S. (2004) *Participation and Working with Boys and Young Men: Guidance for Practitioners and Policy Development.* London: Working with Young Men Publications.

Foster, H. and Brooks-Gunn, J. (2009) Toward a Stress Process Model of Children's Exposure to Physical Family and Community Violence. *Clinical Child and Family Psychological Review*, 12:71–94.

Fowler, P. and Braciszewski, J. (2009) Community Violence Prevention and Intervention Strategies for Children and Adolescents: The Need for Multi-Level Approaches. *Journal of Prevention and Intervention in the Community*, 37 (4):255–259.

Fraser, A., Burman, M., Bachelor, S. and McVie, S. (2010) *Youth Violence in Scoltand: Literature Review*. Edinburgh: The Scottish Centre for Crime and Justice.

Freire, P. (1972) *Pedagogy of the Oppressed*. London: Penguin.

Frosh, S., Phoenix, A. and Pattman, R. (2002) *Young Masculinities: Understanding Boys in Contemporary Society*. London: Palgrave.

Fry, H., Kettridge, S. and Marshall, S, (Eds.) (2009) *A Handbook for Teaching and Learning in Higher Education: Enhancing Academic Practice*, (3rd Ed). Abingdon, Routledge.

Fulcher, L. C. and McGladdery, S. (2011) Re-examining Social Work Roles and tasks with Foster Care. *Child & Youth Services*, 32:19–38.

Fulkerson, J. A., Story, Mary, Mellin, A., Leffert N., Neumark-Sztainer, D. and French, S. A. (2006) Family Dinner Meal Frequency and Adolescent Development: Relationships with Developmental Assets and High-Risk Behaviors. *Journal of Adolescent Health*, 39:337–345.

Furlong, A. (2013) *Youth Studies: An Introduction*. Routledge: Abingdon.

Garrett, P. (1999) Producing the Moral Citizen: The 'Looking after Children' System and the Regulation of Children and Young People in Public Care. *Critical Social Policy*, 19 (3):291–311.

Geldard and Geldard (2010) *Counselling Adolescents: The Proactive Approach for Young People*. (3rd Ed). London: Sage.

Gibson, S. (2004) Social Learning Theory and Implications for Human Resource Development. *Advances in Developing Human Resources*, 6 (2):193–210.

Giddens, A. and Sutton, P. W. (2013) *Sociology*. (7th Ed). Cambridge, UK: Polity Press.

Gillespie, N., Lovett, T. and Garner, W. (1992) *Youth Work and Working Class Youth Culture: Rules and Resistance in West Belfast*. Buckingham: Open University Press.

Gilligan, J. (1996) *Violence: Our Deadliest Epidemic and Its Causes*. New York: Grosset/Putnam.

Gilligan, J. (2000) *Violence: Reflections on Our Deadliest Epidemic*. Philadelphia: Jessica Kingsley Publishers.

Gilling, D. (1997) *Crime Prevention: Theory, Policy and Politics*. London: UCL Press.

Goeke-Morey, M., Taylor, L., Merrilees, C., Cummings, M., Cairns, E. and Shirlow, P. (2013) Adolescents' Educational Outcomes in a Social Ecology of Parenting, Family, and Community Risks in Northern Ireland. *School Psychology International*, 34 (3):243–256.

Goodman, R. (1997) The Strengths and Difficulties Questionnaire: A Research Note. *Journal of Child Psychology and Psychiatry*, 38 (5):581–586.

Gordon, F., McAlister, S., & Scraton, P. (2015). Behind the Headlines: Media Representation of Children and Young People in Northern Ireland: Summary of Research Findings. Queen's University Belfast.

Gough, B. (2007) Real Men Don't Diet: An Analysis of Contempory Newpaper Representations of Men, Food and Health. *Journal of Social Science and Medicine*, 64 (2):326–337.

Grady, R. T. (2003) *An Interpretation of Dewey's Experiential Learning Theory*. ERIC Available at: http://eric.ed.gov/?id=ED481922 accessed 26 March 2015.

Graham, K. (2003) Social Drinking and Aggression. In Mattson, M. (Ed.) *Neuro-Biology of Aggression: Understanding and Preventing Violence*. Totowa, NJ: Humana Press. 253–274.

Graham, I. and Damkat, I. (2014) *Northern Ireland Conviction and Sentencing Statistics 2010–2012*. DOJNI: Northern Ireland.

Gormley-Heenan, C. and Monaghan, R. (2012) Political Reverberations: Northern Ireland's Conflict, Peace Process and Paramilitaries. *Behavioural Sciences of Terrorism and Political Aggression*, 4 (1):1–3.

Gray, A. M., Horgan, G., Leighton, A. and Todd, D. (2014) Policy Brief: Truth about Youth. ARK Northern Ireland Policy Brief. University of Ulster and Queens University.

Haj-Yahia, M. M., Leshem, B. and Guterman, N. B. (2011) Exposure to Community Violence among Arab Youth in Israel: Rates and Characteristics. *Journal of Community Psychology*, 39:136–151.

Haj-Yahia, M. M., Leshem, B. and Guterman, N. (2013) The Rates and Characteristics of Exposure of Palestinian Youth to Community Violence. *Journal of Interpersonal Violence*, 28 (11).

Hall, G. S. (1904) *Adolescence: Its Psychology and Its Relations to Physiology, Anthropology, Sociology, Sex, Crime, Religion, and Education* (Vols. I & II). New York: D. Appleton & Co.

Hall, S. and Jefferson, T. (Eds.) *Resistance through Rituals: Youth Subcultures in Post-War Britain*. London: Hutchinson.

Hallsworth, S. and Young, T. (2004) Getting Real about Gangs. *Criminal Justice Matters*, 55 (1):12–13.

Hansson, U. (2005) *Troubled Youth? Young People, Violence and Disorder in Northern Ireland*. Belfast: Institute for Conflict Research.

Harbom, L., Hogbladh, S. and Wallensteen, P. (2006) Armed Conflict and Peace Agreements. *Journal of Peace Research*, 43 (5):617–719.

Hargie, O. Dickson, D. and Nelson, S. (2003) Working Together in a Divided Society. *Journal of Business and Technical Communication*, 17 (3):285–318.

Harland, K. (1997) *Young Men Talking – Voices from Belfast*, London: Youth Action Northern Ireland and Working With Young Men Publications.

Harland, K. (2009) *Acting Tough: Young Men, Masculinity and the Development of Practice in Northern Ireland*. Derry: Nowhere Man Press.

Harland, K. (2000) *Men and Masculinity: The Construction of Masculine Identities in Inner City Belfast*. Ph.D. Thesis: University of Ulster.

Harland, K. (2001) The Challenges and Potential of developing a more effective Youth Work Curriculum with young men. *Child Care in Practice*, 7 (4): 288–300.

Harland, K. (2011) Violent Youth Culture in Northern Ireland: Young Men Violence and the Challenges of Peacebuilding. *Youth & Society*, 43 (2): 422–430.

Harland, K. and McCready, S. (2007a) Work with Young Men. In Flood, M., Gardiner, J. K., Pease, B. and Pringle, K. (Eds.) *International Encyclopaedia Men & Masculinities*. London: Routledge. 654–656.

Harland, K. and McCready, S. (2007b) Young Men. In Flood, M., Gardiner, J. K., Pease, B and Pringle, K. (Eds.) *International Encyclopedia Men & Masculinities*. London: Routledge. 665.

Harland, K. and McCready, S. (2010) *Finding Positive Responses to Young Men's Experiences of Violence and Personal Safety*. Queen's University, Shared Spaces. Community Relations Council publications. Issue 10. 49–63.

Harland, K. and McCready, S. (2012) *Taking Boys Seriously: A Longitudinal Study into Adolescent Boys' School-Life Experiences in Northern Ireland*. Northern Ireland:

Department of Education/Department of Justice/Centre for Young Men's Publications.

Harland, K. and McCready, S. (2014) Rough Justice: Considerations on the Role of Violence, Masculinity, and the Alienation of Young Men in Communities and Peacebuilding Processes in Northern Ireland. *International Journal of Youth Justice*, 14 (3):269–283.

Harland, K., McCready, S. and Beattie, K. (2005) *Young Men and the Squeeze of Masculinity: The Inaugural Paper for the Centre for Young Men's Studies*. Ulster University. Available at: http://www.ulster.ac.uk/sass/the-centre-for-young-mens-studies-publications/

Harland, K. and Morgan, S. (2003) Youth Work and Young Men in Northern Ireland: An Advocacy Approach. In *Youth and Policy*, 81 Autumn.

Harland, K., Morgan, T. and Muldoon, O. (2005) *The Nature of Youth Work in Northern Ireland: Purpose, Contribution and Challenges*. Belfast: Ulster University and Queens University Publication.

Hawkins, D., Herrenkohol, T., Farrington, D., Brewer, D., Catalino, R. F., Harachi, T. W. and Cothern, L. (2000) *Predictor of Youth Violence. Juvenile Justice Bulletin*. Washington, DC: US Office of Juvenile Justice and Delinquency Prevention (NCJ 179065).

Hawkins, J. D., Catalano, R. F. and Miller, J. Y. (1992) Risk and Protective Factors for Alcohol and Other Drug Problems in Adolescence and Early Adulthood: Implications for Substance Abuse Prevention. *Psychological Bulletin*, 112:64–105.

Haydon, D., McAlister, S. and Scraton, P. (2012) Young People, Conflict and Regulation. *The Howard Journal of Criminal Justice*, 51 (5):503–520.

Haydon, D. and Scraton, P. (2008) Conflict, Regulation and Marginalisation in the North of Ireland: The Experiences of Children and Young People. *Current Issues in Criminal Justice*, 20 (1):59–78.

Hearn, J. (2005) The Hegemony of Men. In Hearn, J. (Ed) *Gender Inequalities: Feminist Theories and Politics*. Los Angeles, USA: Oxford University Press. pp. 221–225.

Hearn, J. and Morgan, D. (1990) The Critique of Men. In Hearn and Morgan (Eds.) *Men, Masculinity and Social Theory*. London: Hyman Unwin. pp. 206–214.

Heilbrun, K., Sevin Goldstein, N. E. and Redding, R. E. (Eds.) (2005) *Juvenile Delinquency: Prevention, Assessment, and Intervention*. New York: Oxford University Press. 368.

Hemphill, S., Smith, R., Toumbourou, J., Herrenkohl, T., Catalano, R., McMorris, B. and Romanuik, H. (2009) Modifiable Determinants of Youth Violence in Australia and the United States: A Longitudinal Study. *Australian and New Zealand Journal of Criminology*, 42 (3):289–309.

Henggeler, S., Schoenwald, S., Bouduin, C., Cunningham, P. and Rowland, M. (2009) *Multisystemic Therapy for Antisocial Behaviour in Children and Adolescents*. New York: Guilford Press.

Henry, B., Feehan, M., McGee, R., Stanton, W. R., Moffitt, T. E. and Silva, P. A. (1993) The Importance of Conduct Problems and Depressive Symptoms in Predicting Adolescent Substance Use. *Journal of Abnormal Child Psychology*, 21 (21):469–480.

Henry, P., Morgan, S. and Hammond, M. (2010) Building Relationships through Effective Interpersonal Engagement: A Training Model for Youth Workers. *Youth Studies Ireland*, 5 (2):Autumn/Winter.

Herek, G. M. (2000) Homosexuality. In Kazdin, A. E. (Ed.) *Encyclopedia of Psychology*. Washington, DC: American Psychological Association & Oxford University Press. pp. 149–153.

Hester and Pearson (1993) J. Hester, C. Pearson; Domestic Violence, Mediation, and Child Contact Arrangements: Issues from Current Research. Children and Youth Services Review.

Hirchi, T. and Gottfredson, M. (2001) Self Control Theory. In Paternoster, R. and Bachman, R. (Eds.) *Explaining Criminals and Crime*. Los Angeles: Roxbury. pp. 81–96.

Hoff-Sommers, C. (2000) The War against Boys. *The Atlantic Monthly*, 285 (5):59–74.

Holstein, J. and Gubrium, J. (2007) *Constructionist Perspectives on Life Course*. *Sociology Compass 1*. Oxford: Blackwell Publishing.

Hong, L. (1998) *Redefining Babes, Booze, and Brawls: Men against Violence—Towards a New Masculinity*. Unpublished doctoral dissertation, Lousiana State University and Agricultural and Mechanical College, Baton Rouge.

Hong, L. (2000) Toward a Transformed Approach to Prevention: Breaking the Link between Masculinity and Violence. *Journal of American College Health*, 48:269–280.

Horgan, G. (2007) *The Impact of Poverty on Young Children's Experience of School*. Joseph Rowntree Foundation. JRF and York Publishing. 78 pp. [Research report (external)]

Horgan, G. (2011) The Making of an Outsider: Growing Up in Poverty in Northern Ireland. *Youth & Society*, 43 (2):453–467.

Horgan, G., Gray, A. M. and Conlon, C. (2014) *Young People Not in Education, Employment or Training*. Ark Policy Brief 3. Available at: http://www.ark.ac.uk/pdfs/policybriefs/policybrief3.pdf Accessed 3 March 2015.

Horgan, J. (2003) Lecturing for Learning. In Fry, H., Ketteridge, S. and Marshall, S. (Eds.) *A Handbook for Teaching & Learning in Higher Education*. London: Kogan Page. pp. 75–90.

Horrocks, R. (1994) *Masculinity in Crisis-Myths, Fantasies and Realities*. London: The Macmillan Press Ltd.

Hughes, K., Bellis, M., Calafat, A., Juan, M., Schnitzer, S. and Anderson, Z. (2008) Predictors of Violence in Young Tourists: A Comparative Study of British, German and Spanish Holiday Makers. *European Journal of Public Health*, 18 Ivan Illich, I. (1971) *Deschooling Society* New York: Harper Row.

International Centre for Prison Studies (2013) World Prison Population List (10th Ed.). Available at: http://www.prisonstudies.org/sites/prisonstudies.org/files/resources/downloads/wppl_10.pdf Accessed 15 February 2015.

Ireland, C. S. and Thommeny, J. L. (1993) The Crime Cocktail: Licensed Premises, Alcohol and Street Offences. *Drug and Alcohol Review*, 12:143–250.

Jackson, C. (2002) Motives for 'Laddishness' at School: Fear of Failure and Fear of the 'Feminine'. *British Educational Research Journal*, 29 (4c):583–598.

Jackson, C. (2006) *Lads and Ladettes in School*. Maidenhead: Open University press.

Jacobson, J., Bhardwa, B., Gyateng, T., Hunter, G. and Hough, M. (2012) *Punishing Disadvantage: A Profile of Children in Custody*. London: Prison Reform Trust.

Jakupcak, M., Tull, M. and Roemer, L. (2005) Masculinity, Shame, and Fear of Emotions as Predictors of Men's Anger and Hostility. *Psychology of Men and Masculinity*, 6 (4):275–284.

James, W. (1995) Peace and Conflict. *Journal of Peace Psychology*, 1 (1):17–26.

Jarman. N. (2004) Demography and Disorder: Changing Patterns of Interface Actions. Institute of Conflict. Belfast. Office for Minister Deputy First Minister. Stormont, Belfast: OFMDFM.

Jarvis, P. (2006) *From Adult Education to the Learning Society: 21 Years from the International Journal of Lifelong Education*. New York: Routledge, Education Heritage Society.

Jeffs, T. and Smith, M. (1999) The Problem of 'Youth' for Youth Work. *Youth & Policy*. 62, Winter.

Jeffs, T. and Smith, M. (Eds.) (2010) *Youth Work Practice*. London: Palgrave MacMillan.

Jenkins, R. (1982) *Hightown Rules: Growing up in a Belfast Housing Estate*. Leicester: National Youth Bureau Publishers.

Jenkins, R. (1983) *Lads, Citizens and Ordinary Kids: Working-Class Youth Life-Styles in Belfast*. London: Routledge.

Jordan, E. (1995) Fighting Boys and Fantasy Play: The Construction of Masculinity in the Early Years of School. *Gender and Education*, 7 (1):69–86.

Kaufman, S. (1993) *Cracking the Armour: Power, Pain and the Lives of Men*. Toronto: Penguin.

Kaufmann, S. (2001) *Modern Hatreds: The Symbolic Politics of Ethnic War*. Ithaca, NY: Cornell University Press.

Keddie, A. (2006) Pedagogies and Critical Reflection: Key Understandings for Transformative Gender Justice. *Gender and Education*, 18 (1):99–114.

Kelly, L. (2012) Representing and Preventing Youth Crime and Disorder: Intended and Unintended Consequences of Targeted Youth Programmes in England. *Youth Justice*, 12:101.

Kennedy, L. (2001) They Shoot Children Don't They?: An Analysis of the Age and Gender of Victims of Paramilitary 'Punishments' in Northern Ireland. Available at: http://cain.ulst.ac.uk/issues/violence/docs/kennedy01.htm Accessed 1 February 2015.

Kerner, J. F. and Hall, K. L. (2009) Research Dissemination and Diffusion: Translation within Science and Society. *Research on Social Work Practice*, 19: 519–530.

Kershaw, C., Nicholas, S. and Walker, A. (2008) *Crime in England and Wales 2007/08*. London: Home Office Statistical Bulletin.

Kessler, S., Ashenden, D. J., Connell, R. W. and Dowsett, D. W. (1985) Gender Relations in Secondary Schooling. *Sociology of Education*, 58:34–48.

Kilpatrick, C. (2013) We Cannot Turn Our Backs on Savagery. *The Belfast Telegraph*, 19 November:4.

Kimmel, M., Hearn, J. and Connell, R. W. (2005) *Handbook of Studies on Men & Masculinities*. London: Sage.

Kimmel, M. and Messner, M. (Eds.) (1995) *Men's Lives*. (3rd Ed.) Boston: Allyn and Bacon.

Kivel, P. (1997) *Unlearning Violence: A Breakthrough Book for Violent Men and All Those Who Love Them*. New York: MJF Books.

Knott, C. and Scragg, T. (2010) Reflective Practice Revisited. In Knott, C. and Scragg, T. (Eds.) *Reflective Practice in Social Work*. (2nd Ed). Learning Matters Ltd: Exeter, pp. 3–12.

Kolb, D. A. and Fry, R. (1975) Toward an Applied of Experiental Learning. In Cooper, G. (Ed) *Theories of Group Processes*. New York: Wiley.

Kolb, D. A. (1984) *Experiential Learning, Experience as the Source of Learning and Development*. Englewood Cliffs, NJ: Prentice Hall.

Krauss, H. (2006) *Perspectives on Violence*. New York Academy of Sciences, 1087.

Lawson, M. (2005) Theoretical Foundation. In Sexton-Radek, K. (Ed.) *Violence in Schools; Issues, Consequences and Expressions*. Westport, Connecticut: Praeger. 3–34.

Lacasse, A. and Mendelson, M. J. (2007) Sexual Coercion among Adolescents. *Journal of Interpersonal Violence*, 22:424–437.

Leonard, M. (2006) Teenagers Telling Sectarian Stories. *Sociology*, 40 (6):1117–1133.

Leverett, S. and Rixon, A. (2011) Reflective Spaces. In Foley, P. and Leverett, S. (Eds.) *Children and Young People's Spaces*. Basingstoke: Palgrave Macmillan. pp. 176–192.

Lingard, R. and Douglas, P. (1999) *Men Engaging Feminisms*. Buckingham: OU Press.

Lipsey, M. W. and Derzon, J. H. (1998) Predictors of Violent or Serious Delinquency in Adolescence and Early Adulthood. In Loeber, R. and Farrington, D. P. (Eds.) *Serious and Violent Juvenile Offenders: Risk Factors and Successful Interventions*. Thousand Oaks, CA: Sage Publications, Inc., pp. 86–105.

Littell, J. H. (2005) Lessons from a Systematic Review of Effects of Multisystemic Therapy. *Children and Youth Services Review*, 27 (4):445–463.

Livingstone, S., Kirwil, L., Ponte, C. and Staksrud, E. (2014) In Their Own Words: What Bother Children Online? *European Journal of Communication*, 29 (3):1–20.

Lloyd, T. (1996) *Young Men's Health. A Youth Work Concern?* Published jointly by Youth Action Northern Ireland and Health Promotion Agency for Northern Ireland.

Lloyd, T. (1997) *Let's Get Changed Lads*. London: Working with Men Publications.

Lloyd, T. (2001) What Works? (Boy's and Young Men's Health) Research Report, Working with Men Publications, London.

Lloyd, T. (2002) Men and Violence: An Evaluation of Three Innovative Projects. YouthNet: Belfast. Available at: http://www.boysdevelopmentproject.org.uk/wp-content/uploads/2013/06/wwm_violencereport-17.pdf

Lloyd, T. (2006) *Young Men and Violence Project: External Evaluation*. Belfast: YouthAction Northern Ireland.

Lloyd, T. (2007) *Young Men and Violence Evaluation*. Belfast: YouthAction Northern Ireland.

Lloyd, T. (2009) *Stuck in the Middle* (Some Young Men's Attitudes and Experience of Violence, Conflict and Safety). Centre for Young Men's Studies Publication: Ulster University. Available at: http://www.ulster.ac.uk/sass/the-centre-for-young-mens-studies-publications/

Loeber, R., Farrington, D. P., Stouthamer-Loeber, M., Moffitt, T. E., Caspi, A. and Lynam, D. (2001) Male Mental Health Problems, Psychopathy and Personality Traits: Key Findings from the First 14 Years of the Pittsburgh Youth Study. *Clinical Child and Family Psychology Review*, 4:273–297.

Lomas, T. (2014) *Masculinity, Meditation and Wellbeing*. London and New York: Palgrave Macmillan.

Lorber, J. (1998) Men's Gender Politics. *Gender and Society*, 12 (4) August:469–477.

Lusher, D. and Robins, G. (2010) Hegemonic and Other Masculinities in Local Social Contexts. *Men and Masculinities*, 11 (4):387–423.

Mac an Ghaill, M. (1994) *The Making of Men: Masculinities, Sexualities and Schooling*. Buckingham: Open University Press.

Mac an Ghaill, M. (1996) What about the Boys?: Schooling, Class and Crisis of Masculinity. *Sociological Review*, 44 (3):381–397.

MacDonald, J., Piquero, A., Valois, R. and Zullig, K. (2005) The Relationship between Life Satisfaction, Risk Taking Behaviours and Youth Violence. *Journal of Interpersonal Violence*, 20 (11):1495–1518.

Macinnes, J. (1988) *The End of Masculinity?* The Confusion of Sexual Genesis and Sexual Difference in Modern Society. Bristol: Open University Press.

McAlister, S., Haydon, D. and Scraton, P. (2013) Violence in the Lives of Children and Young People in Post Conflict Northern Ireland. *Children, Youth and Environments*, 23 (1):1–22.

McAlister, S., Scraton, P. and Haydon, D. (2009) *Childhood in Transition: Experiencing Marginalisation and Conflict in Northern Ireland*. Save the Children, The Princes Trust Publication. Belfast: Queens University Belfast.

McCarry, M. (2007) Masculinity Studies and Male Violence: Critique or Collusion? *Women's Studies International Forum*, 30 (5):404–415.

McCarry, M. (2009 Justifications and Contradictions: Understanding Young People's Views *of* Domestic Abuse. *Men and Masculinities*, 11 (3):325–345.

McCarry, M. (2010) Becoming a 'Proper Man': Young People's Attitudes about Interpersonal Violence and Perceptions of Gender. *Gender and Education*, 22 (1):17–30.

McCready, S. Harland, K. and Beattie, K. (2006) *Violent Victims? Young Males as Perpetrators and Victims of Violence*. Research Update No. 1, Centre for Young Men's Studies Ulster University.

McCready, S. and Harland, K. (2013) *Youth Work as Education*. Curriculum Development News. Belfast: Accessed 21 April 15. Available at: http://www.youthworkni.org.uk/publications/?assetdet40=17211&categoryesctl156292=433, pp. 11–13.

McKenna, M., Harland, K. and Walsh, C. (2006) Young Men and Violence – Practical Ways for Youth Workers to Engage and Support Young Men. A YouthAction Northern Ireland and Centre for Young Men's Studies Publication.

McKinlay, W., Forsyth, A. J. M. and Khan, F. (2009) *Alcohol and Violence among Young Male Offenders in Scotland*. Edinburgh: Scottish Prison Service.

Majors, R. (2001) Cool Pose: Black Masculinities and Sports. In Whitehead, S. and Barrett, F. (Eds.) *The Masculinities Reader*. Cambridge: Polity Press. pp. 209–217.

Marcus, R. F. (2005) Youth Violence in Everyday Life. *Journal of Interpersonal Violence*, 20 (4):442–447.

Maringira, G. (2014) Militarised Minds: The Lives of Ex-Combatants in South Africa. *Sociology*, March: 17, doi:10.1177/0038038514523698.

Martino, W. (2007) Boys and Boyhood. In Flood, M., Gardiner, J. K., Pease, B. and Pringle, K. (Eds.) *International Encyclopedia of Men and Masculinities*. London: Routledge. 46–53.

Mattaini, M. and McGuire, M. (2006) Constructing Non-Violent Cultures with Youth: A Review. *Behaviour Modification*, 30 (2):184–224.

Meghan-Davidson, M. and Canivez, G. (2012) Attitudes toward Violence Scale: Psychometric Properties with a High School Sample. *Journal of Interpersonal Violence*, 27 (18):3060–3682.

Messerschmidt, J. W. (1993) *Masculinities and Crime: Critique and Reconceptualisation of Theory*. Lanham, MD: Rowman and Littlefield.

Milburn, T., Rowlands, C., Stephen, S., Woodhouse, H. and Sneider, A. (2003) *Set It Up: Charting Young People's Progress*. Glascow: University of Strathclyde.

Miller, N. and Dollard, J. (1941) *Social Learning and Imitation*. New Haven: Yale University Press.

Mitchell, W. (2012) *Eighteen and a Half Years Old -Ordinary Young Men, Extraordinary Times: A Biographical Study into the Temporal Life-Histories of Former Loyalist Paramilitaries in the Ulster Volunteer Force and Its Associated Groups*. Unpublished Ph.D. Thesis: University of Ulster.

Miettinen, R. (2000) The Concept of Experiential Learning and John Dewey's Theory of Reflective Thought and Action. *International Journal of Lifelong Education*, 19 (1):54–72.

Moller, M. (2007) Exploiting Patterns: A Critique of Hegemonic Masculinity. *Journal of Gender Studies*, 16 (3):263–276.

Moon, J. A. (2002) *Reflection in Learning & Professional Development*. London: Kogan Page Limited.

Mooney, E., Fitzpatrick, M. and Hewitt, R. (2006) *Outcome Indicators for Looked after Children: Year Ending 30 September 2003*. Belfast: DHSSPS.

Morgan, D. (1992) *Discovering Men*. London: Routledge.

Muldoon, O. (2004) Children of the Troubles: The Impact of Political Violence in Northern Ireland. *Journal of Social Issues*, 6 (3):453–468.

Muldoon, O., Schmid, K., Downes, C., Kremer, J. and Trew, K. (2008) The Legacy of the Troubles: Experiences of the Troubles, Mental Health and Social Attitudes. Available at: http://www.legacyofthetroubles.qub.ac.uk/LegacyOfTheTroublesFinalReport.pdf Accessed 8 February 2015.

Muncie, J. (2009) *Youth and Crime*. (3rd Ed). London: Sage.

Muncie, J. (2015) *Youth and Crime*. (4th Ed). London: Sage.

Murtagh, B. (2003) Territoriality, research and Policy Making in Northern Ireland. In Hargie, O. and Dickson, D. (Eds.) *Researching the Troubles: Social Science Perspectives on the Northern Ireland Conflict*. London: Mainstream Publishing. pp. 209–225.

Nathanson, D. (1992) *Shame and Pride: Affect, Sex, and the Birth of the Self*. New York, NY: Norton.

Nation, M., Crusto, C., Wandersman, A., Kumpfer, K., Seybolt, D., Morrissey-Kane, E. and Davino,K. (2003) What Works in Prevention: Principles of Effective Programs. *American Psychologist*, 59 (6/7):449–456.

NISRA. (2012) *Children in Care in Northern Ireland 2009/10* Statistical bulletin. Belfast: DHSSPS.

Noguera, P. (1995) Preventing and Producing Violence. *Harvard Educational Review*, 65 (2):189–213.

Nolan P. (2014) *Northern Ireland Policing Report*. Belfast: Community Relations Council Number 3.

Northern Ireland Census (2011) Northern Ireland Statistics and Research Agency. Available at: http://www.nisra.gov.uk/Census.html Accessed 21 April 2015.

Oberschall, A. (2007) *Conflict and Peace Building in Divided Societies: Responses to Ethnic Violence.* New York: Routledge.

Office for National Statistics (2015) 8 Facts about Young People. Available at: http://www.ons.gov.uk/ons/rel/uncategorised/summary/facts-about-young-people/sty-facts-about-young-people.html Accessed 11 March 2015.

Olate, R., Salas-Wright, C. and Vaughn, M. (2012) Predictors of Violence and Delinquency among High Risk Youth and Youth Gang Members in San Salvador, El Salvador. *International Social Work,* 55 (3):383–401.

Olsson, T. (2009) Crossing the Quality Chasm? The Short-Term Effectiveness and Efficiency of MST in Sweden: An Example of Evidence Based Practice Applied to Social Work. PhD Dissertation. Lund: Lund University.

Olsson, T. and Roxa, T. (2013) Pedagogical Competence – a Model Promoting Conceptual Change in Higher Education. 4:e Utvecklingskonferensen för Sveriges ingenjörsutbildningar, Tekniska Högskolan vid Umeå universitet, 27 November–28 November 2013. Available at: http://www8.cs.umu.se/utvecklingskonferensen_2013/Session3_A.pdf

Ord, J. (2012) John Dewey and Experiential Learning: Developing the Theory of Youth Work. *Youth & Policy,* 108:55–72.

O'Loughlin, J. (2010) Inter-Ethnic Friendships in Post-War Bosnia-Herzegovina: Sociodemographic and Place Influences. *Ethnicities,* 10 (1):26–53.

Parkes, J. (2007) The Multiple Meanings of Violence: Children's Talk about Life in a South Africa Neighbourhood. *Childhood,* 14 (4):401–414.

Parsons, C. (2010) *Behaviour and Discipline in Schools.* Memorandum Submitted by Carl Parsons, Visiting Professor of Educational and Social Inclusion, Centre for Children, Schools and Families, University of Greenwich.

Parsons, T. (1954) Psychology and Sociology. In Gillin, J. (Ed.) *For a Science of Social Man: Convergences in Anthropology, Psychology, and Sociology.* New York: Macmillan. (Chapter 4). pp. 67–101.

Patton, G. C., Coffey, C., Sawye, S. M., Viner, R. M., Haller, D. M., Bose, K. and Mathers, C. D. (2009) Global Patterns of Mortality in Young People: A Systemic Analysis of Population Health Data. *Lancet,* 374 (9693):881–892.

Perry, C. (2010) Successful Post-Primary Schools Serving Disadvantaged Communities. *Research and Library Services Paper.* Northern Ireland Assembly. Paper 601.

Peterson, J., Rothfleisch, J., Zelazo, P. and Pihl, R. (1990) Acute Alcohol Intoxication and Neuropsychological Functioning. *Journal of Studies on Alcohol,* 51 (2):114–122.

Petrie, P. (2011) Children's Associative Spaces and Social Pedagogy. In Foley, P. and Leverett, S. (Eds.) *Children and Young People's Spaces.* Bristol: Open University Press. pp. 131–144.

Piaget, Jean (1968) *Six Psychological Studies.* Anita Tenzer (Trans.), New York: Vintage Books.

Pike, A., Rodriguez-pose and Tomaney, J. (2006) What Kind of Local and Regional Development and for Whom? *Regional Studies,* 41 (9):1253–1269. (Received November 2006; revised April 2007).

Pitts, J. (2011) Needs or Deeds? Youth Justice in Finland and England and Wales. *Prison Service Journal,* 197, September:15–19.

Plummer, D. C. (2001) The Quest for Modern Manhood: Masculine Stereotypes, Peer Culture and the Social Significance of Homophobia. *Journal of Adolescence,* 24:15–23.

Police Service of Northern Ireland (2014) *Police Recorded Security Situation Statistics: 1st March-2013–28.* February 2014. NISRA.

Polk, K. (1994) *When Men Kill.* Cambridge: University Press.

Postareff, L. (2007) *Teaching in Higher Education. From Content-Focused to Learning-Focused Approaches to Teaching.* Helsinki: Helsinki University.

Poynting, S. (2007) Male Youth Cultures. In Flood, M., Gardiner, J. K., Pease, B. and Pringle, K. (Eds.) *International Encyclopaedia of Men and Masculinities.* London: Routledge. 378–380.

Pringle, K. and Pease, B. (2001) *A Man's World: Changing Men's Practices in A Globalized World.* London: Zed Books.

Pringle, K. (2007) Child Abuse. In Flood, M., Gardiner, J. K. and Pease, B. and Pringle, K. (Eds.) *International Encyclopaedia of Men and Masculinities.* London and New York: Routledge. 55–59.

Proctor, C., Linley, A. and Maltby, J. (2009) Youth Life Satisfaction: A Review of the Literature. *Journal of Happiness Studies,* 10:583–630.

Race, P. (2010): *Making Learning Happen: A Guide for Post-Compulsory Education.* 2nd ed. London: Sage.

Rahman, N. (2007) Patriarchy. In Flood, M., Gardiner, J. K., Pease, B. and Kringle, K. (Eds.) *International Encyclopedia of Men and Masculinities.* London and New York: Routledge. pp. 467–468.

Rajmil, L., Herdman, M., Fernández de Sanmamed, M. J., Detmar, S., Bruil, J., Ravens-Sieberer, U., Bullinger, M., Simeoni, M.-C., Auquier, P., and the Kidscreen group (2004). Generic Health-related Quality of Life Instruments in Children and Adolescents: A Qualitative Analysis of Content. *Journal of Adolescent Health,* 34 (1):37–45.

Reilly, J., Muldoon, O. and Bryne, C. (2004) Young Men as Victims and Perpetrators of Violence in Northern Ireland. *Journal of Social Issues,* 60 (3):469–484.

Renken, B., Egeland, B., Marvinney, D,. Sroufe. L. A. and Mangelsdorf, S. (1989) Early Childhood Antecedents of Aggression and Passive Withdrawal in Early Elementary School. *Journal of Personality,* 57 (2):257–281.

Review of Health and Social Care in Northern Ireland (2011) *Transforming Your Care.* Compton J., Chair of Review: Health and Social Care in Northern Ireland.

Richardson, D. and Hammock, G. (2007) Social Context of Human Aggression: Are We Paying Too Much Attention to Gender? *Aggression and Violent Behavior,* 12 (4):417–426.

Rigby, K. (1996) *Bullying in Schools and What to Do about It.* Melbourne: Australian Council for Educational Research LTD.

Robertson, S. (2007) *Understanding Men and Health.* Buckingham: Open University Press.

Rogers, C. R. (1980) *Way of Being.* Boston: Houghton Mifflin.

Rogers, C. R. (1983) *Freedom to Learn for the 80's.* Columbus, OH: Charles E. Merrill/Macmillan Publications.

Rogers, C. and Freiberg, H. J. (1994) *Freedom to Learn.* (3rd Ed). Columbus, OH: Merrill/Macmillan Publications.

Ruiz, B. (2005) Caring Discourse: The Care/Justice Debate Revisited. *Philosophy Social Criticism,* 31 (11):304–316.

Salisbury, J. and Jackson, D. (1996) *Challenging Macho Values.* Bristol: Falmer Press.

Sampson, R. J. (1997) The Embeddedness of Child and Adolescent Development: A Community-Level Perspective on Urban Violence. In McCord,

J. (Ed.) *Violence and Childhood in the Inner City*. Cambridge: University Press. 31–78.

Santamaria, L. J. and Santamaria, A. P. (2012) *Applied Critical Leadership in Education: Choosing Change*. New York: Routledge.

Savin-Williams Ritch, C. (2001) A Critique of Research on Sexual-Minority Youths. *Journal of Adolescence*, 24 (5):5–13.

Schofield, G., Ward, E., Biggart, L., Scaife, Dodsworth, J., Larsson, B., Haynes, A. and Stone. (2012) *Looked after Children and Offending: Reducing Risk and Promoting Resilience*. Norwich, University of East Angela: Centre for Research on the Child and Family.

Schnitzer, S., Bellis, M. A., Anderson, Z., Hughes, K., Calafat, A., Juan, M. and Kokkevi, A. (2010) Nightlife Violence: A Gender-Specific View on Risk Factors for Violence in Nightlife Settings: A Cross-Sectional Study in Nine European Countries. *Journal of Interpersonal Violence*, 25 (6):1094–1112.

Schoenwald, S., Brown, T. and Henggeler, S. (2000) Inside Multisystemic Therapy: Therapist, Supervisory and Program Practices. *Journal of Emotional and Behavioral Disorders*, 8:113–144.

Schroeder, R. and Mowen, T. (2014) Parenting Style Transitions and Delinquency. *Youth & Society*, 46 (2):228–254.

Schubotz, D. and Devine, P. (2008) *Young People in Post Conflict Northern Ireland: The Past Cannot Be Changed but the Future Can be Developed*. Lyme Regis: Russell House Pub.

Scraton, P. (2004) Streets of Terror: Marginalisation, Criminalisation and Authoritarian Renewal. *Social Justice*, 31 (1):130–158.

Scraton, P. (2008) The Criminalisation and Punishment of Children and Young People: Introduction. *Current Issues in Criminal Justice*, 20 (1):1–13.

Scowcroft, E. (2012) *Suicide Statistics Report 2012: Data for 2008–2010,* Samaritans, February.

Seaton, P. (2007) *Japan's Contested War Memories: The 'Memory Rifts' in Historical Consciousness of World War II*. London: Routledge.

Seidler, V. J. (2007) Masculinities, Bodies, and Emotional Life. *Men and Masculinities*, 10 (1):9–21.

Sempik, J., Ward, H. and Darker, I. (2008) Emotional and Behavioural Difficulties of Children and Young People at Entry into Care. *Clinical Child Psychology and Psychiatry*, 13 (2):91–100.

Shirlow, P. and Coulter, C. (2014) Northern Ireland: 20 Years after the Ceasefires. *Studies in Conflict & Terrorism*, 37:713–719.

Shover, N. (1996) *Great Pretenders: Pursuits and Careers of Persistent Thieves*. Colorado: Westview Press.

Sivarajasingam, V., Wells, J. P., Moore, S., Page, N. and Shepherd, J. P. (2014) *Violence in England and Wales in 2013: An Accident and Emergency Perspective*. Violence and Society Research Group, Cardiff: Cardiff University.

Skinner, D. (2010) *Effective Teaching and Learning in Practice*. London: Continuum International Publishing.

Skuse, D., Morris, J. and Lawrence, K. (2003) The Amygdala and Development of the Social Brain. *New York Academy of Sciences*, 1008:91–101.

Skuse, T. and Ward, H. (2003) *Outcomes for Looked after Children: Children's Views of Care and Accommodation*. Interim Report to the Department of Health. Centre for Child and Family Research. Loughborough University:

Smith, C. A., Susan, B. and Stern, S. B. (1997) Delinquency and Anti-Social Behavior: A Review of Family Processes and Intervention Research. *Social Service Review*, 71:382–420. OJJDP.

Smith, M. K. (1988) Beyond Social Education in Developing Youth Work OU Press.

Smith, M. K. (2002) Social Education – the Evolution of an Idea. *The Encyclopedia of Informal Education*, Available at: http://www.infed.org/biblio/b-soced.htm.

Smith, M. K. (2007) Carl Rogers, Core Conditions and Education (first published 1997) *The Encyclopaedia of Informal Education*. Available at: www.infed.org/thinkers/er-rogers.htm

Smyth, M. and Hamilton, J. (2003) The Human Costs of the Troubles. In Hargie, O. and Dickson, D. (Eds.) *Researching the Troubles: Social Science Perspectives on the Northern Ireland Conflict*. London: Mainstream Publishing. 15–36.

Sobieraj, S. (1998) Taking Control: Toy Commercials and the Social Construction of Patriarchy. In Bowker, L. H. (Ed.) *Masculinities and Violence*. California: Sage Publications. 15–29.

Sommers, J. (2015) Why Northern Ireland's Peace Walls Show No Sign of Following Berlin's Example. *The Huffington Post*. Available at: http://www.huffingtonpost.co.uk/2014/11/03/peace-walls-northern-ireland_n_6093634.html

Spano, R., Rivera, C. and Bolland, J. (2010) Are Chronic Exposure to Violence and Chronic Violent Behavior Closely Related Developmental Processes during Adolescence? *Criminal Justice and Behavior*, 37 (10):1160–1179.

Spano, R., Rivera, C., Bolland, J. (2011) Does Parenting Shield Youth from Exposure to Violence during Adolescence? A 5-Year Longitudinal Test in a High-Poverty Sample of Minority Youth. *Journal of Interpersonal Violence*, 26 (5):930–949.

Spence, J., Devanney, C. and Noonan, K. (2006) *Youth Work: Voices of Practice*. Leicester: The National Youth Agency.

Sukarieh, M. and Tannock, S. (2011) The Positivity Imperative: A Critical Look at the 'New' Youth Development Movement. *Journal of Youth Studies*, 14 (6):675–691.

Summerfield, A. (2012) *Children and Young People in Custody 2010–11. HM Inspectorate of Prisons Youth Justice Board*. London: The Stationary Office.

Sundaram, V. (2013) Violence as Understandable, Deserved or Unacceptable? Listening for Gender in Teenagers' Talk about Violence. *Gender and Education*, 25 (7) 889–906.

Swain, J. (2004) The Resources and Strategies that 10–11-Year-Old Boys Use to Construct Masculinities in the School Setting. *British Educational Research Journal*, 30 (1) February.

Swain, J. (2006a) Reflections on Patterns of Masculinity in School Settings. *Men and Masculinities*, 8:331.

Swain, J. (2006b). The Role of Sport in the Construction of Masculinities in an English Independent Junior School. *Sport, Education and Society*, 11 (4): 317–335.

Swartz, S. and Scott, D. (2013) The Rules of Violence: A Perspective from South African Townships. *Journal of Youth Studies*. DOI: 1080/13676261.2013.815699. 1–19.

Taylor, C. (2003) Justice for Looked after Children? *Probation Journal,* 50 (3):239–251.

The Albemarle Report (1960) *The Youth Service in England and Wales* Chapter 1 of Ministry of Education. London: Her Majesty's Stationery Office.

The Home Office (2013) *Ending Gang and Youth Violence: Annual Report (2013). HM Government.* London: The Stationary Office.

Themner, L. and Wallensteen, P. (2012) Armed Conflict, 1946–2011. *Journal of Peace Research,* 50 (4):509–521.

Tighe, A., Pistrang, N., Casdagli, L., Baruch, G. and Butler, S. (2012) Multisystemic Therapy for Young Offenders: Families' Experiences of Therapeutic Processes and Outcomes. *Journal of Family Psychology,* 26 (2):187–197.

Titley, G. (2003) Youth Work with Boys and Young Men as a Means of Preventing Violence in Everyday Life. Report of the General Rapporteur, Council of Europe.

Tolan, P. H. and Gorman-Smith, D. (1998) Development of Serious, Violent and Chronic Offenders. In Loeber, R. and Farrington, D. (Eds.) *Never to Early, Never to Late: Serious, Violent, and Chronic Juvenile Offenders.* Beverly Hills, CA: Sage. pp. 68–65.

Tolson, A. (1997) *The Limits of Masculinity.* London: Tavistock.

Tolstoy, L. (1967) *Tolstoy on Education* translated by Leo Weiner. Chicago: University of Chicago Press.

Tomlinson, M. (2012) War, Peace and Suicide: The Case of Northern Ireland. *International Sociology,* 20 (14):464–482.

Tomsen, S. (1997) A Top Night: Social Protest, Masculinity and the Culture of Drinking Violence. *British Journal of Criminology,* 37 (1):90–102.

Topping, J. and Byrne, J. (2012) Paramilitary Punishments in Belfast: Policing Beneath the Peace. *Behavioural Sciences of Terrorism and Political Aggression,* 4 (1):41–59.

Trew, K. (1995) Psychological and Social Impact of the Troubles on Young People Growing up in Northern Ireland. In *Growing through Conflict: The Impact of 25 years of Violence on Young People Growing up in Northern Ireland.* The International Association of Juvenile and Family Court Magistrates. Regional Seminar.

Tucker, S. (1994), Changing Times, Changing Roles? An Examination of Contemporary Youth and Community Practice. *Youth & Policy,* 46:5–16.

Turner, M. and Piquero, A. (2002) The Stability of Self Control. *Journal of Criminal Justice,* 20:457–471.

Turner, K., Hill, M., Stafford, A. and Walker, M. (2006) How Children from Disadvantaged Areas Keep Safe. *Health Education,* 106 (6):450–464.

United Nations Development Program (UNDP), B.-H. (2006) *Early Warning System 2006* Second Quarter Report (Web Edition). Sarajevo: United Nations. United Nations Report (February 2015) BBC News. Available at: http://www.bbc.co.uk/news/world-europe-31495099 Accessed 17 February 2015.

United States Department of State (2013) Bosnia and Herzegovina 2013 Crime and Safety. Available at: https://www.osac.gov/pages/ContentReportDetails.aspx?cid=13733

Van Wilsem, J., De Graaf, N. D. and Karin Wittebrood, K. (2003) Cross-National Differences in Victimization: Disentangling the Impact of Composition and Context. *European Sociological Review,* 19:125–142.

Varshney, A. (2001) Ethnic Conflict and Civil Society: India and Beyond. *World Politics*, 53 (3):362–98.

Walker, G. W. (2006) Disciplining Protest Masculinity. *Men and Masculinities*, 9:5–22.

Walden, L. and Beran, T. (2010) Attachment Quality and Bullying Behaviour in School-Aged Youth. *Canadian Journal of School Psychology*, 25: 1–14.

Wallensteen, P. (2002) *Understanding Conflict Resolution: War, Peace and the Global System*. London: Sage.

Weatherburn, D. and Lind, B. (2001) *Delinquent-Prone Communities*. New York: Cambridge University Press.

Weisbach, M. (1999) How Masculine Ought I to Be? Men's Masculinity and Aggression. Sex Roles: *A Journal of Research*, April 2001.

Werner, E. E. (2012) Children and War: Risk, Resilience, and Recovery. *Development and Psychopathology*, 24 (2):553–558.

Westwood, S. (1990) Racism, Black Masculinity and the Politics of Space. In Hearn, J. and Morgan, D. (Eds.) *Men, Masculinities and Social Theory*. London: Unwin Hyman Ltd. 55–72.

Whitehead, A. (2005) Man to Man Violence: How Masculinity Works as a Dynamic Risk Factor. *The Howard Journal*, 44 (4) 411–422.

Whitehead, S. (2007) Patriarchal Dividend. In Flood, M., Gardiner, J. K., Pease, B. and Pringle, K. (Eds.) *International Encyclopaedia Men & Masculinities*. London: Routledge. p. 468.

Whitehead, S. M. (2002) *Men and Masculinities: Key Themes and New Directions*, Cambridge: Polity.

Whitt, S. (2012) Social Norms in the Aftermath of Ethnic Violence: Ethnicity and Fairness in Non-Costly Decision Making. *Journal of Conflict Resolution*, 58 (1) 93–119.

Willis, P. (1997) *Learning to Labour: How Working Class Kids Get Working Class Jobs*. Farnborough: Saxon House.

Woodward, R. (2000) Warrior Heroes and Little Green Men: Soldiers, Military Training, and the Construction of Rural Masculinities. *Rural Sociology*, 65 (2) 640–647.

World Health Organisation (2000) World Health Report 2000. Available at: http://www.who.int/whr/2000/en/

World Health Organization (2002*) First World Report on Violence and Health: Summary*. Geneva. Available at: http://www.who.int/violence_injury_prevention/violence/world_report/en/introduction.pdf

World Health Organisation (2014) Mortality Estimates, Including Deaths Due to Violence. Available at: http://www.who.int/violence_injury_prevention/violence/en/

World Health Organisation Media Centre (2015) Youth Violence: Fact Sheet No 356. Available at: http://www.who.int/mediacentre/factsheets/fs356/en/

Yablonsky, L. (1962) *The Violent Gang*. New York: Macmillan.

Young, J. (1971) *The Drugtakers*. London: Paladin.

Young, K. (2006) *The Art of Youth Work*. 2nd ed Lyme Regis: Russell House Publications.

YouthAction Northern Ireland (2002) *Everyday Life: Young Men, Violence and Developing Youth Work Practice in Northern Ireland*. YouthAction Publications.

Zakowski, H. (2013) Reporting Physical Assault: How experiences with Violence Influences Adolescents' Response to Victimization. *Youth Violence and Juvenile Justice*, 11 (1):44–59.

Zimbardo, P. (2007) *The Lucifer Effect: How Good People Turn Evil*. New York: Random House Group.

Žižek, S. (2008) *Violence: Six Sideways Reflections*. New York: Picador.

Index